T0182893

Lecture Notes
in Business Information Processing 269

Series Editors

Wil M.P. van der Aalst
  Eindhoven Technical University, Eindhoven, The Netherlands
John Mylopoulos
  University of Trento, Trento, Italy
Michael Rosemann
  Queensland University of Technology, Brisbane, QLD, Australia
Michael J. Shaw
  University of Illinois, Urbana-Champaign, IL, USA
Clemens Szyperski
  Microsoft Research, Redmond, WA, USA

More information about this series at http://www.springer.com/series/7911

Dietmar Winkler · Stefan Biffl
Johannes Bergsmann (Eds.)

Software Quality

Complexity and Challenges of Software Engineering in Emerging Technologies

9th International Conference, SWQD 2017
Vienna, Austria, January 17–20, 2017
Proceedings

 Springer

Editors
Dietmar Winkler
Institute of Software Technology
  and Interactive Systems
Vienna University of Technology
Vienna
Austria

Stefan Biffl
Institute of Software Technology
  and Interactive Systems
Vienna University of Technology
Vienna
Austria

Johannes Bergsmann
Software Quality Lab GmbH
Linz
Austria

ISSN 1865-1348   ISSN 1865-1356 (electronic)
Lecture Notes in Business Information Processing
ISBN 978-3-319-49420-3   ISBN 978-3-319-49421-0   (eBook)
DOI 10.1007/978-3-319-49421-0

Library of Congress Control Number: 2016956500

© Springer International Publishing AG 2017
This work is subject to copyright. All rights are reserved by the Publisher, whether the whole or part of the material is concerned, specifically the rights of translation, reprinting, reuse of illustrations, recitation, broadcasting, reproduction on microfilms or in any other physical way, and transmission or information storage and retrieval, electronic adaptation, computer software, or by similar or dissimilar methodology now known or hereafter developed.
The use of general descriptive names, registered names, trademarks, service marks, etc. in this publication does not imply, even in the absence of a specific statement, that such names are exempt from the relevant protective laws and regulations and therefore free for general use.
The publisher, the authors and the editors are safe to assume that the advice and information in this book are believed to be true and accurate at the date of publication. Neither the publisher nor the authors or the editors give a warranty, express or implied, with respect to the material contained herein or for any errors or omissions that may have been made.

Printed on acid-free paper

This Springer imprint is published by Springer Nature
The registered company is Springer International Publishing AG
The registered company address is: Gewerbestrasse 11, 6330 Cham, Switzerland

Message from the General Chair

The Software Quality Days (SWQD) conference and tools fair started in 2009 and has grown to be the biggest conference on software quality in Europe with a strong community. The program of the SWQD conference is designed to encompass a stimulating mixture of practical presentations and new research topics in scientific presentations as well as tutorials and an exhibition area for tool vendors and other organizations in the area of software quality.

This professional symposium and conference offer a range of comprehensive and valuable opportunities for advanced professional training, new ideas, and networking with a series of keynote speeches, professional lectures, exhibits, and tutorials.

The SWQD conference is suitable for anyone with an interest in software quality, such as software process and quality managers, test managers, software testers, product managers, agile masters, project managers, software architects, software designers, requirements engineers, user interface designers, software developers, IT managers, release managers, development managers, application managers, and those in similar roles.

January 2017   Johannes Bergsmann

Message from the Scientific Program Chair

The 9th Software Quality Days (SWQD) conference and tools fair brought together researchers and practitioners from business, industry, and academia working on quality assurance and quality management for software engineering and information technology. The SWQD conference is one of the largest software quality conferences in Europe.

Over the past years, a growing number of scientific contributions were submitted to the SWQD symposium. Starting in 2012 the SWQD symposium included a dedicated scientific program published in scientific proceedings. For the sixth year we received an overall number of 21 high-quality submissions from researchers across Europe, which were each peer-reviewed by three or more reviewers. Out of these submissions, the editors selected four contributions as full papers, yielding an acceptance rate of 19 %. A further seven short papers, representing promising research directions, were accepted to spark discussions between researchers and practitioners at the conference.

Main topics from academia and industry focused on systems and software quality management methods, improvements of software development methods and processes, latest trends and emerging topics in software quality, and testing and software quality assurance.

This book is structured according to the sessions of the scientific program following the guiding conference topic "Complexity and Challenges of Software Engineering in Emerging Technologies":

- Model-Driven Development and Configuration Management
- Software Development and Quality Assurance
- Software Quality Assurance in Industry
- Crowdsourcing in Software Engineering
- Software Testing and Traceability
- Process Improvement

January 2017   Stefan Biffl

Organization

SWQD 2017 was organized by the Software Quality Lab GmbH and the Vienna University of Technology, Institute of Software Technology and Interactive Systems, and the Christian Doppler Laboratory "Software Engineering Integration for Flexible Automation Systems."

Organizing Committee

General Chair

Johannes Bergsmann   Software Quality Lab GmbH

Scientific Program Chair

Stefan Biffl   Vienna University of Technology

Proceedings Chair

Dietmar Winkler   Vienna University of Technology

Organizing and Publicity Chair

Petra Bergsmann   Software Quality Lab GmbH

Program Committee

SWQD 2017 established an international committee of well-known experts in software quality and process improvement to peer-review the scientific submissions.

Miklos Biro	Software Competence Center Hagenberg, Austria
Matthias Book	University of Iceland, Iceland
Ruth Breu	University of Innsbruck, Austria
Maya Daneva	University of Twente, The Netherlands
Oscar Dieste	Universidad Politécnica de Madrid, Spain
Frank Elberzhager	Fraunhofer IESE, Germany
Michael Felderer	University of Innsbruck, Austria
Gordon Fraser	University of Sheffield, UK
Nauman Ghazi	Blekinge Institute of Technology, Sweden
Volker Gruhn	University of Duisburg-Essen, Germany
Jens Heidrich	Fraunhofer IESE, Germany
Frank Houdek	Daimler AG, Germany
Slinger Jansen	Utrecht University, The Netherlands
Marcos Kalinowski	Fluminense Federal University, Brazil
Marco Kuhrmann	University of Southern Denmark, Denmark
Ricardo Machado	CCG-Centro de Computação Gráfica, Portugal
Eda Marchetti	ISTI-CNR, Italy

Emilia Mendes	Blekinge Institute of Technology, Sweden
Paula Monteiro	CCG-Centro de Computação Gráfica, Portugal
Jürgen Münch	University of Helsinki, Finland
Markku Ovio	University of Oulu, Finland
Oscar Pastor Lopez	Universitat Politècnica de València, Valencia, Spain
Dietmar Pfahl	University of Tartu, Estonia
Rick Rabiser	Johannes Kepler University Linz, Austria
Rudolf Ramler	Software Competence Center Hagenberg, Austria
Andreas Rausch	Technical University of Clausthal, Germany
Barbara Russo	Free University of Bozen-Bolzano, Italy
Ina Schieferdecker	Fraunhofer Institute for Open Communication Systems, FOKUS, Germany
Klaus Schmid	University of Hildesheim, Germany
Stefan Wagner	University of Stuttgart, Germany
Dietmar Winkler	Vienna University of Technology, Austria

Additional Reviewers

Boban Celebic
Florian Häser
Rainer Niedermayr
Emmanuel Nowakowski
Jan-Peter Ostberg
Sebastrian Völst
Thomas Ziebermayr

Contents

Keynote

From Pair Programming to Mob Programming to Mob Architecting

Carola Lilienthal[✉]

WPS – Workplace Solutions GmbH,
Hans-Henny-Jahnn-Weg 29, 22085 Hamburg, Germany
Carola.Lilienthal@wps.de

Abstract. The real life of a developer is not about development – it is about maintenance. Today typical programmers do not develop applications from scratch but they spend their time fixing, extending, modifying and enhancing existing applications. The biggest problem in their daily work is that over time maintenance mutates from structured programming to defensive programming: The code becomes too complex to be maintained. We put in code which we know is stupid from an architectural point of view but it is the only solution that will hopefully work. Maintenance becomes more and more difficult and expensive.

In this paper, I will show you how pair programming, mob programming and mob architecting help your team to avoid this apparently inevitable dead end. These three levels of quality improvement start with programming in pairs evolve to programming with the whole team (mob) and finally arrive at improving the architecture with the whole team.

Keywords: Software architecture · Teamwork · Pair programming · Mob programming · Quality improvement · Mob architecting

1 Introduction

Software systems are surely among the most complex constructions of humankind. It is hardly surprising that software projects tend to fail and legacy systems stay untouched because of the fear that they might fall apart when changed. The reasons why software development and maintenance fail can come from various levels: the application area and the organizations involved, the applied technologies, the domain fit of the software systems, or even the qualification of users and developers. In this article, I will focus on different techniques that can help development teams to reduce the technical debts of the software architecture. If the whole team is aware of the architecture and potential technical debts, the software architecture will stay maintainable and extendable with steady costs over a long period.

Let us begin with the typical path that the software architecture of a system takes and then discuss the techniques to prevent these dead ends.

© Springer International Publishing AG 2017
D. Winkler et al. (Eds.): SWQD 2017, LNBIP 269, pp. 3–12, 2017.
DOI: 10.1007/978-3-319-49421-0_1

1.1   From Structural to Defensive Programming

At the beginning of a software development project a team of experienced developers and architects will contribute their best experiences and their collective knowledge in order to design a durable architecture with a low level of technical debts. The term "technical debt" is a metaphor Ward Cunningham coined in 1992 [1]. Technical debts arise when developers and architects consciously or unconsciously make wrong or suboptimal technical decisions. Later, this wrong or suboptimal decisions lead to additional expenses and will delay maintenance and expansion.

Unfortunately, it is not enough to focus on this aim at the beginning of the project. According to the motto: We'll design a long-lasting architecture at the beginning and then everything is and remains good. On the contrary, a development team will only achieve a long living architecture if it constantly keeps an eye on the technical debts. In Fig. 1, you see what will happen when you permit the technical debts to increase over time or, which is much better, if the team is able to reduce them regularly [2].

Imagine a team that always evolves its system in releases or iterations. If we have a quality-conscious team in action, every member of the team will know that they add some new technical debt with each extension (yellow arrow in Fig. 1). During the extension, this team is therefore already thinking about how it could improve the architecture. Following the extension, the technical debt is then reduced again (green arrows in Fig. 1). A continuous sequence of extensions and improvement emerges. If the team follows this path, the system remains in a corridor of low technical debt.

If the team is not working in a steady sequence of renovations of the architecture, the system's architecture will slowly dissolve and maintainability deteriorates. Eventually the software system leaves the corridor of low technical debts (s. red rising arrows in Fig. 1).

The architecture has eroded more and more. Maintenance and extensions of the software are becoming more expensive to the point at which any change will be a painful effort. In Fig. 1 the red arrows are getting shorter and shorter indicating this circumstance. Per unit of time, the team will achieve less and less functionality, bug fixes and adaptations to other quality requirements due to this increasing architecture erosion. The team will become more and more frustrated and demotivated sinding

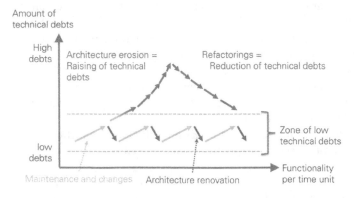

Fig. 1. Technical debts and architecture erosion (Color figure online)

desperate signals to project leadership and management. However, when management hears these warnings, it will usually be too late.

If a team is on the way up the red arrows, the sustainability of the software system decreases continually [3]. The software system will be prone to errors. The development team will be said of being cumbersome. Changes that could previously be done in two days, now will take twice or three times as long. Overall, everything will be going too slowly. "Slow" is in the IT industry a synonym for "too expensive". I agree! Technical debts accumulate and with every change, you have to pay the interest on the technical debts.

The path that leads out of this dilemma of technical debt is to improve the quality of architecture retroactively. This enables the team to gradually bring back their system into the corridor of fewer technical debts (see red arrows descending in Fig. 1). This path is arduous and costs money – therefore, it is a good idea to install techniques that keep a development team within the zone of low technical debts.

1.2   Uniform Structure and Guidelines

Software is in general hard to construct due to the immense number of elements needed in a software system. In my experience, a smart developer is able to overlook about 30,000 lines of code while changing the source code and anticipate the impact of a change in one place to the other parts of the code. Typically, operational software systems are much larger. Their sizes ranges from 200 thousand to 100 million lines of code [2].

These numbers make clear that developers need a software architecture that provides them with two things:

- A **uniform structure** that helps developers to find their way through the existing complexity
- **Guidelines** that restrict the design space and thereby give direction to the development.

If developers have an overview of the existing uniform structure, they probably will make changes to the software correctly. Guidelines will lead all members of the development team into the same direction, while unknown parts of the software are much easier to understand and comprehend. The software system will obtain its uniform structure. This uniform structure will be the basis of common understanding, so maintenance and enhancements will be quicker and more consistent.

Of course, the architects need to document the uniform structure and the guidelines. However, what may even be of higher importance is that all team members know and understand the structure and guidelines. To achieve this, knowledge must be spread throughout the whole team.

2   Spreading Knowledge in Teams

I frequently meet teams that keep their system's architecture under control despite its application area, its size or age. Enhancements and bug fixes are made in an acceptable timeframe. New developers can understand the source code with reasonable effort.

Why are these teams different? How do they manage to live in peace with their software architecture for a long time?

What I realize observing these teams is a heavy use of pair programming and mob programming. With our own teams, we added another technique: mob architecting. In the following, I will present these three techniques and describe the advantages and drawbacks of each of them.

2.1   Pair Programming

Kent Beck proposed pair programming in 1999 as a technique of extreme programming [4]. In pair programming, two programmers work together at one workstation. One, the pilot, has control over the keyboard and writes code. The other, the so-called navigator, reviews the work in progress and discusses his upcoming ideas for improvements and future problems with the chosen solution. The two programmers switch roles continually (Fig. 2).

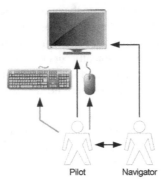

Fig. 2. Pair programming

Pair programming has been evaluated in various scientific experiments [5]. The quality of the code written in a pair is higher, with fewer bugs, better interfaces and less redundancy. Moreover, it is frequently reported that programmers have a higher confidence in their results and enjoy their work more with pair programming. As programmers report, this confidence and enjoyment mainly stems from the fact that as a pair they can work more focused and effectively. The time wasted by doing more than what is sufficient or unnecessarily switching tasks or being interrupted is noticeably reduced.

In our teams, we have equipped our pair programming workstations with two keyboards and two mice. This helps to prevent back pain, but poses a new problem: Pilot and navigator have to be very clear about who is coding. If not, the navigator will start annoying the pilot by interfering with his or her work (Fig. 3).

We have also done distributed pair programming. Two programmers, who were use to work with each other in one place now were located in two different places.

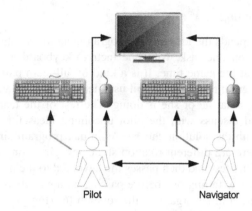

Fig. 3. Pair programming with double equipment

Nevertheless, they worked together sharing the screen and discussing their solutions via VoIP services. This solution showed very good effects on team building in distributed teams, but only worked in our experience if the members of the pair had been working together on-site before (Fig. 4).

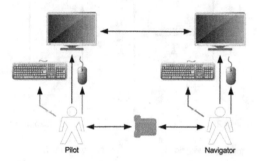

Fig. 4. Pair programming in different locations

Since the pilot in a pair has to explain his ideas and decisions to his counterpart their understanding of the architecture will continuously be challenged. Through programming in a pair, they will deepen and enrich their architectural knowledge of the whole system. Especially if pairs are switch repeatedly, the team members will distribute their knowledge continuously.

Spreading the knowledge and thereby easing incorporation of new team members or overcoming the loss of experienced team members is a big advantage of pair programming. However, the knowledge is distributed on a rather low level, such as by documentation in code. If the task of each pair is fixing a bug or implementing a new feature. The system's architecture will come rarely into focus. Maybe the pair will discuss the architecture but on a local level within the pair and they have no means to visualize the architecture while programming.

2.2   Mob Programming

Mob programming expands the idea of pair programming to an entire team. The whole team works together on one task, with one (active) keyboard and one large screen (usually a projector) at the same time. It is a kind of full-team pair programming [6].

Just as in pair programming, a pilot will use the keyboard and write the code while constantly explaining what he or she is doing. The rest of the team will observe the work in progress and discuss with the pilot upcoming ideas for improvements and potential problems with the solution chosen. As in pair programming, the pilot role is rotated regularly. There are different rotation strategies: ping-pong-pairing means that one pilot writes a failing test and then passes the keyboard to the next pilot who fulfills that test and writes a new failing one before passing on the keyboard. Timer pairing is another strategy where a timer organizes the rotation [6] (Fig. 5).

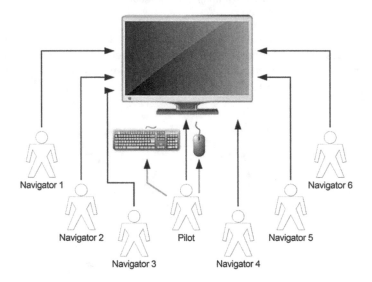

Fig. 5. Mob programming

Up to now, no scientific experiments have been conducted showing the usefulness of mob programming. Therefore, only experience reports of the advantages of mob programming exist. The teams using mob programming claim that they have achieved the maximal possible throughput for their team. Typing obviously is not the bottleneck in software development. The real cost factor is solving the problem with all the cycles of revision and rework typically involved [7].

Mob Programming addresses all these time-consuming issues. Working with all experts on one task is the best and quickest way to finish it. All the knowledge needed is available and the energy of the whole team focuses on one problem. This is the main advantage over pair programming, while all the other advantages of pair programming are also valid for mob programming: fewer bugs, higher quality in code and design and less redundancy.

In our company, we have one team who has started to practice mob programming in their daily work. They have reached the conclusion, that mob programming is the best solution for crucial new features and refactorings that will affect fundamental parts of the architecture. Our team calls this kind of changes "heart surgery". The whole team in a mob always works on these far-reaching tasks. Their goal is to bring together the knowledge of the entire team and to spread the solutions and decisions within the team.

In summary, mob programming takes pair programming one-step further. But still a team only sees the architecture through the code. With mob architecting, this drawback can be finally overcome.

3   Mob Architecting

With mob architecting, the concept of mob programming is taken to a different level. Supported by a consultant and a tool to visualize the architecture the whole team can discuss and improve their system's architecture in a very focussed and holistic manner. How does this work?

Initially, the tool for architecture visualization is loaded with the source code of the system. There are various tools available for architecture visualization and refactoring: for example Lattix, Sonargraph, Sotograph, Structure101. Since these tools are tools for experts, an eternal pilot who has a lot of experience in using the chosen tool typically drives a mob programming session [2].

The external pilot is conducting the development team through the process of mob-architecting (Step 1 to Step 4 in Fig. 6).

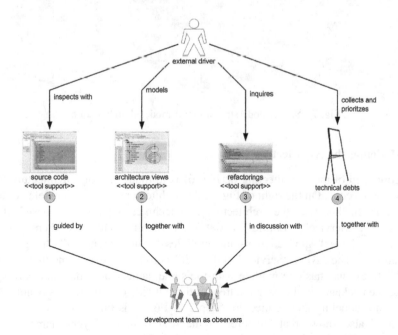

Fig. 6. Mob architecting with the whole team

3.1   Inspecting the Source Code (Step 1)

The first step is to analyze the source code in order to find the mapping of source code to architecture. Tools for architecture visualization can visualize the structures found within the source code and within the build-process tools, such as classes, directories, packages and build units. If the architecture is important for the development team, the main architecture should be detectable in these source code structures and build structures. Build units, packages, or directories should represent technical layers or domain modules.

In Fig. 7 (left side), the source code of an open source java system is presented by the tool Sotograph. The circles represent packages, the triangles represent files and the green arcs represent dependencies. Arcs on the left side of the vertical denote dependencies that go downwards. For example, within the package "plugin" there is a class that needs functionality from a class in the "net"-package. The arcs on the right side of the vertical denote dependencies that go upwards. For example, in the package "util" you will find one or more classes that need functionality from classes in the packages "entities", "controllers" and "security". All the circles (packages in this case) that are marked with a plus contain other packages or classes. The package at the bottom "com. frovi.ss.Tree" is opened completely, showing four classes belonging to this package [2].

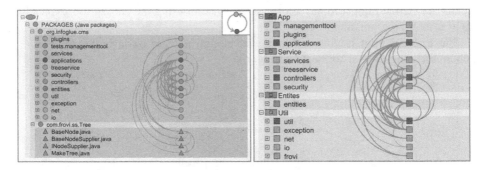

Fig. 7. Source code structure and modeled architecture

3.2   Modeling the Architecture (Step 2)

The second step of mob architecting (s. Fig. 6) is to model various architecture views onto the source code. On the right of Fig. 7, the architecture has been modeled onto the source code. In this case, the architecture is a technical layering composed of four layers "App", "Service", "Entities" and "Util". Within each layer, there a several modules. The layer "App" contains the modules "managementtool", "plugins" and "applications". The layers "Service" and "Util" consist of several modules as well, while "Entities" just has one module with the same name. These modules correspond nicely to the packages in the package tree on the left side of Fig. 7. This is not always the case and modeling the architecture (step 2 in Fig. 6) is time-consuming.

Figure 7 also shows that the three of the four technical layers, namely "App", "Service" and "Util" do not exist in the package tree. The knowledge about these layers exists only in the documentation or in the brains of some members of the development team. Missing matches like this will usually emerge during mob architecting. Then, the team will start to learn about their architecture. New members of the team will begin to catch the overall idea. Old members will be discussing their different ideas about the architecture.

3.3 Inquiring (Step 3) and Collecting (Step 4) Refactorings

In Fig. 7 (right side), some red arcs are shown. These arcs are depicted in red, because these dependencies violate the technical layering. Some classes from the module "util" in the layer "Utils" need some functionality from classes in "Entities" and "Service". Inspecting these red arcs and defining refactorings for these violations is the third step of mob architecting shown in Fig. 6.

The violation between the layer "Service" and "App" will serve as an example to understand how a violation can be refactored. Figure 8 left and right show a filtered view of the source code. Only the classes involved in the violation are visible. Therefore, only some packages are shown and not all their content is displayed.

In Fig. 8 (left side) you can see three classes from the package "org.infoglue. cms.controllers.kernel.impl.simple" that cause the violation (red arc) from the module "controllers" to the module "applications". They all call one method in the class "VisualFormatter.java". The line within the three controller classes perform the following call:

```
value = new VisualFormatter().escapeHTML(value);
```

Since the whole functionality of VisualFormatter is more like a utility than like an application functionality, the team decides that VisualFormatter should belong to the "Util" layer and not to the "App" layer.

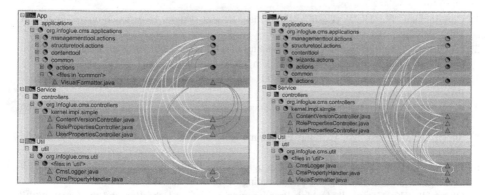

Fig. 8. Violation and refactoring for a very simple problem

The right side of Fig. 8 shows this refactoring. VisualFormatter has been moved to the "Util" layer and the violating dependencies are gone. Of cause, this refactoring is only done virtually in the tool and it is obviously a very simple refactoring.

No classes have to be redesigned and reimplemented. More complicated refactorings cannot be resolved by moving a class in the tool, but will lead to implementation work. As the final step 4 of the process of mob architecting (s. Fig. 6), the external pilot documents the refactoring on a flipchart or a whiteboard.

This process of modeling architecture, inspecting and collecting violations is an iterative process which is repeated several times during mob architecting. Not only the technical layering but also the segmentation of the system into domain modules and the use of patterns can be analyzed. Examinating different architectural views with the entire team stimulates discussion and helps the team inspecting their system quickly and on a high level.

Finally, the collected refactorings are prioritized and the improvements of the software architecture will be scheduled for the subsequent iterations.

4 Summary

In this paper, I have shown how pair programming, mob programming and mob architecting can help your team keeping their system's architecture in good shape without technical debts. Three levels of quality improvements have been presented and the value of each of these techniques have been discussed. Applying these techniques to development teams can help them improving their overall understanding of their software architecture and spark architectural discussions. More information on the various techniques of mob architecting can be found in my book "Langlebige Softwarearchitekturen" an English version is in preparation.

References

1. Cunningham, W.: The WyCash portfolio management system. Experience report, OOPSLA 1992 (1992)
2. Lilienthal, C.: Langlebige Softwarearchitektur, Technische Schulden analysieren, begrenzen und abbauen, dpunkt.verlag (2015). English version in preparation
3. Martin, R.C.: Principle and Patterns (2000). http://www.objectmentor.com/resources/articles/Principles_and_Patterns.pdf
4. Beck, K.: Extreme Programming Explained: Embrace Change. Addison-Wesley, Boston (1999)
5. Succi, G., Marchesi, M.: Extreme Programming Examined (XP). Addison-Wesley, Boston (2001)
6. Jansson, P.: Get a good start with mob programming. https://thecuriousdeveloper.com/2013/09/15/get-a-good-start-with-mob-programming/. Accessed 25 Aug 2016
7. Obermüller, K., Campbell, J.: Mob Programming - the Good, the Bad and the Great. http://underthehood.meltwater.com/blog/2016/06/01/mob-programming/. Accessed 29 Aug 2016

Model-Driven Development
and Configuration Management

Traceability in a Fine Grained Software Configuration Management System

Martin Eyl[1]([✉]), Clemens Reichmann[1], and Klaus Müller-Glaser[2]

[1] Vector Informatik GmbH, Ingersheimer Straße 24, 70499 Stuttgart, Germany
Martin.eyl@vector.com
[2] Karlsruhe Institute of Technology (KIT), 76128 Karlsruhe, Germany

Abstract. Traceability between artefacts from different domains (e.g. requirements management or test data management) is important in the software development process. Therefore modern application lifecycle management solutions support traceability links between these artefacts. But the support of traceability links into the source code is still very rudimentary or does not exist at all, although the source code is of central importance. Traceability links between artefacts in a repository and source code can break very easily when changing the text. To solve this problem we store the source code as Abstract Syntax Tree (AST) in a repository. A special editor for the source code, which supports refactoring, makes robust traceability between the AST artefacts and other artefacts possible. The repository provides the version history of all AST artefacts including their traceability links for a better understanding of changes over time. This paper introduces an implementation of such a system based on Eclipse.

Keywords: Traceability · Fine grained software configuration management system · Abstract syntax tree

1 Introduction

The importance of traceability between development artefacts created during the software development life-cycle is well understood and incorporated in numerous software development standards [1]. Traceability, in particular requirements traceability, has received quite a lot of attention from the research community [2–7]. Traceability links from the requirement into the source code are crucial and can help to answer among others the following questions [6]: Where can I find the source code, which implements this requirement? Do all functional requirements have a concrete implementation? Why has this source code been developed? But not only requirements traceability requires links into the source code. There are more important use cases: Which defects have been fixed in this "if-statement" in the source code (Change Management)? Where can I find the source code for the automated tests which verify this requirement (Test Data Management)? Is there any additional documentation or a UML diagram for this class available (Design and Documentation) [8]?

Some commercial application lifecycle management solutions (e.g. Polarion Software [9] or Rational Team Concert [10]) integrate several domains in one application

© Springer International Publishing AG 2017
D. Winkler et al. (Eds.): SWQD 2017, LNBIP 269, pp. 15–29, 2017.
DOI: 10.1007/978-3-319-49421-0_2

and in one repository. These applications support the creation of traceability links between artefacts of different domains e.g. between test data management and requirement management. But the support of traceability links into the source code is still rudimentary. Very common is the possibility to link a requirement to a set of source code files which has been changed for the requirement. At most traceability links to classes [7] are supported. The reason is that the smallest unit stored in the source code configuration management systems is a file which usually contains a class. A traceability link into the text is difficult to maintain because by changing the text the link can break.

A Java class contains fields and methods. A method contains statements like a "for loop" or an "if statement". At least for all of these artefacts traceability links should be possible. In addition the expectation towards a software configuration management system is that the complete history of these artefacts including the traceability links can be retrieved. Fine granular traceability links are needed because of the following reasons:

- The traceability between a test case and a method of a unit test in the source code is important because of the following reason: If the test case is linked with a requirement (test case tests the requirement), it is possible to find all test methods in the source code which verifies a certain requirement.
- Usually not only one requirement is implemented in a Java class. This would be too restrictive. Different methods might be linked to different requirements. Over time after several changes and refactorings (for example moving statements to another class) there is the need for traceability links between requirements and single statements otherwise we would lose the information why this statement has been developed.
- The software developer is not only interested in the last reason for change of the statement but also the developer wants to know all requirements and defects which caused a statement to be changed over the complete history regardless of how often the statement has already been moved in the source code between different classes and methods.
- Documents (e.g. an activity diagram or an image) which are linked to only parts of a class can provide additional information for a better understanding of the source code. For example a presentation explaining an algorithm can be linked to the "for loop" which implements the algorithm.

In order to support this kind of fine granular traceability links into the source code and to benefit from the links the following concepts are needed:

1. A consistent metamodel which allows us to define traceability links between different artefacts and the source code. This can be achieved by defining a metamodel for the source code.
2. An editor which allows us to change the source code without losing the traceability links into the source code.
3. Very good support for creating and maintaining the traceability links to keep expense low for the developer.
4. Visualization of the traceability links during the development of the source code in the source code editor.

These concepts have been implemented in a prototype called Morpheus. Morpheus is an extension for the Eclipse Integrated Development Environment (IDE) [11]. We did not want to develop a new IDE and therefore one major goal was that the software developer still can use all the powerful features of a standard IDE including the management of the projects and the Java editor.

2 Metamodel

For all domains in the software development process it is useful to define a metamodel with meta classes like requirement, test specification, test case, or ticket and traceability links between these meta classes. Often the following two solutions are used to store traceability links from the artefacts of these domains into the source code:

1. The full qualified name for example in Java the package name, class name and the method name are stored with the artefact. If the developer for example renames the method, all traceability links to this method have to be searched and updated. This can be quite expensive and complex. Also it is not possible to store links to source code which does not have an explicit name for example a "for loop" or an "if statement". As well it is difficult and costly to follow the link from the source code to the artefact.
2. The directory name, the file name and the line number are stored with the artefact. But this information is only valid for a certain version of the file (which also has to be stored with the artefact) because with every change in the file the line number can get invalid. So, we can only follow the traceability link to a certain version of the file in the history and actually we have no information where the link points to in the current version of the file.

Surely it would make a lot more sense if everything including the source code could be defined as one consistent metamodel. Then all traceability links could be handled in the same way whether the traceability link points into the source code or not. The solution is to integrate the Abstract Syntax Tree (AST) of Java into the entire metamodel. The complete model including all requirements, test cases, tickets and all AST artefacts can then be stored into one data backbone. The goal is to define one metamodel for all aspects of the software development process with traceability links between the meta classes. The links are bidirectional and can be traced with little effort.

For Morpheus we used the Meta Data Framework (MDF) of PREEvision [12–14]. MDF is based on the OMG's Meta Object Facility (MOF) Standard [15]. MDF provides an editor for defining the metamodel and to generate the Java source code for the model. We also use the data backbone of PREEvision to persist the model. The client of PREEvision is based on Eclipse and so several plugins of PREEvision are used to load and store the model and to visualize the model in the graphical user interface. Also parts of the metamodel of PREEvision are reused (e.g. requirements or tickets).

2.1   Metamodel Generator

The Java AST metamodel can be derived from the Java Language Specification of Oracle [16]. By doing this manually many errors can creep into such a metamodel. To avoid this we developed a metamodel generator, which allows us to generate a MDF metamodel from the Backus-Naur Format (BNF).

Eclipse has a lot of functionality regarding parsing and processing of Java source code. Eclipse provides a Java AST and an AST parser, which creates an AST from a source code file. To use these and other functions, it is beneficial if the metamodel is very similar to the Eclipse AST. Therefore we extended the metamodel generator so that it is also possible to process the Eclipse Java AST classes as input and to generate a suitable metamodel. With this additional feature of the generator it is now possible to use the MDF metamodel with the Eclipse functionality.

2.2   Traceability into the Source Code

In the first version of Morpheus we have considered the following use cases in the metamodel.

Test Data Management. The *TestSpecification* describes how functional require-ments must be tested in order to ensure the quality of the software (see Fig. 1). It is created in natural language regardless of the test implementation. Typically, the *Tes-tItem*s include different use cases and they are linked to the corresponding *Require-ments* and *Tickets*.

A *Ticket* can be a change request or a defect. To ensure that a defect will not reappear in the next releases and to increase the test coverage of the automated tests it makes sense to create a test for a defect. A *Requirement* represents not the complete requirement specification but only one single requirement within a specification. The requirement has to be specific and it is written in natural language. Usually the requirement is a functional requirement which can be expressed directly in source code.

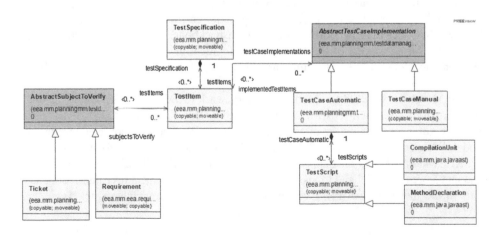

Fig. 1. The metamodel for test data management

The *Requirement*s can be hierarchically structured in requirement packages which build up a complete requirement specification.

Test implementations are provided for the specified test items, which can be brought to execution. A test implementation is a manual test which is executed by a human tester (*TestCaseManual*) or an automated test (*TestCaseAutomatic*). The automated tests can then be linked to a compilation unit (e.g. unit test class) or a method of a compilation unit. The meta classes *CompilationUnit* and *MethodDeclaration* are AST artefacts. The *MethodDeclaration* is contained below a *CompilationUnit*. If the software developer renames or moves a test method to another unit test class the traceability link to the test case and therefore also to the *Requirement* or *Ticket* survives. The *TestCaseAutomatic* is linked to the *CompilationUnit* or the *MethodDeclaration* because the complete test class or the test method can be executed during automated test execution.

Traceability links can be traced in both direction and so it is possible to find all automated test code for a requirement or ticket and it is possible to see which requirement or ticket is tested by a certain test method or test class.

Requirement and Change Management. The meta class *ASTNode* is the base class of all AST artefacts in the metamodel (see Fig. 2). When the developer changes the source code, already existing AST artefacts are changed or deleted and new AST artefacts are created. This set of AST artefacts is put into the *ChangedArtefactSet* which is connected to a *Requirement* or *Ticket*. Therefore traceability between the reason for change (requirement and ticket) and the changed source code is possible in both directions.

With every change of an AST artefact a traceability link to a requirement or ticket is created. There can be more than one requirement because the source code can be relevant for different requirements. For the requirements all test methods can be identified. All this information together (source code – requirement – test method) can be used to determine which automated tests should be executed when source code (AST artefacts) has been changed. This test selection strategy can be very useful during Continuous Integration (CI) to determine which automated tests shall be executed for the committed source code [17].

Documentation. The source code can be documented by comments in the source code text. But the software developer can only use characters. Some formatting is possible with HTML tags but editing is difficult. It is not possible to use images, diagrams,

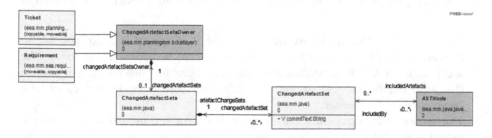

Fig. 2. The metamodel for requirement and change management

spreadsheets, or presentations. Traceability links between any kind of document containing documentation for the source code and the source code itself is a substantial improvement. Design documents can also be linked to all relevant AST artefacts.

The metamodel of MDF has the special meta class called *FileAttachment* which makes it possible to store files with the model in the data backbone (see Fig. 3). The meta class *FileAttachment* supports any document format, e.g. WinWord, Powerpoint or Excel document. The file attachment can be placed in a *SourceCodePackage* or in a *FileAttachmentPackage* contained in a *SourceCodePackage* independent from the AST artefacts. The software developer can then link the file attachment with any AST artefacts via the meta class *ModelContext* to express the relevance of the file attachment for this source code. Additional documentation stored in a *FileAttachment* can be useful for any AST artefact for example a class, a method, a statement or a field declaration. Moving the source code to another class will not break the traceability link.

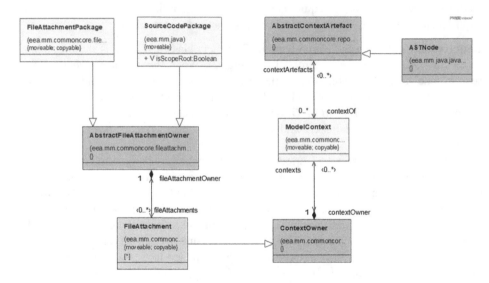

Fig. 3. The metamodel for documentation

2.3   Implications of the AST Model

The following implications have to be considered when using an AST model instead of text.

1. For editing the AST model we need a special AST editor. It is not possible to convert the AST into text and to change the text in any text editor and to convert the text back to an AST because then we could lose traceability links to the source code (for more details see next section). Therefore we need a special text editor or a complete new AST editor.
2. The syntax of Java can change with every new Java version and so a new metamodel is needed for a new Java version. The source code of Java 1.8 cannot be

stored in the metamodel for Java 1.7. Usually the changes are backwards compatible so that the source code must not be changed and a migration of the model via a model to model transformation [18] is not necessary. The metamodel will only be extended.

3. Whatever the user enters in the editor must be convertible to an AST so that it can be stored in the model. Therefore it is not possible to store certain kinds of syntax errors in the model.

4. If the user temporarily comments source code out e.g. for testing purpose, traceability links could get lost. It is of course possible to save the comment in the AST, but the original AST artefacts with possible traceability links are then deleted. After removing the comment and thereby restoring the original source code the AST artefacts are newly created without any traceability links. For such a use case a special support is needed. Here is potential for improvement for Morpheus.

3 Java Editor

A special Abstract Syntax Tree (AST) editor is needed for editing the AST model. The Java Editor of Eclipse is very powerful with many functions like syntax highlighting, code assistant, quick fix, integrated debugging and more. So, we wanted to reuse this editor and only extend the functionality for editing the AST. We call this editor "Java AST Editor".

The input and output of the Java editor is text. Therefore the AST has to be converted to text before editing and the text has to be converted to an AST after editing. Thereby the following problem has to be solved (shown as an example for renaming a method): If the developer renames a method and saves the source code in the AST model, a new method declaration is created and the existing method declaration is deleted including all traceability links to this method. During saving it is impossible to know whether the developer has renamed the method or deleted a no longer needed method and created a new one. This is determined by how the user has changed the text: The developer changes the name of the method in the text or the developer deletes the text of the method and starts writing a new method. Therefore we have to keep track of the AST artefacts in the text. This is accomplished by the following features of the Java AST Editor:

- During opening the Java AST Editor the AST artefacts from the model are converted to text. For each AST artefact the start position and the length in the created text is determined and stored in the editor as mapping information. So, the editor knows for each position in the editor which AST artefacts are located on this position.
- If the developer enters new characters or deletes characters, the start position and length of the AST artefacts have to be corrected. If the changed text is located at the position of the AST artefact, the length has to be corrected. For all other AST artefacts behind the changed position, the start positions have to be adapted.
- If the developer moves text in the editor (e.g. per drag and drop), removes text via the clipboard command cut or adds text via the clipboard command insert, the start position and length of all relevant AST artefacts have to be adapted.

- If the developer copies source code text into the clipboard via the clipboard command cut, not only the text itself is put into the clipboard but also all AST artefacts contained in the text and their start positions and lengths. If the developer pastes the text back into the editor, the developer can decide whether only the text or the AST artefacts shall be used. In the first case new AST artefacts are created. In the second case the list of AST artefacts stored in the editor is updated with the information from the clipboard. So, it is possible to move source code from one class to another without losing any traceability links to the moved AST artefacts.

When the text of the editor is saved, the text is converted back to AST artefacts. These AST artefacts are then merged into the model. Why cannot the new created AST artefacts from the editor just replace the original AST artefacts in the model? The reason is that the AST artefacts from the editor do not have any traceability links which might exist in the model and these traceability links have to be merged. MDF provides a powerful merge engine which is used for this purpose. The merge engine uses the mapping information of the editor (the AST artefacts from the model and their current position in the current text) so that the AST artefacts from the editor can be matched to the AST artefacts in the current model and so a merge can be executed. The AST artefacts in the current model are then modified during the merge.

With the Java AST Editor the developer can just edit the source code as before without knowing that the source code is stored as AST artefacts in a model. But the Java AST Editor cannot really know what the developer intends to do. Does the developer want to modify a method although the developer deletes the text of the method and creates a new one with the same name? Does the developer want to create a new method although the developer just changes the name of the method? So the developer must be aware that AST artefacts with traceability links are edited and the developer must understand when a method will be created, changed or deleted: As long as the developer is not deleting the text of the method and is only changing text, no new method is created and the current method will be changed. With this knowledge the developer can change the text in the proper way according to his or her intentions.

Via the clipboard it is possible to copy source code. In this case new AST artefacts are created. The developer can decide whether to take over the traceability links from the copied source code or not.

4   Traceability Link Creation and Visualization

In the first version of Morpheus the focus was on supporting the software developer for traceability link creation and visualization. For the roles test manager, product manager or project manager additional functionality and additional reports are possible and useful.

4.1   Test Data Management and Documentation

Traceability Link Creation. PREEvision provides a view called "Model View" (1) (see Fig. 4) which shows all artefacts of the currently loaded model. This view is

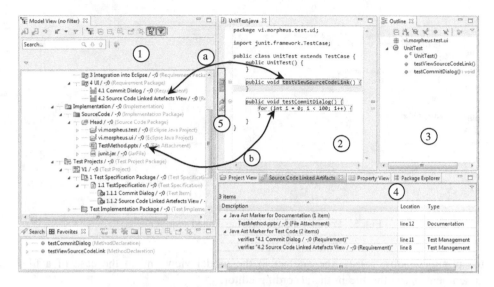

Fig. 4. Support of drag and drop to create links

integrated into the Eclipse Integrated Development Environment (IDE). The Java AST Editor (2) knows for every cursor position the corresponding Abstract Syntax Tree (AST) artefact. Therefore drag and drop into the editor or out of the editor is possible.

If the developer wants to document that the newly created method "testView-SourceCodeLink" verifies the requirement "Source Code Linked Artefacts View", then the developer drags the requirement from the model view into the editor and drops it onto the method (a). Alternatively the developer can also drag the text with the name of the method onto the requirement in the model view. It is also possible to use the "Outline" view (3) as drop target or as a starting point of a drag and drop operation. After dropping the requirement on the test method declaration Morpheus creates automatically a test specification (if not already existing), a test item and a test case in the model and links all the artefacts including the method declaration. Of course the developer can also use an existing test item or test case for the drag and drop operation.

A similar drag and drop operation can be executed with the file attachment with the difference that the file attachment can be dropped on any AST artefact and not only on a method declaration (b). Again both directions from model view into the Java AST Editor or from the Java AST Editor into the model view are possible.

Traceability Link Visualization. For the traceability link visualization in the Java AST Editor the marker functionality of Eclipse has been used. The traceability link markers are shown in the "Source Code Linked Artefacts" view (4) and on the marker bar (5) in the editor area (see Fig. 4). By double clicking on a traceability link marker in the view the according source code text is highlighted and the linked artefact in the model view is selected. By clicking on the icon in the marker bar a list of all linked artefacts is displayed in a popup window and a tool tip for each artefact provides additional, detailed information (see Fig. 5). Double clicking on the linked artefact in

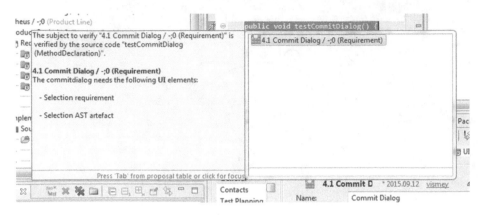

Fig. 5. Popup window showing linked requirements

the popup window selects the artefact in the model view and in the case of a file attachment opens the file in the according editor.

The relevant information (requirement, ticket or document) for the method or the current line of source code is directly available without switching to a different application and without searching for the information. The deletion of a traceability link can be done via a context menu in the "Source Code Linked Artefacts" view.

4.2   Requirement and Change Management

Traceability Link Creation. For the traceability between requirement and the source code implementing the requirement, links are needed between these artefacts. Similarly traceability links can be created between tickets and the changed source code which solves the ticket. Morpheus handles requirement and ticket equally. So, in this section the term requirement can also be replaced by ticket.

The effort to link these artefacts can be enormous if it is done after the development task has already been finished. The best time to create this traceability link is during the commit of the changed source code [7]. The commit stores the changes in the data backbone and makes them available for all users. The developer has to provide the reason for change by selecting the requirement which can be done in the commit dialog. Additionally a commit comment can be entered. If the developer works in parallel on several requirements, the developer has to select more than one requirement and has to decide which changed AST artefact belongs to which requirement. This can also be done in the commit dialog.

Mylyn [19] is used to simplify this task for the developer. Mylyn is a task management tool for software developers integrated into Eclipse. The tasks are usually imported from an application lifecycle management repository. In our case each requirement or ticket in the model represents a task and they are imported into Mylyn if these artefacts are assigned to the current developer. The developer can activate a task in

Mylyn at the beginning of his or her work. Mylyn keeps then track of all touched artefacts by creating a context for this task. During the commit Morpheus retrieves this information from Mylyn (each task with its touched artefacts) and determines the correct mapping between requirements and the relevant changed AST artefacts. If the developer uses Mylyn then there is no additional effort during the commit of the source code.

With every commit of source code a *ChangedArtefactSet* is created with the following information: author, date of commit, commit comment and all changed AST artefacts. Morpheus links the *ChangedArtefactSet* with the selected requirement or ticket.

Traceability Link Visualization. Eclipse provides the functionality to display an annotation bar in the editor area. In the Java editor this annotation bar is used to show information about the last modifications in the source code. This information is retrieved from the Software Configuration Management (SCM) system. Besides the author and the change date also the commit comment is displayed in a popup window. The color of the annotation represents the author (different colors for different authors) or the date (newer changes are displayed in a lighter color).

For Morpheus the annotation bar has been modified in such a way that the necessary information is now retrieved from the model. The traceability link from the source code to the requirement or ticket can now be used to retrieve title and content of these artefacts which are displayed in the annotation bar (1) and in a popup window (2) in addition to author, change date and commit comment (see Fig. 6). Different colors are used for different requirements or tickets.

The annotation bar of the Java editor can only show information about the last modification for a line in the source code text. Although it is possible to compare two

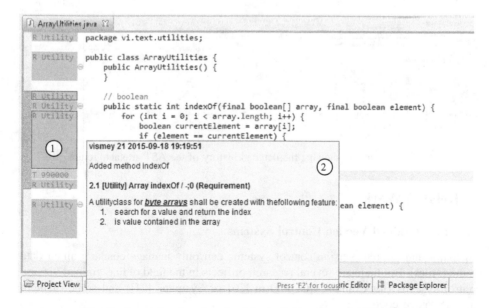

Fig. 6. Annotation bar showing history information of AST nodes

arbitrary file versions from the history, a single AST artefact in two versions cannot be compared. Eclipse is not able to find the matching AST artefacts because position and/or name in the file might have changed. A typically use case is the following: the developer wants to know when, why and who has changed the "for loop" in the last two years. By comparing different versions of the file the developer can try to find the "for loop" in the older versions of the file which can be very time-consuming and difficult. If the "for loop" has been moved from one file to another file then the developer has to check all committed files to find the "for loop". The more changes (beside the change in the "for loop") have been made in the different versions of the file the more difficult it is to find the relevant source code text.

Morpheus knows the exact history of any AST artefact because not only the latest version is stored in the data backbone but also every committed version can be retrieved from the data backbone. Via the context menu in the annotation bar or directly in the editor the developer can receive detailed information about the history of an AST artefact (see Fig. 7). In the popup window every commit, where the AST artefact has been changed, is displayed in a list (in this example for the "return" statement) with the information who has changed it and when was it changed. A tool tip window contains information about the linked requirements and tickets with the reason for change.

Two entries in the list (two versions of the AST artefact) can be selected and can then be compared. For this the complete compilation unit, where the AST artefact is contained, is loaded from the data backbone and converted to source code text for both selected versions. The source code text can then be displayed in the compare editor of Eclipse. If the AST artefact has been moved from one compilation unit to another, two different compilation units are loaded and compared with the AST artefact in two different versions.

Fig. 7. Popup window showing the detailed history of the AST artefact "return −1"

5   Related Work

5.1   Fine-Grained Version Control Systems

All major and popular version control systems can only manage coarse grained data chunks (files). But there are several research projects in the field of fine-grained version control systems (for example COOP/Orm [20] or Sysiphus [21]) and some of them support source code.

MolhadoRef [22] is a refactoring-aware software configuration management system. It stores program entities (classes, fields and methods) in nodes, slots and attributes and records the refactoring operations that change them. A node represents a program entity and a slot holds the values. Attributes map nodes to slots. The recorded operations are replayed to transform one version to another. So, the history of refactored program elements can be tracked. The generic versioned data model of MolhadoRef allows storing programs in different languages. A concrete implementation for Java with an integration into Eclipse has been developed. MolhadoRef does not support AST artefacts below a method and provides no traceability functionality.

Stellation [23] is a software configuration system which supports fine (method level) storage granularity by using so called fragments. One key feature is the multi-dimensional program organization which allows multiple overlapping viewpoints of the fragments instead of having only one viewpoint which is dominated by the layout in source code files. Therefore Stellation provides a query language which allows the developer to search the repository for relevant fragments and present the result in a source-file like form. Stellation (as well as MolhadoRef) does not support traceability to requirements, tests or documentation and does not include any AST artefacts below a method.

5.2 Traceability

UNICASE Trace Client [6] is a tool which provides a traceability information model consisting of artefacts from requirements engineering, project management and source code and traceability links between these artefacts. The capturing of the traceability links between requirements, work items and code has been solved similar to Morpheus and is done during the commit of the source code into the software configuration management system. Refactoring of a class (rename, delete, split up or unite classes) is supported. UNICASE Trace Client supports only traceability links to classes. Links below class level are not possible.

5.3 Domain-Specific Language (DSL) Development Environment

JetBrains Meta Programming System (MPS) [24] is an environment for language engineering which allows to create own domain-specific languages. MPS can also be used for Java. The editor of MPS is called a projectional editor because the Abstract Syntax Tree (AST) is edited and not text. The developer is not completely free to enter any text. The entered text must be transformable to an AST. Every AST artefact has a unique identifier and refactoring is possible without losing the identity of the AST artefact. The development environment stores the AST of one software module in an XML file on the hard disc or in a software configuration management system (for example Subversion [25]). The history of an AST artefact is expensive to calculate and traceability links are not supported. The support of traceability links would be difficult because the AST artefacts exist only inside the XML files.

6 Conclusion and Future Work

In this paper we presented Morpheus as an extension of Eclipse which allows the software developer to create fine granular traceability links into the source code to support traceability between source code and requirements, defects, test cases and documentation. Morpheus supports refactoring of the source code (e.g. renaming or moving of source code) so that the traceability links will not break. This is achieved by integrating the Abstract Syntax Tree (AST) of Java into the model and by using a text editor which is aware of the AST artefacts. The model can be stored in a data backbone. With Morpheus integrated into Eclipse all features of Eclipse can still be used as usual.

We are currently working on the following improvements: Firstly, syntax errors in the source code stored in the data backbone shall be prevented. Without any syntax errors in the model the application can always be built and continuous integration will no longer fail because of syntax errors. Some types of syntax errors are not possible because the source code is stored as AST. But other syntax errors can even exist in an AST for example a method invocation with wrong parameter types.

Secondly, we plan to avoid the effort for merging source code. When several developers change the same code, they have to merge their changes and this is costly and error-prone.

References

1. Cleland-Huang, J., Gotel, O., Zisman, A.: Software and Systems Traceability, vol. 2. Springer, Heidelberg (2012)
2. Gotel, O.C.Z., Finkelstein, A.C.W.: An analysis of the requirements traceability problem. In: Proceedings of the First International Conference on Requirements Engineering. IEEE (1994)
3. Pinheiro, F.A.C.: Requirements traceability. In: do Prado Leite, J.C.S., Doorn, J.H. (eds.) Perspectives on Software Requirements. Kluwer International Series in Engineering and Computer Science, pp. 91–114. Springer, Heidelberg (2004)
4. Bacchelli, A., Lanza, M., Robbes, R.: Linking e-mails and source code artifacts. In: Proceedings of the 32nd ACM/IEEE International Conference on Software Engineering, vol. 1. ACM (2010)
5. Corley, C.S., et al.: Recovering traceability links between source code and fixed bugs via patch analysis. In: Proceedings of the 6th International Workshop on Traceability in Emerging Forms of Software Engineering. ACM (2011)
6. Egyed, A., Grunbacher, P.: Automating requirements traceability: beyond the record & replay paradigm. In: 17th IEEE International Conference on Proceedings of the Automated Software Engineering, ASE 2002. IEEE (2002)
7. Delater, A., Paech, B.: Tracing requirements and source code during software development: an empirical study. In: 2013 ACM/IEEE International Symposium on Empirical Software Engineering and Measurement. IEEE (2013)
8. Marcus, A., Maletic, J.: Recovering documentation-to-source-code traceability links using latent semantic indexing. In: 25th International Conference on Proceedings of the Software Engineering. IEEE (2003)

9. Inc., Siemens: Application Lifecycle Management (ALM), Requirements Management, QA Management | Polarion Software (2016). http://www.polarion.com/. Accessed 30 July 2016
10. IBM: IBM - Rational Team Concert (2016). http://www-03.ibm.com/software/products/de/rtc. Accessed 30 July 2016
11. Foundation, Eclipse: Eclipse Neon (2016). http://eclipse.org. Accessed 30 July 2016
12. Vector Informatik GmbH: PREEvision – Development Tool for model-based E/E Engineering (2016). https://vector.com/vi_preevision_en.html. Accessed 30 July 2016
13. Matheis, J.: Abstraktionsebenenübergreifende Darstellung von Elektrik/Elektronik-Architekturen in Kraftfahrzeugen zur Ableitung von Sicherheitszielen nach ISO 26262. Shaker (2010)
14. Zhang, R., Krishnan, A.: Using delta model for collaborative work of industrial large-scaled E/E architecture models. In: Whittle, J., Clark, T., Kühne, T. (eds.) MODELS 2011. LNCS, vol. 6981, pp. 714–728. Springer, Heidelberg (2011). doi:10.1007/978-3-642-24485-8_52
15. OMG: OMG's MetaObject Facility (MOF) Home Page (2016). http://www.omg.org/mof/. Accessed 30 July 2016
16. Oracle: Java SE Specifications (2016). https://docs.oracle.com/javase/specs/. Accessed 30 July 2016
17. Eyl, M., Reichmann, C., Müller-Glaser, K.: Fast feedback from automated tests executed with the product build. In: Winkler, D., Biffl, S., Bergsmann, J. (eds.) SWQD 2016. LNBIP, vol. 238, pp. 199–210. Springer, Heidelberg (2016). doi:10.1007/978-3-319-27033-3_14
18. Reichmann, C.: Grafisch notierte Modell-zu-Modell-Transformationen für den Entwurf eingebetteter elektronischer Systeme. Shaker (2005)
19. Kersten, M.: Eclipse Mylyn Open Source Project (2016). http://www.eclipse.org/mylyn/. Accessed 30 July 2016
20. Asklund, U.: Configuration management for distributed development in an integrated environment. Lund University (2002)
21. Bruegge, B., Dutoit, A.H., Wolf, T.: Sysiphus: Enabling informal collaboration in global software development. In: International Conference on Global Software Engineering, ICGSE 2006. IEEE (2006)
22. Dig, D., et al.: MolhadoRef: a refactoring-aware software configuration management tool. In: Companion to the 21st ACM SIGPLAN Symposium on Object-Oriented Programming Systems, Languages, and Applications. ACM (2006)
23. Chu-Carroll, M.C., Wright, J., Shields, D.: Supporting aggregation in fine grained software configuration management. In: Proceedings of the 10th ACM SIGSOFT symposium on Foundations of software Engineering. ACM (2002)
24. JetBrains: MPS overview (2016). https://www.jetbrains.com/mps. Accessed 30 July 2016
25. Collins-Sussman, B., Fitzpatrick, B., Pilato, M.: Version Control with Subversion. O'Reilly Media Inc., Sebastopol (2004)

Software Development and Quality Assurance

From Agile Development to DevOps: Going Towards Faster Releases at High Quality – Experiences from an Industrial Context

Frank Elberzhager[1(✉)], Taslim Arif[1],
Matthias Naab[1], Inge Süß[2], and Sener Koban[2]

[1] Fraunhofer Institute for Experimental Software Engineering IESE,
Fraunhofer-Platz 1, 67663 Kaiserslautern, Germany
{frank.elberzhager, taslim.arif,
matthias.naab}@iese.fraunhofer.de
[2] Fujitsu Enabling Software Technology GmbH,
Schwanthalerstraße 75A, 80336 Munich, Germany
{inge.suess, sener.koban}@est.fujitsu.com

Abstract. DevOps promises advantages, such as faster time-to-market or higher quality. A company transforming itself towards DevOps needs guidance in order to ask and answer relevant questions and not waste time and effort. We state four key issues that companies should discuss before they start introducing DevOps concepts. Furthermore, we report on a project conducted by Fujitsu Enabling Software Technology GmbH (Fujitsu EST) and Fraunhofer IESE where the introduction of DevOps for one product was accompanied for roughly one year. We present the concrete goals, the procedure, first results, as well as observations and lessons learned. To the best of our knowledge, this is one of the first contributions that describe practical experiences in introducing DevOps, without concealing that a lot of thinking, tailoring, and learning is still required to further improve DevOps in the environment.

Keywords: Continuous delivery · Continuous integration · DevOps · Deployment pipeline · DevOps introduction · DevOps culture · Industrial experience · Software architecture

1 Introduction

DevOps is an artificial word, composed of Development and Operations. DevOps became famous in 2009 after it was first coined by Patrick Debois during the so-called DevOpsDays [3]. Its main intention is to remove the barriers between development and operations. Thompson and Shafter call this the "wall of confusion" that has to be removed [1]. Idena et al. [2] describe a study where they derived 66 issues between development and IT operations, and narrowed them down to six severe problems, including poor communication and unsatisfactory test environments. By addressing such problems, DevOps promises several benefits, such as faster time to market, better communication, less friction, or high-quality products [10]. Cultural change is one important factor that has to be considered in order to be able to achieve the benefits of

© Springer International Publishing AG 2017
D. Winkler et al. (Eds.): SWQD 2017, LNBIP 269, pp. 33–44, 2017.
DOI: 10.1007/978-3-319-49421-0_3

DevOps; here, the whole organization has to think about how to realize such a change in its mindset. Of course, this is a rather long-term process, which is why it is important to think carefully about how to achieve this. Furthermore, several technical concepts and tools that support DevOps have to be considered, as well as process changes for development, operations, and quality assurance, and even changes in the software product itself, especially the architecture.

An analysis of the current state-of-the-art and the state-of-the-practice revealed that the number of articles describing the introduction of DevOps is rather low. For example, a literature study by Erich et al. in 2014 resulted in only 25 relevant papers, listed and classified according to different DevOps topics (e.g., culture, automation, or measurement) [4]. Balalaie, for example, presents practical experiences from a migration to a microservice architecture in order to enable DevOps [7], but such articles are rare.

DevOps is not the same for all organizations. We identified four key questions that an organization has to answer before launching DevOps activities on a larger scale: (1) What are the goals to be achieved with DevOps in our organization? (2) What is our introduction strategy for DevOps? (3) What should be developed and operated by whom? (4) What is the impact on our architecture? Not dealing with these questions will nearly always lead to a waste of time and money. In this paper, we will describe the four key questions in more detail and share experiences from the specific context of Fujitsu EST, where such a DevOps journey was initiated. We will derive lessons learned to share our main experiences from which others can also learn.

Section 2 sketches the preparation and gives answers to the four mentioned questions. Section 3 explains the concrete industrial context and shows the main results. Section 4 concludes the paper with a summary and outlook.

2   Guiding the Introduction of DevOps with Key Questions

When starting with DevOps, many aspects have to be kept in mind, and companies often do not know how to start with their DevOps journey. If the motivation and several other facets regarding the project, the product, and the organization are not clearly understood, the journey might be a failure or a waste of resources. In this section, we will present four key questions that need to be clearly understood and answered before starting DevOps, without claiming that these are the only ones. They will help companies to define a structured way of introducing DevOps. These questions were defined at the beginning of our joined project, and we learned how to answer them in detail during our experiences made throughout the project.

2.1   Q1: What Are the Goals to Be Achieved in Our Organization with DevOps?

The first thing to make explicit is why you want to implement DevOps. The reasons might vary greatly from project to project and from one organization to the next. Moreover, the measures needed to address the problem would also vary drastically.

For example, one company might want to handle the pressure to release applications more quickly, whereas another company might want to improve the quality and performance of the application. It is quite obvious in both cases that the necessary measures would also be different. Identifying the problem and establishing the goal would help to identify appropriate practices, measures, and means for measuring success.

2.2   Q2: What is Our Introduction Strategy for DevOps?

To introduce DevOps in an organization, it is necessary to understand the current status of four topic areas and align them to support the DevOps goals (Table 1):

Table 1. Four topic areas to be considered for the introduction of DevOps

Topic area	Description
Processes	These include all the activities performed during the overall software development and delivery, for example development, quality assurance, release management, configuration management, or product management
Tools	This comprises all software, services, and platforms used in the overall process to deliver software. Tools are indispensable in DevOps as they help to automate activities, resulting in continuous delivery
Organization	This means the company that is building the product, its internal structure, team characteristics, decision making process, and overall culture
Architecture	This is the blueprint of the system. In particular, the decomposition of the system, the assignment to teams, and the integration of components are relevant to DevOps

The introduction of DevOps requires a systemic approach considering everything from goals and business models to the required investments, changes, and time. The introduction strategy has to cover how all areas can be established or changed, knowing that this cannot be done in a big-bang approach but in an incremental way of continuous alignment.

2.3   Q3: What Should Be Developed and Operated by Whom?

In DevOps, the key issue is to remove the barriers between stakeholders, especially between development and operation. Therefore, it is important to know the overall development and operation chain and also to identify who is responsible for which part. We identified four main dimensions that will help companies to understand the context clearly. These dimensions are DevOps activity, responsibility, products, and customers. DevOps activities include development, operation of the infrastructure, operation of the platform, and operation of the application. Each activity can be done by different parties (responsibility). For example, everything could be done by the company itself, or parts could be outsourced; it could even be done by the customer or outsourced by the customer. Another dimension is the product. If the company has multiple products, the first two dimensions might vary from product to product. Therefore, it is necessary to decide for which product DevOps will be implemented. The final dimension is the customer. Every product might have several customers and for every customer the situation might be different in terms of system integration business. It is crucial to identify the initial scope of DevOps and characterize it clearly.

2.4   Q4: What is the Impact on Our Architecture and the Environment?

Achieving the goals of fast release cycles requires delivering different system components developed by separate teams independently. Otherwise, they always need to synchronize, which slows down the delivery. Conway's Law [5] is seeing a renaissance in the era of DevOps as a stronger separation of components is needed for independent delivery. So-called microservices are an architectural style that supports the goals of DevOps, but they also come with tradeoffs like potential redundancy and higher development cost. In the case of an existing software product, a detailed analysis is needed as to the degree to which it can support the goals to be achieved with the DevOps approach.

Furthermore, an environment has to be created where the defined goals can be achieved. This incorporates, for instance, understanding of DevOps and goals to be achieved, introduction of tools to improve the degree of automation, new technologies, or a changed mindset of developers and operators. For this, measurement goals should be defined and concrete qualitative and quantative data be gathered and evaluated.

3   Experiences at Fujitsu EST

For about one year, Fraunhofer IESE accompanied Fujitsu EST on its way towards DevOps, following an action research approach [9]. We discussed concepts and procedures in meetings (face-to-face and telephone meetings) and observed the progress. Furthermore, a questionnaire was provided to capture qualitative feedback about the success at the end of the project. While general goals were defined at the beginning, concrete goals, the procedure, and specific DevOps topics and technologies were selected very flexibly later. The results we present are of course only one data point, but the procedure we followed and the four questions are universal.

In the following sections, we first describe the background, then we present concrete experiences according to the four questions introduced in Sect. 2.

3.1   Fujitsu EST's Background

Fujitsu EST is a subsidiary of Fujitsu Limited, based in Munich. Its mission is to develop innovative middleware and applications for public, private, and hybrid Cloud. On the one hand, this context requires a high degree of agility and flexibility with short delivery cycles. On the other hand, the strict and substantial quality standards of Fujitsu need to be ensured and maintained in the software products.

In 2009, Fujitsu EST started to use agile methods (SCRUM) for the development of its products. The development processes and environment as well as the product management and release processes were continuously improved in the following years with the result that releases fulfilling the quality requirements could be made available basically every month.

Apart from the general goal to further improve its processes and environment, the following three events in the last two years caused Fujitsu EST to take the DevOps approach:

1. With its products, Fujitsu EST got increasingly involved in open-source and OpenStack [6] activities and projects. This resulted in requirements for even more agility, more frequent deliveries, and easy-to-use artifacts such as Docker containers.
2.1. Development of a new product, Fujitsu Cloud Service PICCO[1] (PICCO), was started. PICCO is a service offering for controlling and governing the usage and costs of services and resources in the Cloud.
2.2. Apart from selling the product to customers, Fujitsu EST intended to operate PICCO on its own as a service in the Cloud. Operation topics thus became much more important.
2.3. As the development of PICCO started from scratch under the sole responsibility of Fujitsu EST, there was a high degree of flexibility as to the product itself (architecture, features), its artifacts, delivery, and operation environment, and the team of people taking care for it. Bringing together development and operation became an option that had not been possible before.
3. With more and more companies talking about DevOps, Fujitsu as a modern IT company also started activities in this area. Fujitsu EST intended to contribute to these activities with an approach based on practical experience.

3.2   Goals (Question 1)

Together with Fraunhofer IESE, Fujitsu EST started the journey towards DevOps, with the following goals:

- Obtain a common understanding of DevOps based on state-of-the-art and state-of-the-practice analyses.
- Implement and use a DevOps environment at Fujitsu EST, including the required tooling and processes.
- Based on this practical experience, become an incubator for the Fujitsu group regarding DevOps procedures and practices.
- Provide quantitative evidence (KPIs) of how DevOps affects the performance and output of the teams, and that DevOps does not have a negative impact on the quality of the products.

---

[1] https://www.cloudservicepicco.com/.

The existing agile processes, development environment, and quality assurance procedures at Fujitsu EST were a good starting point for the DevOps activities. From the history of Fujitsu EST, the focus of these existing mechanisms was on the development area. Thus, it was clear from the beginning that improvements and changes would be required in particular in the operations part and in bringing together development and operations.

3.3   Introduction Strategy and Dimensions (Questions 2 and 3)

We started small, selecting one of four available products and their development environments at Fujitsu EST, namely PICCO. PICCO's core and data collectors were developed in Java, its front-end and UI in Angular JS. A microservice architecture was discussed: At the beginning of a project, a microservice architecture is usually less productive as it requires a significant amount of effort to create the foundation and the supporting organizational structure. But as time passes and the complexity of the product increases, the productivity of a monolithic application decreases more than that of a microservice application. As a monolithic architecture is currently in place, discussions centered on whether to change to a microservice architecture, and if so, when to do this. A final decision has not been made yet, but awareness was increased and the consequences were made clearer.

On the other hand, it was soon decided to provide and operate the product in Docker containers since these promised the flexibility required to support different environments. The team taking care of PICCO consisted of three core developers, four front-end and UI specialists, and one dedicated person for operations.

Next, business cases had to be defined, which were only sketched in our context due to PICCO being a new product where several things were still unclear. We then identified the current status of the existing development, deployment, and operations environment, identified factors that support DevOps practices as well as factors where we saw improvement potential, and derived a concrete migration plan. We decided mainly to focus on the implementation of an almost fully automated deployment pipeline and to address some further topics, such as improving quality assurance, introducing microservices, or monitoring. Based on existing best practices and experiences from other environments, we started changing the processes, selected tools, and implemented them. Based on initial experiences and feedback, we further adapted the processes and improved the environment.

Of course, not every aspect could be defined at the very beginning to a large extent, but experience had to be made first based on the described starting point and those aspects that we were able to define.

3.4   Impact on the Environment by the DevOps Introduction (Question 4)

At the beginning, we aimed at a common understanding to increase the awareness of DevOps in the given environment. Fujitsu EST wanted to introduce DevOps. However, their understanding of DevOps was not comprehensive and more information about

DevOps was gathered in order to determine the focus for concrete improvements. Existing processes and tool chains at Fujitsu EST were well documented and Fujitsu EST was well aware of how their processes were being conducted, which helped us to understand the initial situation. Fujitsu EST wanted to explore the current state of the practice and was especially interested in how other companies are using DevOps successfully. Results from an extensive collection of available and consolidated material about several topics, such as what DevOps is about, the Ops part, drivers and benefits of DevOps, the CALMS principles, a deployment pipeline, and tools, created a baseline understanding for Fujitsu EST regarding DevOps and formed the basis for further narrowing down the focus for subsequent project activities.

Not only in the specific team that started using DevOps principles and practices, but also in other teams and on the management level did the awareness for DevOps increase continuously. This was also supported by several workshops where different Fujitsu EST stakeholders discussed the current progress and possible ways for further improvement.

In the PICCO context, development and operations engineers worked together towards shared responsibility of the product. This was an important cultural change. Management and business employees were also involved with the DevOps team. Changes in the organizational structure aimed at living DevOps more strongly is a future issue.

A major result was a new deployment pipeline. Figure 1 shows the deployment pipeline we defined after the context had been evaluated. It is rather simple, as it only contains four steps:

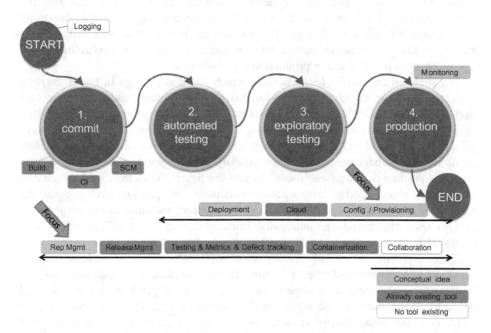

Fig. 1. Deployment pipeline with tool categories

1. Commit: Once any developer commits something to the source version control system, this stage starts. It invokes the continuous integration server that builds the application and generates artifacts. The artifacts are stored and reused in the subsequent stages. If the build fails, the developer is notified and this commit does not progress.
2. Automated Testing: The artifact that is generated in the previous stage is deployed to a testing environment. Automatic testing is done for all aspects of the software. The environment is also provisioned and configured automatically. If the tests fail, this artifact does not progress any further.
3. Exploratory Testing: Once the automatic testing stage has been passed, the artifact is deployed to an exploratory testing environment for manual testing. The environment is again created automatically. Once the tests are finished, the artifact can go to the next stage; otherwise it stops here.
4. Production: After the exploratory testing stage, the artifact is deployed to the final production environment and users can use it directly. The production environment is also created automatically. The environment is monitored. If something goes wrong, the system rolls back to a previous release. All these deployments are done following a deployment strategy. Users should ideally not experience any downtime and the transition from one release to another should be smooth.

We were aware that this could only be a starting point, but it helped the team to identify gaps in the current pipeline and to select new tools based on the collected tool requirements. We considered two explicit quality assurance steps to enforce high quality. One important point in the newly introduced DevOps process is that the artifacts are created only once and are reused across several stages. Another important improvement is that in several stages, the environment is created automatically. This is done by coding the infrastructure and the configurations. The testing environments are kept as close as possible to the production environment.

We analyzed the current tool situation, which can also be seen in Fig. 1. Several tool categories have already been considered in the environment, and specific tools do support the pipeline, such as Jenkins for CI or Docker for Containerization. Tools that are relevant in such a tool chain, but which were not being used at the time, were collected and selected based on the requirements from the concrete context. Especially a configuration management tool and a repository management tool needed to be used to get the pipeline running (see "focus" arcs in the figure). With this, we were able to achieve an almost completely automated deployment pipeline (of course, the exploratory testing step is still done manually). During the time of the project, the DevOps team also introduced automated frontend testing in PICCO, which is now integrated in the pipeline in step 2 (see Fig. 1).

Faster deployments with high quality are now possible with these implementations. About 10 min are required from a commit to the completion of automated testing. Deployment to the production stage takes about 20 min, depending on the time used for exploratory testing and the upload to the production environment in the Cloud.

Other topics being discussed were monitoring and customer feedback. Several possibilities were evaluated, e.g., feedback via surveys, feedback boxes, community groups, or analysis of social media channels. Furthermore, tools supporting app analytics that analyze, for example, click, movement, or time behavior, were presented and first experiences were made with Piwik[2].

The changes resulting from the introduction of DevOps practices, especially the new deployment pipeline, led to much faster releases, which then resulted in much faster feedback. This had a positive effect on the quality of the product, as bugs can now be found earlier by testers and new feature requests can be implemented faster. Furthermore, development and operation engineers collaborate more strongly. This led to requirements from operations that can now be considered and incorporated earlier, and to an overall better understanding of the different viewpoints. This again supports high quality of the product, less friction in the processes, and greater motivation of the employees. The mindset changes from silo thinking, where everybody mainly focuses on achieving his goals and optimizing his tasks, to team thinking, where the customer is more in the focus and where people share responsibilities so that everybody takes care of a high-quality product. Some actual statements from the DevOps team members substantiate this:

- "Development and Operations work directly together ensuring that fixes or releases can be deployed in production almost instantly."
- "The close collaboration automatically contributes to technology transfer among the team members."
- "The different perspectives are very helpful in finding new and creative solutions."

On the opposite side, there are still some obstacles to overcome.

- "[Still], DevOps is understood very differently among the people asked to define it. There are many different, and sometimes false expectations in DevOps."
- "The close collaboration tends to blur responsibilities. A shared code of conduct, a formal roles assignment, and clear and simple processes may help."
- "While living a close collaboration between development and operations, the rest of the team may not understand the new culture (e.g., requirements management, project management, product management, quality management)."
- "A different understanding of the goals to be achieved with DevOps within a project may end up in chaos and frustration."

In order to measure improvements resulting from the introduction of DevOps, metrics were defined to get a better understanding of what changed and how it changed. We started with 76 metrics from several sources (e.g., literature, own experiences), which were classified into the six categories culture, product, process, people, business, and customer. We continually refined them until we had a set of 6 top-ranked candidate metrics (see Table 2), as the initial set was too large and had to be further reduced towards the measurement goals. The refinement was done by a selection by both parties, i.e., Fujitsu EST and Fraunhofer IESE experts, considering the likelihood of a fast implementation and the goal contribution.

---

[2] http://piwik.org/.

Table 2. Selected metrics and categories

Category	Metric
Process	Deployment time and frequency
Process	Mean time to recover
People	Developer productivity
Business	Time to market for new feature
Business	Expense
Customer	Feedback cycle

Concrete calculation rules were defined for each metric. Besides product metrics, which are already in place and visualized on a dashboard, the next step is to implement the six new metrics and to gather concrete data to measure improvements. We expect concrete data soon, which will help Fujitsu EST to judge the current status and to adjust further the initiated changes towards DevOps.

As cultural aspects were considered important, but are difficult to calculate via metrics, we decided to gather such feedback directly via a questionnaire. This questionnaire consisted of three parts: (a) general information (e.g., experience with development, operations, interest in the topic), (b) DevOps-specific statements to be rated on a 5-point Likert scale, and (c) free-text fields for further feedback (e.g., experience made, risk seen). Part b consisted of 36 statements in five categories. These statements were partly taken from the standardized UTAUT questionnaire [8], but some individual statements were added gathered from people working in the Fujitsu EST PICCO environment. Eleven people filled out the questionnaire, and the overall impression regarding DevOps was rather positive.

As an example, Fig. 2 shows an excerpt, where 5 means "strongly agree" and 1 means "strongly disagree". Of the 36 DevOps statements, only two statements were rated lower than three on average, and about ten statements were rated four or higher on average. An average value of four or higher demonstrates that there was an agreement to the statement, and every value higher than three tends towards a positive perception. Many statements have at least one maximum value of 5 (i.e., strong agreement). The high median shows that many people rated rather positive, and only some negative.

DevOps statement	average	max	min	median
I find DevOps useful in my work.	4,10	5,00	3,00	4,00
Using DevOps helps me to produce better product quality.	3,82	5,00	3,00	4,00
Collaboration in our DevOps team is very good.	4,18	5,00	3,00	4,00
If there is a problem, everybody in the DevOps team takes care of it.	4,00	5,00	3,00	4,00
If there is a new customer request, everybody in the DevOps team takes care of it.	3,89	5,00	2,00	4,00
We do not live borders between Dev and Ops.	3,64	5,00	1,00	4,00
Communication within the whole DevOps team is very good.	4,09	5,00	2,00	4,00
We share responsibilities for the success of our product.	4,30	5,00	4,00	4,00
High frequency of personnel changes in the DevOps team does not affect my performance negatively.	2,64	4,00	1,00	3,00

Fig. 2. Questionnaire excerpt with summarized values showing a rather positive impression about DevOps in the Fujitsu EST environment.

Based on these results, further improvement ideas were derived (e.g., to reduce staff turnover), which are currently being discussed.

4 Summary and Outlook

DevOps has become more and more popular in the last six years. Several success cases exist, especially from large companies such as Netflix or IBM. However, shifting to DevOps is no easy task for a company, as many unanswered questions exist at the very beginning: What is the goal? What should be developed and operated by whom, and what does this mean for the architecture? What is the introduction strategy?

We discussed these questions in this paper and presented concrete results from the Fujitsu EST environment. After clarifying the initial questions, a deployment pipeline was introduced and additional DevOps practices were discussed and implemented in part.

Our main lessons learned are the following:

1. Clarification of the direction of the DevOps journey at the beginning is an indispensable step in order to ensure a structured and goal-directed procedure: The four questions we raised in this paper can provide great support for this start.
2. A common understanding of DevOps makes it easier to determine the direction for the DevOps journey: Though DevOps has several different facets, it is worthwhile discussing the topic within the company to share understanding, limitations, and opportunities of DevOps and thus avoid wrong perceptions.
3. Starting with small changes and selecting a manageable context supports the introduction of DevOps: Think about a reasonable migration plan and evaluate DevOps practices in the context of a small project.
4. Clear requirements for tools and procedures to be used in the DevOps environment must be gathered: This allows finding and choosing the appropriate tools and processes from the multitude that exist already and that newly emerge in the market and in the Cloud.
5. Criteria for measuring success need to be defined: To understand the benefits better, it is worthwhile thinking about how to measure an improvement and to use something like a dashboard to make these metrics and data visible.
6. Not only Dev and Ops, but management as well as further stakeholders must be involved: This helps to really start living the DevOps culture and increases acceptance of cultural changes.
7. Several DevOps practices serve to achieve high quality: explicit automated and manual testing steps in a deployment pipeline, strong communication between development and operations, early consideration of operations requirements, knowledge sharing in a joint DevOps team, high automation of several tasks, and high motivation of DevOps team members.

With all the enthusiasm about DevOps, it must be kept in mind that the introduction does not come for free. Sometimes, time constraints occurred in our context due to daily work duties, and not every concept was implemented right now. DevOps is also not suitable for every product or environment. Particularly with products that are installed and operated on premise at a customer site, there may be boundaries between development and operations that cannot be overcome. For legacy products with a monolithic structure or for products with many manual tests but only a few automated ones, the costs of introducing DevOps may outweigh the benefits by far. The level of maturity of a company in agile development practices and environments is also a decisive factor in the introduction of DevOps. The lower this level is, the more costs and efforts are required for setting up the processes and deployment pipelines for DevOps. These aspects must be analyzed before starting the journey towards DevOps as not to waste time and money.

In the Fujitsu EST context, we plan to further implement DevOps practices and to measure the success in order to have a profound basis for determining how to continue the DevOps journey.

Acknowledgment. We would like to thank all people from the Fujitsu EST DevOps team for their participation, and Torsten Lenhart and Sonnhild Namingha for proofreading.

References

1. http://dev2ops.org/2010/02/what-is-devops. Accessed June 2016
2. Idena, J., Tessemb, B., Päivärintac, T.: Problems in the interplay of development and IT operations in system development projects: a Delphi study of Norwegian IT experts. IST J. **53**(4), 394–406 (2011)
3. www.devopsdays.org. Accessed June 2016
4. Erich, F., Amrit, C., Daneva, M.: Cooperation between software development and operations: a literature review. ESEM (2014). Article no. 69
5. Newman, S.: Demystifying Conway's Law (2014). https://www.thoughtworks.com/de/insights/blog/demystifying-conways-law. Accessed June 2016
6. www.openstack.org. Accessed June 2016
7. Balalaie, A., Heydarnoori, A., Jamshidi. P.: Microservices architecture enables DevOps: an experience report on migration to a cloud-native architecture. IEEE Softw. (2016)
8. Venkatesh, V., Morris, M.G., Davis, G.B., Davis, F.D.: User acceptance of information technology: toward a unified view. MIS Q. **27**(3), 425–478 (2003)
9. Runeson, P., Höst, M.: Guidelines for conducting and reporting case study research in S.E. Empir. Softw. Eng. J. **14**(2), 131–164 (2009)
10. Zhu, L., Bass, L., Champlin-Scharff, G.: DevOps and its practices. IEEE Softw. **33**, 32–34 (2016)

Learning to Rank Extract Method Refactoring Suggestions for Long Methods

Roman Haas[1]([✉]) and Benjamin Hummel[2]

[1] Technical University of Munich, Lichtenbergstr. 8, Garching, Germany
roman.haas@tum.de
[2] CQSE GmbH, Lichtenbergstr. 8, Garching, Germany
hummel@cqse.eu

Abstract. Extract method refactoring is a common way to shorten long methods in software development. It improves code readability, reduces complexity, and is one of the most frequently used refactorings. Nevertheless, sometimes developers refrain from applying it because identifying an appropriate set of statements that can be extracted into a new method is error-prone and time-consuming.

In a previous work, we presented a method that could be used to automatically derive extract method refactoring suggestions for long Java methods, that generated useful suggestions for developers. The approach relies on a scoring function that ranks all valid refactoring possibilities (that is, all *candidates*) to identify suitable candidates for an extract method refactoring that could be suggested to developers. Even though the evaluation has shown that the suggestions are useful for developers, there is a lack of understanding of the scoring function. In this paper, we present research on the single scoring features, and their importance for the ranking capability. In addition, we evaluate the ranking capability of the suggested scoring function, and derive a better and less complex one using learning to rank techniques.

Keywords: Learning to rank · Refactoring suggestion · Extract method refactoring · Long method

1 Introduction

A long method is a bad smell in software systems [2], and makes code harder to read, understand and test. A straight-forward way of shortening long methods is to extract parts of them into a new method. This procedure is called 'extract method refactoring', and is the most often used refactoring in practice [16].

The process of extracting a method can be partially automated by using modern development environments, such as Eclipse IDE or IntelliJ IDEA, that can put a set of extractable statements into a new method. However, developers still need to find this set of statements by themselves, which takes a considerable amount of time, and is error-prone. This is because even experienced developers sometimes select statements that cannot be extracted (for example, when several

© Springer International Publishing AG 2017
D. Winkler et al. (Eds.): SWQD 2017, LNBIP 269, pp. 45–56, 2017.
DOI: 10.1007/978-3-319-49421-0_4

output parameters are required, but are not supported by the programming language) [11].

The refactoring process can be improved by suggesting to developers which statements could be extracted into a new method. The literature presents several approaches that can be used to find extract method refactorings. In a previous work, we suggested a method that could be used to automatically find good extract method refactoring candidates for long Java methods [3]. Our first prototype, which was derived from manual experiments on several open source systems, implemented a scoring function to rank refactoring candidates. The result of our evaluation has shown that this first prototype finds suggestions that are followed by experienced developers. The results of our first prototype have been implemented in an industrial software quality analysis tool.

Problem statement. The scoring function is an essential part of our approach to derive extract method refactoring suggestions for long methods. It is decisive for the quality of our suggestions, and also important for the complexity of the implementation of the refactoring suggester. However, it is currently unclear how good the scoring function actually performs in ranking refactoring suggestions and how much complexity will be needed to obtain useful suggestions. Therefore, in order to enhance our work, we need a deeper understanding of the scoring function.

Contribution. We do further research on the scoring function of our approach to derive extract method refactoring suggestions for long Java methods. We use learning to rank techniques in order to learn which features of the scoring function are relevant, to get meaningful refactoring suggestions, and to keep the scoring function as simple as possible. In addition, we evaluate the ranking performance of our previous scoring function, and compare it with the new scoring function that we learned. For the machine learning setting, we use 177 training and testing data sets that we obtained from 13 well-known open source systems by manually ranking five to nine randomly selected valid refactoring candidates.

In this paper, we show how we derived better extract method refactoring suggestions than in our previous work using learning to rank tools.

2   Fundamentals

We use learning to rank techniques to obtain a scoring function that is able to rank extract method refactoring candidates, and use normalized discounted cumulative gain (NDCG) metrics to evaluate the ranking performance. In this section, we explain the techniques, tools and metrics that we use in this paper.

2.1   Learning to Rank

Learning to rank refers to machine learning techniques for training the model in a ranking task [4].

There are several learning to rank approaches, where the pairwise and the listwise approach usually perform better than common pointwise regression approaches [8]. The pairwise approach learns by comparing two training objects and their given ranks ('ground truth'), whereas in our case the listwise approach learns from the list of all given rankings of refactoring suggestions for a long method. Liu et al. [8] pointed out that the pairwise and the listwise approaches usually perform better than the pointwise approach. Therefore, we do not rely on a pointwise approach but use pairwise and listwise learning to rank tools.

Qin et al. [12] constructed a benchmark collection for research on several learning to rank tools on the Learning To Rank (LETOR) data set. Their results support the hypothesis that pointwise approaches perform badly compared with pairwise and listwise approaches. In addition, listwise approaches often perform better than pairwise. However, *SVM-rank*, a pairwise learning to rank tool by Tsochantardis et al. [14], performs quite well and the first experiments on our data set showed that *SVM-rank* may lead us to interesting results. We set the parameter -c to 0.5 and the parameter -# to 5,000 as a trade-off between time consumption and learning performance.

Beside SVM-rank, we used a listwise learning to rank tool, *ListMLE* by Xia et al. [17]. In their evaluation, they showed that ListMLE performs better than ListNet by Cao et al. [1], which was also considered to be good by Qin et al.. Lan et al. [7] improved the learning capability of ListMLE, but did not provide binaries or source code; so we were unable to use the improved version.

ListMLE needs to be assigned a tolerance rate and a learning rate. In a series of experiments we performed, we found that the optimal ranking performance on our data set was with a tolerance rate of 0.001 and a learning rate of 1E-15.

2.2   Training and Testing

The learning process consisted of two steps: training and testing. We applied cross-validation [13] with 10 sets, that is, we split our learning data into 10 sets of (nearly) equal size. We performed 10 iterations using these sets, where nine of the sets were considered to be training data and one set was used as test data.

Test data is used to evaluate the ranking performance of the learned scoring function by comparing the grade of a refactoring candidate determined by the learned scoring function with its grade given by the learning data. We use NDCG metric to compare different scoring functions and their performances.

NDCG is the normalized form of the discounted cumulative gain (DCG), which is described in more detail by Järvelin and Kekäläinen [5], and measures the goodness of the ranking list (obtained by the application of the scoring function). Mistakes in the top-most ranks have a bigger impact on the DCG measure value. This is useful and important to us because we will not suggest all possible refactoring candidates, but only the highest-ranked ones. Given a long method, m_i, with refactoring candidates, C_i, suppose that π_i is the ranking list on C_i and y_i, the set of manually determined grades, then, the DCG at position k is defined as $DCG(k) = \sum_{j:\pi_i(j) \leq k} G(j)D(\pi_i(j))$, where $G(\cdot)$ is an exponential gain function, $D(\cdot)$ is a position discount function, and $\pi_i(j)$ is the position of refactoring candidate, $c_{i,j}$, in π_i. We set $G(j) = 2^{y_{i,j}} - 1$ and $D(\pi_i(j)) = \frac{1}{\log_2(1+\pi_i(j))}$. To normalize the DCG, and to make it comparable with measures of other long methods, we divide this DCG by the DCG that a perfect ranking would have obtained. Therefore, the NDCG for a candidate ranking will always be in $[0, 1]$, where the NDCG of 1 can only be obtained by perfect rankings (see Hang [4] for further details). In our evaluation, we consider the NDCG value of the last position so that all ranks are taken into account.

3   Approach

We discuss our approach to improve the scoring function in order to find the best suggestions for extract method refactoring.

3.1   Extract Method Refactoring Candidates

In our previous work [3], we presented an approach to derive extract method refactoring suggestions automatically for long methods. The main steps are: generating valid extract method refactoring candidates, ranking the candidates, and pruning the candidate list.

In the following, a *refactoring candidate* is a sequence of statements that can be extracted from a method into a new method. The *remainder* is the method that contains all the statements from the original method after applying the refactoring, plus the call of the extracted method. We aim for suggestions that help to improve the readability of the code and reduce its complexity, because these are main reasons for developers to initiate code refactoring [6].

We derived refactoring candidates from the control and data flow graph of a method using the Continuous Quality Assessment Toolkit (ConQAT[1]) open source software. We filtered out all invalid candidates, that is those that violate preconditions that need to be fulfilled for extract method refactoring (for details, see [11]). The second step of our approach was to rank the valid candidates using a scoring function. Finally, we pruned the list of suggestions by filtering out very similar candidates, in order to obtain essentially different suggestions.

In the present paper, we focus on the ranking of candidates, and especially on the scoring function that defines that ranking.

3.2   Scoring Function

We aimed for an optimized scoring function that is capable of ranking extract method refactoring candidates, so that top-most ranked candidates are most likely to be chosen by developers for an extract method refactoring. The scoring function is a linear function that calculates the dot product of a coefficient vector, c, and a feature value vector, f, for each candidate. Candidates are arranged in decreasing order of their score.

---

[1] www.conqat.org.

```
1  public class Example {
2    public void complex(int a, boolean b) {
3      callA(a);
4      callB(a);
5      if (a == 0)
6        callC(a);
7
8      // do something complex
9      for (int i = 0; i < a; i++) {        C1
10       if (b) {
11         if (a < 5) {
12           callD();                        C2
13         }
14       } else {
15         callE(i);
16         Object c = new Object();
17         System.out.println(c);
18       }
19     }
20   }
21 }
```

Fig. 1. Example method with nesting area of statements and example candidates

Table 1. Features and values in example

#	Feature	Type	C_1 ll 9 – 19	C_2 ll 10 – 18
1	LoC Red (abs)	int	8	8
2	Token Red (abs)	int	33	43
3	Stmt Red (abs)	int	5	6
4	LoC Red (rel)	double	0.42	0.42
5	Token Red (rel)	double	0.36	0.47
6	Stmt Red (rel)	double	0.38	0.46
7	Nest Depth Red	int	0	1
8	Nest Area Red	int	1	6
9	# Read Var	int	4	4
10	# Written Var	int	1	1
11	# Used Var	int	4	4
12	# Input Param	int	2	3
13	# Output Param	int	0	0
14	∃ Introd Com	bool	1	0
15	# Introd Com	int	2	0
16	∃ Concl Com	bool	0	0
17	# Concl Com	int	0	0
18	Same T Before	bool	0	0
19	Same T After	bool	0	0
20	# Branch Stmt	int	3	2

In this paper, we use a basis of 20 features for the scoring function. In the following, we give a short overview about the features. There are three categories of feature: complexity-related features, parameters, and structural information.

We illustrate the feature values with reference to two example refactoring candidates (C_1 and C_2) that were chosen from the example method given in Fig. 1. The gray area shows the nesting area, which is defined below. The white numbers specify the nesting depth of the corresponding statement (Fig. 1).

Complexity-related features. We mainly focused on reducing complexity and increasing readability. For complexity indicators, we used length, nesting and data flow information. For length-related features, we implemented six different metrics to measure the reduction of the method length (with respect to the longest method after the refactoring). We considered length based on the number of lines of code (LoC), on the number of tokens, and on the number of statements – all of them as both absolute values and relative to the original method length.

We consider highly nested methods as more complex than moderately nested ones, and use two features to represent the reduction of nesting: reduction of nesting depth and reduction of nesting area. The nesting area of a method with statements S_1 to S_n, each having a nesting depth of d_{S_i}, is defined to be $\sum_{i=1}^{n} d_{S_i}$. The idea of nesting area comes from the area alongside the single statements of pretty printed code (see the gray areas in Fig. 1).

Dataflow information can also indicate complexity. We have features representing the number of variables that are read, written or read and written.

Parameters. We considered the number of input and output parameters as an indicator of data coupling between the original and the extracted methods, which we want to keep low using our suggestions. The more parameters that are needed for a set of statements to be extracted from a method, the more the statements will depend on the rest of the original method.

Structural information. Finally, we have some features that represent structural aspects of the code. A design principle for code is that methods should process only one thing [9]. Methods that follow this principle are easier to understand. As developers often put blank lines or comments between blocks of code that process something else, we use features representing the existence and the number of blank or commented lines at their beginning, or at their end. Additionally, for first statement of the candidate, we check to see whether the type of the preceding is the same; and for the last statement, we check to see whether the type of the following statement is the same. Our last feature considers a structural complexity indicator – the number of branching statements in the candidate.

3.3   Training and Test Data Generation

To be able to learn a scoring function, we need training and test data. We derived this data by manually ranking approximately 1,000 extract method refactoring suggestions. To obtain this learning data, we selected 13 Java open source systems from various domains, and of different sizes. We consider a method to be 'long' if it has more than 40 LoC. From each project we randomly selected 15 long methods. For each method, we randomly selected valid refactoring candidates, where the number of candidates depended on the method length.

Our approach seeks to find suggestions that do not introduce new smells into the code. Therefore, in the pruning step of our approach, we usually filter out candidates that need more than three input parameters, thus avoiding the 'long parameter list' mentioned by Fowler [2]. To avoid learning that too many input parameters are bad, we considered only candidates that had less than four input parameters.

We ranked the selected candidates manually with respect to complexity reduction and readability improvement. The higher the ranking we gave a candidate, the better the suggestion was for us.

Some of the randomly selected methods were not suitable for an extract method refactoring. That was most commonly the case when the code would not benefit from the extract method, but from other refactorings. In addition, for some methods, we could not derive a meaningful ranking because there were only very weak candidates. That is why we did not use 18 of the 195 randomly selected long methods to learn our scoring function.[2]

---

[2] On http://cqse.eu/swqd17data we provide our rankings and the corresponding code bases from which we generated the refactoring candidates.

4   Evaluation

In this section, we present and evaluate the results from the learning procedure.

4.1   Research Questions

RQ1: What are the results of the learning tools? In order to get a scoring function that is capable of ranking the extract method refactoring candidates, we decided to use two learning to rank tools that implement different approaches, and that had performed well in previous studies.

RQ2: How stable are the learned scoring functions? To be able to derive implications for a real-world scoring function, the coefficients of the learned scoring function should not vary a lot during the 10-fold cross evaluation procedure.

RQ3: Can the scoring function be simplified? For practical reasons, it is useful to have a scoring function with a limited number of features. Additionally, reducing the search space may increase the performance of the learning to rank tools – resulting in better scoring functions.

RQ4: How does the learned scoring function compare with our manually determined one? In our previous work, we derived a scoring function by manual experiments. Now we can use our learning data set to evaluate the ranking performance of the previously defined scoring function, and to compare it with the learned one.

4.2   Study Setup

To answer RQ1 and RQ2, we used the learning to rank tools SVM-rank and ListMLE to perform a 10-fold cross validation on our training and test data set of 177 long methods, and a total of 1,185 refactoring candidates. We illustrate the stability of the single coefficients by using box plots that show how the coefficients are distributed over the ten iterations of the 10-fold cross validation.

To answer RQ3, we simplified the learned scoring function by omitting features, where the selection criterion for the omitted features is preservation of the ranking capability of the scoring function. Our initial feature set contained six different measures of length. For the sake of simplicity, we would like to have only one measure of length in our scoring function. To find out which measure best fits in with our training set, we re-ran the validation procedure (again using ListMLE and SVM-rank), but this time with only one length measurement, using each of the length measurements one at a time. We continued with the feature set reduction until only one feature was left.

4.3   Results

The following paragraphs answer the research questions.

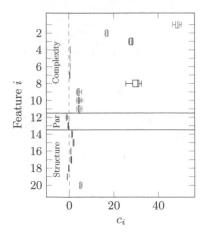
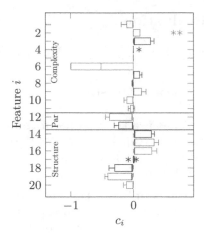

Fig. 2. Learning result from ListMLE with all features

Fig. 3. Learning result from SVM-rank with all features

Table 2. Coefficients of variation for learned coefficients

	ListMLE	SVM-rank
| AVG CV |	0.0087	22.522
| Min CV |	0.0053	0.8970
| Max CV |	0.5767	451.2

RQ1: What are the results of the learning tools? Figs. 2 and 3 show the results of the 10-fold cross validation for ListMLE and for SVM-rank, respectively. For each single feature, i, there is a box plot of the corresponding coefficient, c_i.

The average NDCG values of the learned scoring function for ListMLE is 0.873, whereas for SVM-rank it is 0.790. Therefore, the scoring function found by ListMLE performed better than the scoring function found by SVM-rank.

RQ2: How stable are the learned scoring functions? Table 2 shows the average, minimum and maximum coefficients of variation (CV) for the learned coefficients for ListMLE and for SVM-rank. Small CVs indicate that in relative terms the results from the single runs in the 10-cross fold procedure did not vary a lot, whereas big CVs indicate big differences between the learned coefficients. As the CVs of the single features from ListMLE are much smaller than those of SVM-rank, the coefficients of ListMLE are much more stable compared with SVM-rank. SVM-rank shows coefficients with a big variance between the single iterations of the validation process; that is, despite the heavy overlapping of the training sets, the learned coefficients vary a lot and can hardly be generalized.

RQ3: Can the scoring function be simplified? Fig. 4 shows a plot of the averaged NDCG measure for all 12 runs. Remember that we actually had three length

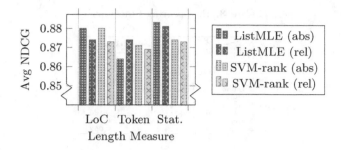

Fig. 4. Averaged NDCG when considering only one length measure

measures, and we considered the absolute and the relative values for all of them. As the reduction of the number of statements led to a higher NDCG for ListMLE (which outperformed SVM-rank with respect to NDCG), we chose to use it as our length measure. In practice, that seems sensible since, while LoC also count empty and commented lines, the number of statements only counts real code.

We iteratively identified a set of features that had no or only small influence on the ranking performance and removed it in the next iteration. A scoring function that only considered the number of input parameters and length and nesting area reduction still had an average NDCG of 0.885.

RQ4: How does the learned scoring function compare with our manually determined one? The scoring function that we presented in [3] achieved a NDCG of 0.891, which is better than the best scoring function learned in this evaluation.

4.4 Discussion

Our results show that, in the initial run of the learning to rank tools, features indicating a reduction of complexity are much more relevant for the ranking, and therefore have a comparatively high impact. Furthermore, the stability of ListMLE is higher on our data set than the stability of SVM-rank. For SVM-rank there is a big variance in the learned coefficients, which might also be a reason for the comparatively lower performance measure values.

The results for RQ3 show that it is possible to achieve a great simplification without big reductions in the ranking performance. The biggest influences on the ranking performance were the reduction of the number of statements, the reduction of nesting area (both are complexity indicators), and the number of input parameters.

Manual improvement As already mentioned, the learned scoring functions did not outperform the manually determined scoring function from our previous work. Obviously, the learning tools were not able to find optimal coefficients for the features. To improve the scoring function from our previous work, we did manual experiments that were influenced by the results of ListMLE and SVM-rank, and evaluated the results using the whole learning data set.

We were able to find several scoring functions that had only a handful of features and a better ranking performance than our scoring function from previous

Table 3. Best scoring functions

# Feature \ Fct	Previous	Learned	Improved
1 LoC (abs)	0.036	-	-
3 Stmt (abs)	-	0.681	0.066
7 Nesting Depth	0.362	-	-
8 Nesting Area	0.724	0.731	0.895
12 # Input P.	-0.362	-0.024	-0.331
13 # Output P.	-0.362	-	-
14 ∃ Introd Com.	0.181	-	0.166
15 # Introd Com.	0.181	-	0.166
16 ∃ Concl Com.	0.090	-	0.166
17 # Concl Com.	0.090	-	0.052
AVG NDCG	0.891	0.885	0.894

work (column 'Previous' in Table 3). In addition to the three most important features that we obtained in the answer to RQ3 (features #3, #7, #10), we also took the comment features (#14–17) into consideration. The main differences between the previous scoring function and the manually improved one from this paper are the length reduction measure, the omission of nesting depth, and the number of output parameters.

By taking the results of ListMLE and SVM-rank into consideration, we were able to find a coefficient vector such that the scoring function achieved a NDCG of 0.894 (see Table 3). That means that we were able to find a better scoring function when we combined the findings of our previous work with the learned coefficients from this paper.

5 Threats to Validity

Learning from data sources that are either too similar or too small means that there is a chance that no generalization of the results is possible. To have enough data to enable us to learn a scoring function that can rank extract method refactoring candidates, we chose 13 Java open source projects from various domains and from each project we randomly selected 15 long methods. We manually reviewed the long methods, and filtered out those that were not appropriate for the extract method. From the 177 remaining long methods, we randomly chose five to nine valid refactoring suggestions, depending on the method length. We ensured that our learning data did not contain any code clones to avoid learning from redundant data.

The manual ranking was performed by a single individual, which is a threat to validity since there is no commonly agreed way on how to shorten a long method, and therefore no single ranking criterion exists. The ranking was done very carefully, with the aim of reducing the complexity and increasing the readability and understandability of the code as much as possible; so, the scoring function should provide a ranking such that we can make further refactoring suggestions with the same aim.

We relied on two learning to rank tools, which represents another threat to validity. The learned scoring functions heavily depend on the tool. As the learned scoring functions vary, it is necessary to have an independent way of evaluating the ranking performance of the learned scoring functions. We used the widely used measure NDCG to evaluate the scoring functions, and applied a 10-fold cross validation procedure to obtain a meaningful evaluation of the ranking performance of the learned scoring function.

A threat to external validity is the fact that we derived our learning data from 13 open source Java systems. Therefore, results are not necessarily generalizable.

6   Related Work

In our previous work [3], we presented an automatic approach to derive extract method refactoring suggestions for long methods. We obtained valid refactoring candidates from the control and dataflow graph of a long method. All valid refactoring candidates were ranked by a manually-determined scoring function that aims to reduce code complexity and increase readability. In the present work, we have put the scoring function on more solid ground by learning a scoring function from many long methods, and manually ranked refactoring suggestions.

In the literature, there are several approaches that learn to suggest the most beneficial refactorings – usually for code clones. Wang and Godfrey [15] propose an automated approach to recommend clones for refactoring by training a decision-tree based classifier, C4.5. They use 15 features for decision-tree model training, where four consider the cloning relationship, four the context of the clone, and seven relate to the code of the clone. In the present paper, we have used a similar approach, but with a different aim: instead of clones, we have focused on long methods.

Mondal et al. [10] rank clones for refactoring through mining association rules. Their idea is that clones that are often changed together to maintain a similar functionality are worthy candidates for refactoring. Their prototype tool, *MARC*, identifies clones that are often changed together in a similar way, and mines association rules among these. A major result of their evaluation on thirteen software systems is that clones that are highly ranked by MARC are important refactoring possibilities. We used learning to rank techniques to find a scoring function that is capable of ranking extract method refactoring candidates from long methods.

7   Conclusion and Future Work

In this paper, we have presented an approach to derive a scoring function that is able to rank extract method refactoring suggestions by applying learning to rank tools. The scoring function can be used to automatically rank extract method refactoring candidates, and thus present a set of best refactoring suggestions to developers. The resulting scoring function needs less parameters than previous scoring functions but has a better ranking performance.

In the future, we would like to suggest sets of refactorings, especially those that remove clones from the code.

We would also like to find out whether the scoring function provides good suggestions for object-oriented programming languages other than Java and whether other features need to be considered in that case.

Acknowledgments. Thanks to the anonymous reviewers for their helpful feedback. This work was partially funded by the German Federal Ministry of Education and Research (BMBF), grant "Q-Effekt, 01IS15003A". The responsibility for this article lies with the authors.

References

1. Cao, Z., Qin, T., Liu, T.-Y., Tsai, M.-F., Li, H.: Learning to rank: from pairwise approach to listwise approach. In: 24th ICML (2007)
2. Fowler, M.: Refactoring: Improving the Design of Existing Code. Addison-Wesley Object Technology Series. Addison-Wesley, Reading (1999)
3. Haas, R., Hummel, B.: Deriving extract method refactoring suggestions for long methods. In: Winkler, D., Biffl, S., Bergsmann, J. (eds.) SWQD 2016. LNBIP, vol. 238, pp. 144–155. Springer, Heidelberg (2016). doi:10.1007/978-3-319-27033-3_10
4. Hang, L.: A short introduction to learning to rank. IEICE Trans. Inf. Syst. **94**(10), 1854–1862 (2011)
5. Jrvelin, K., Keklinen, J.: IR evaluation methods for retrieving highly relevant documents. In: 23rd SIGIR (2000)
6. Kim, M., Zimmermann, T., Nagappan, N.: A field study of refactoring challenges and benefits. In: 20th International Symposium on the FSE (2012)
7. Lan, Y., Zhu, Y., Guo, J., Niu, S., Cheng, X.: Position-aware ListMLE: a sequential learning process for ranking. In: 30th Conference on UAI (2014)
8. Liu, T.-Y.: Learning to rank for information retrieval. Found. Trends Inf. Retrieval **3**(3), 225–331 (2009)
9. Martin, R.C.: Clean Code: A Handbook of Agile Software Craftsmanship. Robert C. Martin Series. Prentice Hall, Upper Saddle River (2009)
10. Mondal, M., Roy, C.K., Schneider, K.: Automatic ranking of clones for refactoring through mining association rules. In: CSMR-WCRE (2014)
11. Murphy-Hill, E., Black, A.P.: Breaking the barriers to successful refactoring: observations and tools for extract method. In: 30th ICSE (2008)
12. Qin, T., Liu, T.-Y., Xu, J., Li, H.: Letor: a benchmark collection for research on learning to rank for information retrieval. Inf. Retrieval **13**(4), 346–374 (2010)
13. Sammut, C. (ed.): Encyclopedia of Machine Learning. Springer, New York (2011)
14. Tsochantaridis, I., Joachims, T., Hofmann, T., Altun, Y.: Large margin methods for structured and interdependent output variables. J. Mach. Learn. Res. **6**, 1453–1484 (2005)
15. Wang, W., Godfrey, M.W.: Recommending clones for refactoring using design, context, and history. In: ICSME (2014)
16. Wilking, D., Kahn, U.F., Kowalewski, S.: An empirical evaluation of refactoring. e-Informatica **1**(1), 27–42 (2007)
17. Xia, F., Liu, T.-Y., Wang, J., Zhang, W., Li, H.: Listwise approach to learning to rank: theory and algorithm. In: 25th ICML (2008)

A Portfolio of Internal Quality Metrics for Software Architects

Miroslaw Staron[1](✉) and Wilhelm Meding[2]

[1] Computer Science and Engineering, University of Gothenburg, Gothenburg, Sweden
miroslaw.staron@gu.se
[2] Ericsson AB, Stockholm, Sweden
wilhelm.meding@ericsson.com

Abstract. Evolving the architecture of the software together with the evolution of the design is one of the key areas in maintaining the high quality. In this paper we present a portfolio of indicators addressing a set of three areas of information needs for large software development companies of embedded software. The portfolio is a result of our studies of literature and at Software Center (nine companies and five universities) with the goal to identify the main information needs and quality metrics for the role of software architects. As a result of our studies we could elicit such information needs as architecture measures, design stability, and technical debt/risk. Nine information needs with one corresponding indicator each fulfill these information needs were identified in literature and through the interviews and workshops with the practitioners.

Keywords: Metrics · Software architecture

1 Introduction

Software architecting as an area has gained increasing visibility in the last two decades as the software industry recognized the role of software architectures in maintaining high quality and ensuring longevity and sustainability of the software products [21]. Even though this recognition is not new, there is still no consensus how to measure various aspects of software architectures beyond the basic structural properties of the software architecture as a design artifact. In the literature we can encounter studies applying base measures for object-oriented designs to software architectures [9] and studies designing low level software architecture measures such as number of interfaces [18]. However, an architect is often faced with the problem which high-level measures (indicators) should he/she use when monitoring the architecture during one software development project, addressing such information needs like – when is the architecture stable? or when is the architecture mature enough to start system testing?

In this paper we set off to identify which measures can be used for the above purpose by reviewing some of the most common measures of internal quality of software architectures and evaluate their applicability in industrial contexts in

© Springer International Publishing AG 2017
D. Winkler et al. (Eds.): SWQD 2017, LNBIP 269, pp. 57–69, 2017.
DOI: 10.1007/978-3-319-49421-0_5

the Software Center research program which consists of five universities and nine companies. The goal of our study was to address the following research question:

Which software architecture measures fulfill the information needs of software architects of large software products?

The goal is to suggest a new measurement set and the result from our studies is a portfolio of measures and indicators addressing three elicited areas of information needs – architectural measures, design stability, and technical debt/risk. Each of these areas have three information needs with one indicator linked to each information need such as architecture changes, internal and external coupling, system complexity. The portfolio is accompanied with the visualization methods for each of these indicators which helps the architects to maintain a consistent overview of the indicators across projects and products. The portfolio can be extended by the architects to add new measures and indicators which address more specific information needs (e.g. at a specific point of time in the project).

This paper is structured as follows. Section 2 describes the most relevant related work to our study. Next, Sect. 3 outlines the research process in this study. Section 4 present the architecture measures identified in our literature study, which is followed by the description of the subset of the measures identified as important for the software architects in the studied companies in Sect. 5. Finally we present the summary and conclusions in Sect. 6.

2   Related Work

One of the most popular methods for evaluating software architectures in general is to use qualitative methods like ATAM [7] where the architecture is analyzed based on scenarios or perspectives. These methods are used for final assessments of the quality of the architectures, but as they are manual they need effort and therefore cannot be conducted in a continuous manner. However, as many of contemporary projects are conducted using Agile methodologies, Lean software development [16] or using the minimum viable product approach [17], these methods are not feasible in practice. Therefore the architects are willing to trade-off the quality of the evaluation to the speed of the feedback on their architecture, which leads to more extensive use of measure-based evaluation of software architectures.

Wagner et al. [29] presented a method for aligning quality models with the measurements and their goals where the gap between the abstract level of the goals and the concrete level of the measures is bridged. Our approach is a similar attempt but based on a specific scope (software architecture) and including the visualization of the results, thus our approach can be seen as an instantiation of Wagner et al.'s approach in a specific context.

One of the tools and methods supporting the architects' work with measures is the MetricViewer [27] which augments software architecture diagrams expressed in UML with such measures as coupling, cohesion or depth of inheritance tree. This augmentation is important to reason about the designs, but they are not linked to the information needs of the stakeholders to monitor attainment of their goals, which otherwise require them to conduct the same analyses manually.

Similarly to Tameer et al., Vasconcelos et al. [28] propose a set of metrics for measuring architectures based on low level properties of software architectures, such as number of possible operating systems or the number of secure components. Our work complements their study by focusing on internal quality properties related to the design and not quality in use.

The ISO/IEC 25000 Software Quality Requirements and Evaluation (SQuaRE) standard provides a set of reference measures for software designs and architectures. As per time of writing of this book the standard is not fully adopted but the main part are already approved and the work is fully ongoing regarding the measures, their definitions and usage. The standard presents the following set of measures related to product, design and architecture in one or its chapters – ISO/IEC 25023 - Software and Software Product Quality Measures [5]. The measures related to the execution of the product and do not focus on the internal quality of the product with such example measures as the size (e.g. number of components) or the complexity (e.g. control flow complexity). Therefore we need to turn to scientific literature to understand the measures and indicators related to software architectures. There we can find measures which are of interest for software architects.

Finally, the software engineering standard ISO/IEC 15939:2007 [14] provides a normative specification for the processes used to define, collect, and analyze quantitative data in software projects or organizations. The central role in the standard is played by the information product which is a set of one or more indicators with their associated interpretations that address the information need – an insight necessary for a stakeholder to manage objectives, goals, risks, and problems observed in the measured objects. These measured objects can be entities like projects, organizations, software products, etc. characterized by a set of attributes. We use the following definitions: (i) base measure – measure defined in terms of an attribute and the method for quantifying it; (ii) derived measure – measure that is defined as a function of two or more values of base measures; (iii) indicator – measure that provides an estimate or evaluation of specified attributes derived from a model with respect to defined information needs and (iv) information product – one or more indicators and their associated interpretations that address an information need. The view on measures presented in ISO/IEC 15939 is consistent with other engineering disciplines, the standard states at many places that it is based on such standards as ISO/IEC 15288:2007 (System lifecycle processes), ISO/IEC 14598-1:1999 (Information technology – Software product evaluation), ISO/IEC 9126-x, ISO/IEC 25000 series of standards, or International vocabulary of basic and general terms in metrology (VIM) [12].

3   Research Process

The research process in our study is a mix of a literature study, interview and workshop. The goal of the study was to identify the most important information needs of software architects and to provide the reference measurement system to fulfill these needs. We combined the research methods as follows:

- We conducted a literature review using snowballing and following the principles of systematic mapping of Petersen et al. [15]. It resulted in identifying 54 measures that can be applied to software architectures and three areas of information needs were elicited.
- We organized the measures according to the ISO/IEC 15939 standard's measurement information model [14] into base measures, derived measures and indicators.
- After that, we grouped them into three areas based on the information needs of software architects elicited from the literature study. We evaluated the applicability of the measures through an interview with an architect from one of the automotive companies. The architect was pointed out as an expert by the company representatives and worked in the area for a number of car projects before.
- We finally designed the portfolio of indicators which fulfill these information needs (presented in this paper).
- We presented to the architects and project managers at the defense company where we obtained feedback on the feasibility of this portfolio. In total two architects, two project managers and two quality managers took part.

The results from the evaluations were that the portfolio is promising and we are currently working on its full fledged implementation as a measurement system for the companies in Software Center.

4   Architecture Measures in Literature

We use the ISO/IEC 15939 measurement information model to organize the measures used for quantifying properties of software architectures. Conceptually

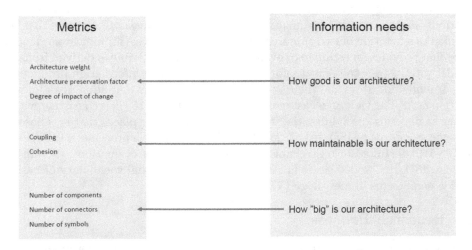

Fig. 1. Higher level measures correspond to more advanced information needs – an example.

we can also consider the fact the higher in the model the measure is, the more advanced information need it fulfills. In Fig. 1 we can see a number of measures divided into three levels – the more basic ones at the bottom and the more complex one at the top.

The more advanced information needs are related to the work on the architects whereas the more basic ones are more related to the architecture as an artifact in software development. So, now that we have the model, let's look into one of the standards where the software measures are defined – ISO/IEC 25000.

Let's start with the base measures which quantify the architecture as shown in Table 1 – we can quickly notice that the list of these measures correspond to the entity they measure. Their measurement method (the algorithm how to

Table 1. Base measures for software architectures

Measure	Description
Number of components [26]	The basic measure quantifying the size of the architecture in terms of its basic building block – components
Number of connectors [26]	The basic measure quantifying the internal connectivity of the architecture in terms of its basic connectors
Number of processing units [10]	The basic measure quantifying the size of the physical architecture in terms of the processing units
Number of data repositories [10]	The complementary measure quantifying the size in terms of data repositories
Number of persistent components [10]	Quantifies the size in terms of the needs for persistency
Number of links [10]	Quantifies the complexity of the architecture, similarly to the McCabe cyclomatic complexity measure. It is sometimes broken down per type of link (e.g. asynchronous – synchronous, data – control)
Number of types of communication mechanisms [10]	Quantifies the complexity of the architecture in terms of the need to implement multiple communication mechanisms
Number of external interfaces [6]	Quantifies the coupling between the architectural components and the external systems
Number of internal interfaces [6]	Quantifies the coupling among the architectural components
Number of services [6]	Quantifies the cohesion of the architecture in terms of how many services it provides/fulfills
Number of concurrent components [6]	The measure counts the components which have concurrent calculations as part of their behavior
Number of changes in the architecture [2]	The measure quantifies the number of changes (e.g. changed classes, attributes) in the architecture
Fanout from the simplest structure [3]	The measure quantifies the degree of the lowest complexity of the coupling of the architecture

calculate the base measure) is very similar and is based on counting entities of a specific type. The list in Table 1 shows a set of example of such base measures.

Collecting the measures presented in the table provides the architects with the understanding of the properties of the architecture, but the architects still need to provide the context to these numbers in order to reason about the architectures. For example the number of components by itself does not provide much insight, however, if put together with a timeline and plotted as a trend allows to extrapolate the information and therefore allow the architects to assess if the architecture is overly large and should be refactored.

In addition to the measures for the architecture we can also find many measures which are related to software design in general – e.g. object-oriented measures or complexity measures. Examples of these are presented in Table 2.

Table 2. Base measures for software design

Measure	Description
Weighted methods per class [1]	The number of methods weighed by their complexity
Depth of inheritance tree [1]	The longest path from the current class to its first predecessor in the inheritance hierarchy
Cyclomatic complexity [11]	Quantifying the control path complexity in terms of the number of independent execution paths of a program. Used often as part of safety assessment in ISO/IEC 26262
Dependencies between blocks/modules/classes [25]	Quantifying the dependencies between classes or components in the system
Abstractness of a Simulink block [13]	Quantifies the ration of the contained abstract blocks to the total number of contained blocks

Once again these examples show that the measures are related to the design the quantification of its properties. Such measures as the *abstractness of a Simulink block*, however, are composed of multiple other measures and therefore are classified as derived measures and as such are closer to the information need of architects. In the literature we can find a large number of measures for designs and their combinations and therefore when choosing measures it is crucial to start from the information needs of the architects [19] since these information needs can effectively filter out measures which are possible to collect, but not relevant for the company (and as such could be considered as waste).

In the next section we identify which measures from the above two groups are to be included in the portfolio and which areas they belong to.

5   Metrics Portfolio for the Architects

The measures presented so far can be collected but as the measurement standards prescribe – they need to be useful for the stakeholders in their decision processes [14,20]. Therefore we organize these measures into three areas corresponding to the information needs of software architects. As architecting is a process which involves the software architecture artifacts we recognize the need of grouping these indicators into areas related both to the product and the process.

5.1 Areas

In our portfolio we group the indicators into three areas related to the basic properties of the design, the stability of it and the quality of it:

Area: architecture measures. Architecture measures – this area groups the product-related indicators that address the information need about *how to monitor the basic properties of the architecture like its component coupling.*

Area: design stability. Design stability – this area groups the process-related indicators that address the information need about *how to ascertain controlled evolution of the architectural design.*

Area: technical debt/risk. Technical debt/technical risk – this area groups the product-related indicators that address the information need about *how to ascertain the correct implementation of the architecture.*

In the following subsections we present the measures and the suggested way to present them. One of the criteria for each of these areas in our study was the upper limit of the number of indicators to be four. The limitations are based on the empirical studies of the cognitive aspects of measurement such as the ability to take in information by the stakeholders [24].

5.2 Area: Architecture Measures

In our portfolio we could identify 14 measures as applicable to measure the basic properties of the architecture. However, when discussing these measures with the architects the majority of the measures seemed to quantify the basic properties of the designs. However, the indicators found in the study in this area are:

Software architecture changes. To monitor and control changes over time the architects should be able to monitor the trends in changes of software architecture at the highest level [2]. Based on our literature studies and discussions with practitioners we identified the following measure to be a good indicator of the changes – *number of changes in the architecture per time unit (e.g. week)* [3,4,8].

Complexity. To manage module complexity the architects need to understand the degree of coupling between components as the coupling is perceived as cost-consuming and error-prone in the long-term evolution of the architecture. The identified indicator is *Average squared deviation of actual fanout from the simplest structure.*

External interfaces. To control the degree of coupling on the interface level (i.e. a subset of all types of couplings) the architects need to observe the number of internal interfaces –*number of interfaces.*

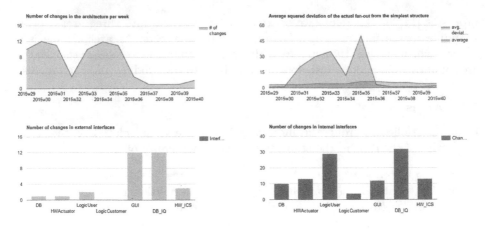

Fig. 2. Visualization of the measures in the architecture property area

Internal interfaces. To have control of the external dependencies of the product the architects need to monitor the coupling of the product to external software products – *number of interfaces.*

The suggested presentation of these measures is presented in Fig. 2.

5.3   Area: Design Stability

The next area which is of importance for the architects is related to the need for monitoring the large code base for stability. Generally, in this area we used the visualizations from our previous research into code stability [22, 23]. We identified the following three indicators to be efficient in monitoring and visualizing the stability:

Code stability. To monitor the code maturity over the time the architects need to see how much code has been changed over time as it allows them to identify code areas where more testing is needed due to recent changes. The measure used for this purpose is *number of changes per module per time unit.*

Defects per modules. To monitor the aging of the code the architects need to monitor defect-proneness per component per time, using a similar measure as the code stability – *number of defects per module per time unit (e.g. week).*

Interface stability. To control the stability of the architecture over its interfaces the architects measure the stability of the interfaces – *number of changes to the interfaces per time unit.*

We have found that in this view it is important to be able to visualize the entire code/product base in one view and therefore the dashboards which visualizes the stability is based on the notion of heatmaps [22]. In Fig. 3 we present such a visualization with three heatmaps corresponding to these three stability indicators. Each of the figures is a heatmap which visualizes different aspects,

Code stability heatmap

Defects per module heatmap

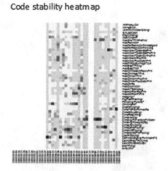
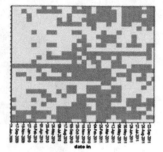

Defects per module heatmap

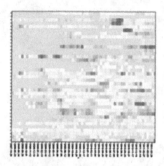

Fig. 3. Visualization of the measures in the architecture stability area

but each of them is organized in the same way – columns designate the weeks, rows designate the single code modules or interfaces and the intensity of the color of each cell designates the number of changes to the module or interface during the particular week.

5.4 Area: Technical Debt/Risk

The last area in our portfolio is related to the quality of the architecture over a longer period of time. In this area we identified the following two indicators:

Coupling. To have manageable design complexity the architects need to have a possibility to quickly overview the coupling between the components in the architecture – measured by *number of explicit architectural dependencies*, where the explicit dependencies are links between the components which are introduced by the architects.

Implicit architectural dependencies. To monitor where the code deviates from the architecture the architects need to observe whether there are no additional dependencies introduced during the detailed design of the software – this is measured by *number of implicit architectural dependencies*, where the implicit dependencies are such links between the components which are part of the code, but not introduced in the architecture documentation diagrams [25].

Fig. 4. Visualization of the measures in the architecture technical debt/risk

The visualization of the architectural dependencies shows the degree of coupling and is based on the circular diagrams as presented in Fig. 4 where each area on the border of the circle represents a component and a line shows the dependencies between the components.

6   Conclusions

In this paper we set off to investigate which measures of software architectures could fulfill information needs of software architects in large software development companies in the embedded software development. We have reviewed a number of measures available in the standard (like ISO/IEC 25023) and available in the literature, shortlisting 54 measures clearly applicable for the role of software architect. The proposed portfolio of measures and indicators is applicable for the context where they were studied. However, as our studies were based on literature we can see that these results can also be applicable to other domains, which is one of the directions of our study.

In our future work we plan to conduct a full fledged evaluation of the portfolio by applying it to complex software development projects in the area of Internet of Things in our partner companies at Software Center.

Acknowledgment. This research has been partially carried out in the Software Centre, University of Gothenburg, Ericsson AB, and Volvo Car Group.

References

1. Chidamber, S.R., Kemerer, C.F.: A metrics suite for object oriented design. IEEE Trans. Soft. Eng. **20**(6), 476–493 (1994)
2. Durisic, D., Nilsson, M., Staron, M., Hansson, J.: Measuring the impact of changes to the complexity and coupling properties of automotive software systems. J. Syst. Soft. **86**(5), 1275–1293 (2013)
3. Durisic, D., Staron, M., Nilsson, M.: Measuring the size of changes in automotive software systems and their impact on product quality. In: Proceedings of the 12th International Conference on Product Focused Software Development and Process Improvement, pp. 10–13. ACM (2011)
4. Durisic, D., Staron, M., Tichy, M., Hansson, J.: Quantifying long-term evolution of industrial meta-models-a case study. In: 2014 Joint Conference of the International Workshop on Software Measurement and the International Conference on Software Process and Product Measurement (IWSM-MENSURA), pp. 104–113. IEEE (2014)
5. ISO/IEC. ISO/IEC 25023 - Systems and software engineering - Systems and software Quality Requirements and Evaluation (SQuaRE) - Measurement of system and software product quality. Technical report (2016)
6. Kalyanasundaram, S., Ponnambalam, K., Singh, A., Stacey, B.J., Munikoti, R.: Metrics for software architecture: a case study in the telecommunication domain. In: 1998 IEEE Canadian Conference on Electrical and Computer Engineering, vol. 2, pp. 715–718. IEEE (1998)
7. Kazman, R., Klein, M., Clements, P.: Atam: method for architecture evaluation. Technical report, DTIC Document (2000)
8. Kuzniarz, L., Staron, M.: Inconsistencies in student designs. In: the Proceedings of the 2nd Workshop on Consistency Problems in UML-Based Software Development, San Francisco, CA, pp. 9–18 (2003)
9. Lindvall, M., Tvedt, R.T., Costa, P.: An empirically-based process for software architecture evaluation. Empirical Softw. Eng. **8**(1), 83–108 (2003)

10. Lung, C.-H., Kalaichelvan, K.: An approach to quantitative software architecture sensitivity analysis. Int. J. Soft. Eng. Knowl. Eng. **10**(01), 97–114 (2000)
11. McCabe, T.J.: A complexity measure. IEEE Transa. Soft. Eng. **4**, 308–320 (1976)
12. International Bureau of Weights and Measures. International vocabulary of basic and general terms in metrology. International Organization for Standardization, Genve, Switzerland, 2nd edn. (1993)
13. Olszewska, M.: Simulink-specific design quality metrics. Turku Centre for Computer Science (2011)
14. International Standard Organization and International Electrotechnical Commission: software and systems engineering, software measurement process. Technical report, ISO/IEC (2007)
15. Petersen, K., Feldt, R., Mujtaba, S., Mattsson, M.: Systematic mapping studies in software engineering. In: 12th International Conference on Evaluation and Assessment in Software Engineering, vol. 17, pp. 1–10 (2008)
16. Poppendieck, M.: Lean software development. In: Companion to the Proceedings of the 29th International Conference on Software Engineering, pp. 165–166. IEEE Computer Society (2007)
17. Ries, E.: The Lean Startup: How Today's Entrepreneurs Use Continuous Innovation to Create Radically Successful Businesses. Random House LLC, New York (2011)
18. Sant'Anna, C., Figueiredo, E., Garcia, A., Lucena, C.J.P.: On the modularity of software architectures: a concern-driven measurement framework. In: Oquendo, F. (ed.) ECSA 2007. LNCS, vol. 4758, pp. 207–224. Springer, Heidelberg (2007). doi:10.1007/978-3-540-75132-8_17
19. Staron, M., Meding, W., Karlsson, G., Nilsson, C.: Developing measurement systems: an industrial case study. J. Softw. Maintenance Evol. Res. Pract. **23**(2), 89–107 (2010)
20. Staron, M.: Critical role of measures in decision processes: managerial and technical measures in the context of large software development organizations. Inf. Soft. Technol. **54**(8), 887–899 (2012)
21. Staron, Miroslaw: Software engineering in low-to middle-income countries. In: Knowledge for a Sustainable World: a Southern African-Nordic Contribution, p. 139 (2015)
22. Staron, M., Hansson, J., Feldt, R., Henriksson, A., Meding, W., Nilsson, S., Hoglund, C.: Measuring and visualizing code stability-a case study at three companies. In: 2013 Joint Conference of the 23rd International Workshop on Software Measurement and the 2013 Eighth International Conference on Software Process and Product Measurement (IWSM-MENSURA), pp. 191–200. IEEE (2013)
23. Staron, M., Kuzniarz, L., Wallin, L.: Case study on a process of industrial mda realization: determinants of effectiveness. Nordic J. Comput. **11**(3), 254–278 (2004)
24. Staron, M., Meding, W., Hansson, J., Höglund, C., Niesel, K., Bergmann, V.: Dashboards for continuous monitoring of quality for software product under development. In: System Qualities and Software Architecture (SQSA) (2013)
25. Staron, M., Meding, W., Hoglund, C., Hansson, J.: Identifying implicit architectural dependencies using measures of source code change waves. In: 2013 39th EUROMICRO Conference on Software Engineering and Advanced Applications (SEAA), pp. 325–332. IEEE (2013)
26. Stevanetic, S., Javed, M.A., Zdun, U.: Empirical evaluation of the understandability of architectural component diagrams. In: Proceedings of the WICSA 2014 Companion Volume, p. 4. ACM (2014)

27. Termeer, M., Lange, C.F.J., Telea, A., Chaudron, M.R.V.: Visual exploration of combined architectural and metric information. In: 3rd IEEE International Workshop on Visualizing Software for Understanding and Analysis, 2005, VISSOFT 2005, pp. 1–6. IEEE (2005)
28. Vasconcelos, A., Sousa, P., Tribolet, J.: Information system architecture metrics: an enterprise engineering evaluation approach. Electron. J. Inf. Syst. Eval. **10**(1), 91–122 (2007)
29. Wagner, S., Lochmann, K., Heinemann, L., Kläs, M., Trendowicz, A., Plösch, R., Seidl, A., Goeb, A., Streit, J.: The quamoco product quality modelling and assessment approach. In: Proceedings of the 34th International Conference on Software Engineering, pp. 1133–1142. IEEE Press (2012)

Validating Converted Java Code via Symbolic Execution

Harry M. Sneed[1(✉)] and Chris Verhoef[2]

[1] Technical University of Dresden, Dresden, Germany
Harry.Sneed@T-Online.de
[2] Department of Computer Science, VU Amsterdam,
Amsterdam, The Netherlands
x@cs.vu.nl

Abstract. The testing approach described here has grown out of migration projects aimed at converting procedural programs in COBOL or PL/1 to object-oriented Java code. The code conversion itself is now automated but not completely. The human reengineer still has to make some adjustments to the automatically generated code and that can lead to errors. These may also be subtle errors in the automated transformation. Therefore, converted code must be tested to prove that it is functionally equivalent to the original code. Up until now converted programs have been tested manually and their results compared, but that is a very labor intensive approach. Besides, it only shows which results differ and not where the code differs. It can be extremely difficult to trace differences in the results back to differences in the code. Such regression testing drives up the costs of migration, causing users to disregard this alternative. If they have to spend so much on testing a conversion they might as well redevelop the software. This paper describes how converted code can be validated at a much lower cost by symbolically executing it and comparting the execution paths. The theory behind this approach is that no matter how statements are statically reordered, dynamically they must still execute in the same sequence to produce the same result.

Keywords: Code conversion · Object-oriented migration · Functional equivalence · Source code animation · Symbolic execution · Dynamic comparison · Verification paths

1 Background and Motivation for This Work

Since the early 1990s both authors have been working on the transformation of procedural legacy code into object-oriented code. This normally entails a change of language. The fact that there are so many languages to be handled only complicates the issue as pointed out by the second author, who also demonstrates that every automated conversion is more or less unreliable [1]. At the beginning the target language was usually C++ or Object Cobol, later it became Java. Each legacy statement is converted on a 1:1 or 1:n basis. For each legacy statement an equivalent Java statement or set of statements is generated. Control statements like "if", "evaluate" and "perform until" can be converted one to one. Also most basic assign statements such as "move",

© Springer International Publishing AG 2017
D. Winkler et al. (Eds.): SWQD 2017, LNBIP 269, pp. 70–83, 2017.
DOI: 10.1007/978-3-319-49421-0_6

"compute" and "transform", etc. can be converted on a one to one basis. However there are some complex statements such as the COBOL "string", the COBOL "perform thru" and the PL/I "substring" where there is no equivalent Java statement. The legacy statement must be replaced by a set of Java statements. These statement sets are best defined as a method in a standard super class from which they can be inherited by the converted class. In the converted class they appear as a method invocation. This also applies to the GOTO statements which have to be simulated in Java with a label variable as the name of the method to be invoked [2]. For a Java developer the converted statements may appear to be awkward but they are functionally equivalent, i.e. there result is the same as the original legacy statement. For instance, Cobol/ASM370/PL/I code is placed into methods that simulate old native constructs so that the code looks like the old code but is compilable in the new language. What is not certain is that the converted Java statements will be executed in the exact same order as the original ones. This has to be demonstrated by testing.

The greater problem in converting procedural code is that of converting the procedural structure of the legacy programs into an object-oriented one which is far removed from the original procedural architecture. This entails not only the reordering of the data declarations, but also the reordering of the procedural statements. The latter can be avoided by placing the entire procedural code into a single control class with a method for each COBOL paragraph or PL/I internal procedure. This approach was originally suggested by Yang, who referred to the control class as a God class [3]. It is also practiced by many conversion tool vendors who want to avoid the problems of objectification. However, in so doing, they create Java components which are not really object-oriented. Only the data is split up into classes, the procedures are left as one big procedural class. The end result is a COBOL or a PL/1 program with Java syntax. One can then really question whether it is not better to leave the code as it was and to wrap it behind a Java wrapper [4].

The God class solution may be acceptable for users only interested in using the Java development and runtime facilities and in producing portable byte code which will compile once and run everywhere, but it is not a long term solution which can serve as a basis for further development. For that the procedural code has to be objectified, by splitting it up into methods and assigning those methods to the data objects they process. Locality of reference is one of the fundamental principles of object-orientation [5]. It is the rationale for encapsulation. Operations should be kept together with the data they process. If code is to be considered object-oriented it must adhere to this principle. Therefore, the operations in the procedural code of the legacy programs should be assigned to the classes whose data they reference most. That is the approach favored by the first author from the very beginning and which has been implemented in the CodeTran code transformation workbench [6].

The greatest obstacle to converting legacy code to Java remains the handling of GO TO branches, a problem which has been addressed in a previous paper by the same authors [7]. Legacy code, whether it be COBOL, PL/I or C, is usually full of GO TO branches for which there is no equivalent in Java. There have been many approaches suggested to remove the GO TO branches by restructuring the code prior to conversion with tools such as XTRAN (see: http://www.xtran-llc.com/cblstr.html), but this can lead to bloated and deeply indented code. The restructured programs are also inevitably error prone as discovered in many restructuring projects. The U.S. National Standards Institute made a study of governmental restructuring projects in the early 1990s to discover that most such projects failed to achieve their goals because of restructuring errors [8]. This must not be the case as demonstrated in a large scale industrial project in the Netherlands [10], however, the safest and least code bloating method is to return a label variable to a central controller and have it invoke the next method referred to in the GO TO statement. That technique is referred to as label variable branching and was originally suggested by a research team at Oxford University [12]. Either way the problem is solved it effects the control flow execution of the code branches and can alter the execution sequence. Thus, in objectifying procedural code, there are two problems to deal with:

- eliminating GO TO branches and
- redistributing procedural code units.

Any solution to these two problems is subject to being error prone. The removal or replacement of the GO TO constructs may cause methods to be left out or executed in a wrong sequence. The redistribution of the procedural code blocks among the data objects entails a static reordering of the statements. This too can lead to serious errors in the execution sequence. Therefore, there is a definite need to demonstrate that the converted Java code is executed in the same sequence as the original COBOL code, since any variation in that sequence is an indication of a transformation error.

2   Symbolic Execution as a Means of Testing

The symbolic execution of software source code has a long tradition. It grew out of the attempt to prove the correctness of a program without actually executing it. Program proving was very much in fashion in the 70's as an alternate to testing. Proving was considered the mathematical systematic approach to demonstrating correctness, whereas testing was looking down upon as the empirical haphazard approach. There were many scientific disputes between the testers on one side and the provers on the other. In the end, the testers won out because the provers were only able to make a proof of very small program samples and even that required a tremendous effort. Manfred Broy, now a leading professor on software engineering in Germany, spent over two years trying to prove the correctness of a simple text editor and finally had to give up [11]. In the U.S. Prof. William Howden at the University of Southern California spent an equally long time in proving the correctness of a FORTRAN mathematical subroutine library. In doing this he developed a tool named Dissect to record the symbolic execution of the code [14]. He was able to express all of the operations performed on variables in terms of symbolic data as in algebra, therefore the term symbolic execution. Instead of using real numbers he used algebraic symbols and combined them together in compound expressions. The compound expressions were then compared against the specified expressions to determine equivalence. The specified expressions were referred to as the Oracle.

The problem with this approach is that it is recursive. There is no way to prove that the Oracle is correct other than verifying it against another higher oracle. So proofing turned out to be an endless loop. One proof is dependent upon another. This dilemma persists in software testing. Here too testers are dependent upon an oracle to ascertain program correctness. A test is always a test against something else, a comparison of two hypotheses as to what is right. This lead to Howden's landmark work on functional testing, marking the beginning of a black box test technology [15].

Today the problem remains that there must be some oracle to test against. In developing a new application that oracle is most often the requirement specification, but we all know how unreliable most such specifications are. Rich and Waters came to the conclusion in their automatic programming research project at M.I.T. that it is much easier to write an executable program than it is to prepare a complete and consistent specification of that program [16]. This being the case, specifications inevitably remain inaccurate descriptions of what might be a correct solution to a selected problem. In the end, researchers concluded that the only complete and accurate description of a program is the program itself [17]. This insight leads to the diverse programming approach to ensure the reliability of safety critical software. Several different program solutions to the same problem are tested back to back against each other and their states compared at regular intervals. Any deviation in the states of the redundant solutions is an indication of a fault [18]. In this way, programs are tested against one another to demonstrate correctness. This goes to show that there is no such thing as absolute correctness. Software correctness is relative to what we assume to be correct. If all program versions happen to produce the exact same result, we assume that to be correct. In the experience of both authors, many old errors are brought to the surface by code transformation, which are then repaired during the project. To preserve consistency the original system must also be corrected. In practice, this is too expensive, raising the question of correctness: what is the oracle if the upgraded code is indeed different from the original? Light weight checks such as those made by Veerman might help here [9, 10].

In the case of regression testing the existing software version is the oracle. It is assumed to be correct because the users have accepted the results it produces. These results may be in fact incorrect in terms of their original specification, as the first author witnessed in a reengineering project for the Bavarian water works. Customers were billed one tariff level higher that what they should have been billed according to government regulation, due to a one off-by-one error in processing the tariff table. When it came to converting the Assembler program into COBOL this error was discovered but never corrected because the users never complained. They had accepted the higher tariff level. Thus, correct is that what exists and has been accepted to be correct. This is the biggest advantage of legacy software. It is assumed to be correct and can be used as an oracle.

The greatest problem with the development of new software is this lack of an oracle. There is nothing to test against except the requirements, which are usually at a too high a level of abstraction to be used for testing. For the specification to be used as a test reference, it has to be at the same semantic level as the code. The decisions made in the code have to be defined as rules in the specification, for instance as OCL statements or as decision tables. Then the test is comparing to the Java statements with the OCL statements. However, there is no way to prove that the OCL statements are correct. At most one can only claim that the Java code does not match with the OCL rules, therefore one of them or both must be wrong [19].

In retesting a converted program it is assumed that the original code is right. Therefore any deviation on the side of the converted code is considered an error. Such is the case in the following Java code where in COBOL the value of variable TXL1-3 is moved to the target variables USR-IDENT, USR-ID, R223-LID. In Java there should be three assignment statements, but there are only two. The setting of the last target item R223-LID is missing, due to some error in the conversion routine. A normal module test will only reveal the missing statement after the test by comparing all of the variable states. By comparing the execution paths at test time the missing statement will be noticed immediately since the path through the Java code will be shorter than the path through the COBOL code.

```
//   MOVE TXL1-3 TO USR-IDENT USR-ID R223-LID
IAB6.WORK.USR_IDENT.setUSR_IDENT(IAB6.INPUT.RTX_STORAGE.getTXL
1_3());
IAB6.WORK.IAB6_WORKING.setUSR_ID(IAB6.INPUT.RTX_STORAGE.getTX
L1_3());
//IAB6.DB.R223.setR223_LID(USR_ID(IAB6.INPUT.RTX_STORAGE.getTXL1_3
());
//Is missing!
```

Normally, such an error would eventually be found in the regression test by comparing the new R223 SQL table with the old data record R223. There it would come out that the attribute R223-LID does not match. However, considering that several programs are using that record, it would be extremely difficult and time consuming to locate the missing statement. By comparing the two trace paths the tester will immediately see that the one path is longer than the other. To make this possible such compound statements must be split up into several statements with one per variable assignment.

```
MOVE TXL1-3 TO USR-IDENT   = setUSR_IDENT(IAB6.INPUT.RTX_STORAGE.getTXL1_3());
MOVE TXL1-3 TO USR-ID      = setUSR_ID(IAB6.INPUT.RTX_STORAGE.getTXL1_3());
MOVE TXL1-3 TO R223-LID    = no equivalent
```

If the variable R223-LID is later used as a conditional operand in an "*if*" statement there would also be a deviation in the control flow since the COBOL variable R223-LID has another value than the Java equivalent. Missing statements are one of the main sources of error in program transformation.

3   Demonstrating Functional Equivalence

Proving functional equivalence is an open research issue. Principally it could be done, by comparing the two sources and matching their algorithms. But this is very difficult and has yet to be solved. Therefore functional equivalence is generally demonstrated by testing. There are two ways of demonstrating functional equivalence

(1) by comparing the results
(2) by comparing the execution sequences.

Comparing the results means that the contents of the screens, interfaces, files and database tables produced by the legacy system have to be compared data item for data item with the contents of the web pages, interfaces, files and database tables produced by the converted system. Any deviation in the data is to be regarded as an error [20].

If the conversion is taking place offline at a remote location this presents a problem. The converters can compile the converted code, but they cannot readily test it, since they don't have access to the complete target environment. It may not be ready yet, or they may not be able to access it for security reasons. More often the necessary test data will not be available until later in the migration project [21].

Simulating the target environment with test drivers and stubs is another possible solution, but this also requires a significant effort to achieve. For every framework function or library class referred to by the converted code, a stub has to be created which simulates the behavior of that function. In the end, the tester may wind up rewriting the whole framework. In any case, the effort required to demonstrate functional equivalence in an artificial test environment is prohibitive. The cost of regression testing becomes many times more than the cost of automatically converting the code. This drives up the price of the conversion approach and makes it less attractive compared to a redevelopment or a wrapping solution [22].

In order to keep the costs down, a testing approach is needed which demonstrates functional equivalence with a minimum of effort. The approach proposed here is animation. Both the old and the new sources are animated and their animation paths compared with one another. Any deviation in the statement execution sequence is an indication of an error in the conversion process. There may still be errors in the converted code due to other factors such as incompatible data types, but the errors

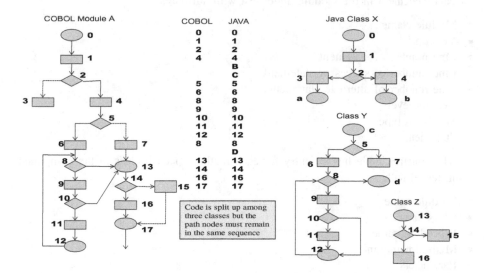

Fig. 1. Equivalent control flow paths

caused by restructuring the control flow will come to the surface. The advantage of this approach is that it can be applied as soon as the source code is compiled and that it requires neither an elaborate test environment nor test data. It forces the conversion specialist to steer the same execution path simultaneously through both the original and the converted versions of the code and in this way to recognize the deviations. If there is a difference in the control flow sequence he will recognize it immediately as the paths do not match [23].

As shown in the graph in Fig. 1, the Java nodes are split up among three classes and additional nodes inserted, but the nodes must still be executed in the same order as the COBOL nodes for the code to be functionally equivalent.

4   Implementing Parallel Source Animation

The process of demonstrating functional equivalence by parallel source animation consists of the three steps:

- pre processing
- processing
- post processing.

4.1   Preprocessing the Code

In the first step both the original code and the converted code are processed to produce a statement, a data and a function table. No change is made to the original code, however it is copied over into a statement table. Thus, we are not animating the original code but a copy of that code which may be distorted. The statement table has an entry for each statement in the module under test with attributes:

- Module Name
- Version
- Line number of statement
- Line number of successor statement
- Line number of alternate statement
- Nesting level
- Statement type
- Statement

The function table has an entry for each method of each class in the component being tested with.

- Module name
- Class name,
- Procedure name
- Method name and
- Parameters

The module and procedure names are taken from the legacy code in COBOL, PL/1 or C. The Class and Method names are taken from the converted Java code. There is a data table for each object class with an entry for each data attribute declared with the

- Class or structure in which the data is contained
- data type
- data name
- location of assignment
- assignment rule

These three tables are created for every converted component in two versions

- a version for the original legacy code and
- a version for the converted object-oriented code

Since individual components are seldom larger than 2000 statements, the tables have a limited size and can be preserved in main storage and accessed via a binary search algorithm. The statements are ordered by source name and statement number, the functions by function name and the data by data name.

4.2   Comparing Data Assignment

The data variables of a module are collected together in a module data table with their names and types and rules which are yet to be defined. The rules are verified at test time by the statement animated. If a value is assigned to a variable then that assignment is recorded in the rule clause of that variable. For instance if the variable X is assigned to the sum of Y and Z, then the rule for X is

$$X = Y + Z;$$

If the variable X is also assigned the value of b, then the rule of X is extended to be

$$X = Y + Z \ \& \ B;$$

If the variable X is alternately assigned the value C then the rule for X is extended to be

$$X = Y + Z \ \& \ B \ ! \ C;$$

As shown here, if the assignment is conditional it is added to the rule with an "!" sign. If the assignment is unconditional it is added to rule with the "&" sign. In this way the rules are extended. If a large number of operations is performed upon a single variable, the rule can become long and difficult to read, but it is mainly intended for automatic comparison.

The names of variables in the legacy code are carried over into the converted Java code. The difference lies in the qualification. In the Java code the variables are qualified by the class names. The whole class hierarchy is reflected in the qualification of the variable names, but the names themselves remain the same. This allows them to be linked to one another and allows for the rules to be compared. The rule of the variable x in module a can be compared to the rule of variable x in class a derived from class s. Thus x of a is equivalent to $s.a.x$. When the rules are displayed together the tester can compare them and verify their correctness. They can also be compared automatically by tool. If the rules do not match, an error condition is generated. Thus, the rule validation can be made both manually and automatically by comparing the assignment as depicted below:

$$\text{COBOL R223.R223−MSID } = \text{ IAB6.IAB6−P5 } (+\text{TX3})$$
$$\text{JAVA R223.R223\_MSID} = \text{ IAB6.IAB6\_P5}(-\text{TX3})$$

The tool will notice that in the method IAB6-P5 in the class IAB6 the variable TX3 is subtracted from the data attribute R223_MSID whereas in COBOL it is added to it. Such subtle conversion errors are very difficult to track down in regression testing but here they are exposed at the location where they occur.

4.3   Processing the Code

In comparing the two source versions with one another the user is presented two windows, one with the original source and one with the converted source. They are positioned next to one another. By scanning the source the user can find an entry-point from which he wants to start. In a COBOL module it is normally the first paragraph after the Procedure Division declaration. In a PL/I module it is the Procedure Main. Since the entry-point in the new source may be at a different place other than in the old source, the tool will scan the converted source to find the first method. From this point on control is taken over by the animation tool. It jumps automatically from one statement to the other in the original code and does the same for the converted Java code. The path thru the legacy code is replicated automatically in the converted Java version. It is based on the next statement entry in the two parallel statement tables. When the control flow comes to a decisional statement with more than one successor statement such as ifs, loops or case statements, the user is requested to select one. In the case of an "if" statement, he must select between the then and the else clause. In a loop statement he must choose whether to continue the loop or to terminate it. With an "evaluate" or "select" statement he is presented a list of the cases and can choose which case should be executed. In this way he animates the flow of control thru the code of the COBOL, C or PL/1 module. That control flow is mirrored in the converted Java code transcending class boundaries. The tester can follow the parallel flow thru the two sources. The tool ensures that the two paths are synchronized. The equivalent to the next node of the path thru the legacy code is looked for in the path thru the Java code. In animating the code the two statement tables are joined into one for comparison. (see Sample 1).

```
Ver ;Line ;Dest ;Alt    ;Lev;Type ;Statement
--------------------------------------------------------------------------------------
Old ;0076;0077;         ;0  ;label  ;SEMIP0.
new;0100;0101;          ;0 ;method;public  String  RRE3_SEMIP0() {
new;0101;0102;          ;1 ;        ;String xNextMethod = Spaces;
Old ;0077;0078;         ;1 ;assign ;MOVE "00" TO STATUS-KEY IN OUTPUT-MSG.
new;0102;0103;          ;1 ;assign ;RRE3.OUTPUT.OUT_OUT_MSG.setSTATUS_KEY("00");
Old ;0078;0079;0084;1 ;if        ;IF NOT (DESTINATION-ID-3 = "TEI" OR "GAT" OR "LAD")
new;0103;0104;0113;1 ;if        ;if
!(RRE3.OUTPUT.MSG.getDESTINATION_ID_3().trim().equals("TEI") ||
new;0103;         ;  ;          ;
RRE3.OUTPUT.MSG.getDESTINATION_ID_3().trim().equals("GAT") ||
new;0103;         ;  ;          ;
RRE3.OUTPUT.OUT_MSG.getDESTINATION_ID_3().trim().equals("LAD")))   {
Old ;0079;0080;0083;2 ;if        ;IF (NOT (DESTINATION-ID-1 = "S" AND (DESTINATION-ID-4 =
"A")))
Old ;0079;         ;  ;          ;OR DESTINATION-ID-3 = "SYN" OR "SAL" OR "SAI"
```

Sample 1: Combined Statement Table

When a "GO TO" occurs in the legacy code the animator will jump to that target label. In the Java source it will return to the controller and from there be redirected to the method corresponding to the COBOL or PL/I label. That method may be in the same or another class, but it must follow in the same dynamic sequence as in the original procedural code. If not then an error condition is raised. If a paragraph or procedure is performed the path is directed to the target label. In Java it will jump to the corresponding method. Should the same method be contained in several modules or classes, i.e. polymorphic methods, the user is requested to select which one should be the target. For this purpose a menu with all the method versions qualified by their module, i.e. class, name is presented. The selection of a label in the legacy module will cause a branch to the method with that name in the object oriented version. Here again the two versions are synchronized.

In the case of a method invocation, the interface of the called method is displayed together with the parameters of the calling statement so the tester can check if they are compatible. Then the control continues through the called functions until it comes to a return. From there it goes back to the next statement after the perform statement. Functions may be nested so that the called function may call another. The animator tool maintains a stack to return to the last calling statement. The same applies to the call statement. Only here the animator tool reads in the source of the called module together with the source of the corresponding Java class. The step wise animation of the code then continues within the called source until it reaches a return statement.

In this manner, the user follows the flow of control through both source versions from the common entry-point to a final return-point. If the control logic of the converted source has been converted correctly, the two flows should be the same according to the law of dynamic invariance. The statements on the two paths will be traversed in the same order. If not, there has been an error in the conversion. Even where GOTO statements have been replaced by a return to the central controller for invoking the next method the new methods will follow in the same sequence as the original program labels. Deviations in the control flow can be detected immediately and reported [24].

The simultaneous simulation of the execution paths through two source versions can be repeated for each potential path. Since complex components have a large number of potential paths, it is not possible to trace them all. That would require too much time. Therefore, the tester has to select paths to simulate based on two factors:

- that they are representative of other paths and
- that they are most likely to reveal conversion errors

The static analysis tool which processes the COBOL code prior to conversion documents the possible paths through the COBOL code from which the tester can choose. This is done by displaying the source and highlighting the statement traversed by the path. There are better solutions to this problem using a directed graph of the abstract syntax tree. The goal is to emulate as many paths as possible in the time available. The responsible conversion specialist should be confident that the source has been converted correctly before passing it on the users for the final acceptance test.

4.4   Post Processing the Code

When the execution of the two source versions is simulated, the animation tool records the labels of all paragraphs, procedures, methods and modules traversed by the two paths. The resulting label lists serve to document the execution paths. The labels of the set and get methods in the converted object-oriented source are left out purposely to keep the paths equivalent. For the same reason the labels of the controller and the inserted access routines are suppressed, as are all labeled methods inserted by the source transformation, so that the label list of the converted source contains only those labels that were in the original source. A deviation in the two executed label lists will only appear if there is a conversion error. By comparing the two label lists, a separate control step is implemented in addition to the visual control performed by the conversion engineer when simulating the execution. If he oversees a deviation, it will be caught by this path comparison routine. This ensures if not code equivalence at least trace equivalence.

A second, useful post processing function is that of coverage measurement. In pre processing, a table of function labels is created for the two source versions. It contains the labels of every module, procedure and method. After the source execution has been simulated, there exists a label list for every path simulated. By comparing the labels of each path with the labels of the source as a whole, all labels not traversed by a path are recognized and reported in a label coverage report. This report also shows what percent of the labels have been covered. This coverage technique was originally proposed by Cimitile and Fasolino at the ICSM conference in 1993 [25]. Label coverage is here equivalent to code coverage. With the help of this report, the conversion engineer can decide if the simulated test is sufficient to demonstrate functional equivalence. If the coverage is too low, more paths have to be simulated to bring it up.

A third purpose of the source animation described here is to help the responsible maintenance engineer in debugging the code. By tracing the paths thru the source, he can better understand what is going on in the sources and find out where errors occur without having to execute the code, which is not always possible. This was the original purpose of Howden when he introduced symbolic execution back in 1977 [26].

The challenge is to discover as many conversion errors as possible as early as possible. The earliest moment is immediately upon compilation. That is where the source animator is engaged. If there are syntax errors in the conversion, the compiler will find them. If there are logic errors in the restructuring of the code, the animator will find them. An earlier source animator COBRETEST was developed in the late 90's and used to test converted COBOL programs at a Swiss bank. It was very helpful in finding restructuring errors before the program went to the system testers, but the main purpose was to create a dynamic trace documentation to compare with the original program documentation. This approach to comparing test documentation with the original design documentation had been proposed by Parnas and Peters [27].

The current source animator has only recently been implemented for testing converted Java and C# sources against the original COBOL, PL/1 and C sources. It is planned to make this tool publically available after a year. The first usage was to compare converted Java sources with the legacy COBOL code from which they were derived. The use of the tool proved to be very helpful. More than 80 conversion errors could be detected and corrected in the 300.000 lines of converted code before the actual regression test began. Considering the fact that it costs an average of two person days to correct an error found by the testers in system testing, that represent a saving of 160 person days. This is significant in a project calculated on the basis of 1.50 Euros per original line. In fact it amounts to about 14 % of the total cost.

The use of parallel animation to compare source code versions is not restricted to conversions. It applies equally well to refactoring projects where the language remains the same but the structure changes. By factoring out nested logic to new methods, there will be additional methods, but the execution of the original methods will remain invariant. Animation will demonstrate that the refactoring has no undesired side effects on the control flow. This usage is planned for the reengineering of C++ and C# as well as for Java code. Some preliminary work on this has already has been tested at the university where the first author teaches software maintenance. Students are required there to test the sources they have refactored. Animation makes it possible for the students to check the correctness of their refactoring without having to setup an extensive test environment. Animating the code also helps them to become more familiar with the code, as pointed out by the first author in a previous paper [28]. A similar approach is suggested by Cornelissen, Zaidman and van Deursen in their controlled experiment on program comprehension via trace visualization. The emphasis of their approach is on understanding one program whereas the main goal here is to match one program against another [29].

5 Conclusion and Further Work

The conclusion to be made is that there is a need to test reengineered code independently of the target environment for which it is intended. Testing in the target environment is expensive and time consuming. Besides it occurs very late in the reengineering or conversion process. The goal is to find conversion errors as soon after the conversion as possible so the conversion engineer can make the necessary corrections to the conversion tools. Source animation is a good way of achieving this. It is inexpensive and practical. It also forces the conversion engineers to think through the logic of the converted code and to compare it with the original code. Thus it supports dynamic code inspection as proposed by Gilb and Graham already in 1993 [30].

Further work on the comparison tool will be directed toward the verification of refactored code. Both procedural and object-oriented code can be refactored. Statements are cut out and moved to other locations, for instance in subordinate methods or higher level classes. Variables can also be moved up to a higher level class or collected together in a common class. However, regardless of this shifting around the statements must still be executed in the same dynamic order and the variables must be assigned the same values. Symbolic execution thru animation is a good way of demonstrating that a refactored component still behaves in the exact same way as the original one. Symbolic execution via source animation is a good way to minimize the test effort [31].

The next steps are to improve path comparison techniques and to check the usage of the data types. The second author has been working on research in this area for a long time and this research continues in the direction of source code comparison. By comparing the original data types with the new ones it is possible to detect such data anomalies. There still remains much work left to do until source code can be safely and predictably transformed from one form into another. Much of this work has to do with ensuring that transformation algorithms are correct, a topic which the second author has already published on [32].

References

1. Terekhov, A., Verhoef, C.: Realities of language conversion. IEEE Softw. **17**(6), 111 (2000)
2. Sneed, H.: Migrating from COBOL to Java – a report from the field. In: IEEE Proceedings of 26th ICSM, p. 122. Computer Society Press, Temesvar, September 2010
3. Yang, H., Zedan, H.: Abstraction – a key notion for reverse engineering in a system reengineering approach. J. Softw. Maint. **12**(4), 197 (2000)
4. Sneed, H.: Encapsulating legacy software for reuse in client-server systems. In: IEEE 3rd WCRE, p. 104. Computer Society Press, Monterey (1996)
5. Meyer, B.: Object-oriented Software Construction, p. 12. Prentice-Hall International, Hertfordshire (1988)
6. Sneed, H.: Transforming procedural program structures to object-oriented class structures. In: IEEE Proceedings of 18th ICSM, p. 286. Computer Society Press, Montreal, October 2001
7. Sellink, A., Sneed, H., Verhoef, C.: Restructuring of COBOL/CICS legacy systems. Sci. Comput. Program. **45**(2–3), 193 (2002)
8. Ruhl, M., Gunn, M.: Software reengineering – a case study and lessons learned, pp. 500–193. NIST Special Publication, September 1991
9. Veerman, N.: Revitalizing modifiability of legacy assets. J. Softw. Maint. Evol. **16**, 219 (2004)
10. Veerman, N.: Towards lightweight checks for mass maintenance transformations. Sci. Comput. Program. **57**(2), 129–163 (2005)
11. Broy, M.: Zur spezifikation von programmen für die textverarbeitung. In: Wossido, P. (ed.) Textverarbeitung und Informatik. Informatik Fachberichte, vol. 30, p. 75. Springer, Heidelberg (1980)

12. Lano, K., Breuer, P., Haughton, H.: Reverse engineering of COBOL via formal methods. J. Softw. Maint. **5**(1), 13 (1993)
13. Howden, W.: Symbolic testing with the DISSECT symbolic evaluation system. IEEE Trans. **1**(4), 266 (1977)
14. Howden, W.: Functional program testing. IEEE Trans. **6**(3), 162 (1980)
15. Rich, C., Waters, R.C.: The programmer's apprentice: a research overview. IEEE Comput. Mag. **21**(11), 10–25 (1988)
16. Swartout, V., Balzer, R.: On the inevitable intertwining of specification and implementation. Commun. ACM **25**(7), 438–440 (1982)
17. Basili, V., Selby, R.: Comparing the effectiveness of software testing strategies. IEEE Trans. **13**(12), 1278 (1987)
18. El-Fakih, K., Yevtushenko, N., Bochmann, G.: FSM-based incremental conformance testing methods. IEEE Trans. **30**(7), 425 (2004)
19. Sneed, H.: Validating functional equivalence of reengineered programs via control path, result and data flow comparison. Softw. Test. Verif. Reliab. **4**(1), 33 (1994)
20. Sneed, H.: Risks involved in reengineering projects. In: IEEE Proceedings of 6th WCRE, p. 204. Computer Society Press, Atlanta, October 1999
21. Leung, N., White, L.: Insights into regression testing. In: IEEE Proceedings of 5th ICSM, p. 60. Computer Society Press, Miami, November 1989
22. Weyuker, E.: The cost of data flow testing – an empirical study. IEEE Trans. **16**(2), 121 (1990)
23. Korel, B., Laski, J.: Dynamic slicing of computer programs. J. Syst. Softw. **13**(3), 187 (1990)
24. Stevens, S.: Intelligent interactive video simulation of a code inspection. Commun. ACM **32** (7), 832 (1989)
25. Cimitile, A., Fasolino, A.: Reuse reengineering and validation via concept assignment. In: IEEE Proceedings of 9th ICSM, p. 216. Computer Society Press, Montreal, September 1993
26. Howden, W.: Reliability of the path analysis testing strategy. IEEE Trans. **1**(4), 208 (1976)
27. Peters, D., Parnas, D.: Using test oracles generated from program documentation. IEEE Trans. **24**(3), 161 (1998)
28. Sneed, H.: Source animation as a means of program comprehension for object-oriented systems. In: Proceedings of 8th IEEE International Workshop on Program Comprehension, p. 179. Computer Society Press, Limerick, June 2000
29. Cornelissen, B., Zaidman, A., van Deursen, A.: A controlled experiment for program comprehension through trace visualization. IEEE Trans. **37**(3), 341 (2011)
30. Gilb, T., Graham, D.: Software Inspection Techniques. Addison-Wesley, Wokingham (1993)
31. Verhoef, C.: Towards automated modification of legacy assets. Ann. Softw. Eng. **9**, 315 (2000)
32. Klusener, S., Lämmel, R., Verhoef, C.: Architectural modifications to deployed software. Sci. Comput. Program. **54**, 143 (2005)

Software Quality Assurance in Industry

Software Quality Assurance During Implementation: Results of a Survey in Software Houses from Germany, Austria and Switzerland

Michael Felderer[✉] and Florian Auer

Institute of Computer Science, University of Innsbruck, Innsbruck, Austria
{michael.felderer,florian.auer}@uibk.ac.at

Abstract. *Context:* Quality assurance performed during the implementation phase, e.g., by coding guidelines, static analysis or unit testing, is of high importance to ensure quality of software, but there is a lack of common knowledge and best practices on it. *Objective:* The goal of this paper is to investigate the state-of-practice of quality assurance during the implementation phase in software houses. *Method:* For this purpose, we conducted a survey in Germany, Austria, and Switzerland where 57 software houses participated. The questionnaire comprised questions regarding techniques, tools, and effort for software quality assurance during implementation as well as the perceived quality after implementation. The results were complemented by interviews and results from other surveys on software quality in general. *Results:* Results from the survey show that the most common software quality assurance techniques used during implementation are unit testing, code reviews and coding guidelines. Most tool support is used in the areas of bug tracking, version control and project management. Due to relationships between the used tool types, it seems that the introduction of one tool leads to the adoption of several others. Also quality assurance techniques and tools are correlated. Bug fixing takes a significant ratio of the overall project effort assigned to implementation. Furthermore, we found that the more developers a software company has, the more effort is spent on bug fixing. Finally, more than half of all companies rated the quality after implementation as rather good to good. *Conclusion:* For the most important quality assurance techniques and supporting tool types clear usage patterns can be seen and serve as a basis to provide guidelines on their application in practice.

Keywords: Software quality assurance · Implementation · Software development · Software quality · Software houses · Survey

1 Introduction

Quality assurance performed during the implementation phase, e.g., by coding guidelines, static analysis or unit testing, is critical to create software of high quality [1]. According to the ISO/IEC/IEEE Standard 24765 implementation or

© Springer International Publishing AG 2017
D. Winkler et al. (Eds.): SWQD 2017, LNBIP 269, pp. 87–102, 2017.
DOI: 10.1007/978-3-319-49421-0_7

coding is defined as "the process of translating a design into hardware components, software components, or both" [2]. The respective phase in the software development life cycle, i.e., the implementation phase, is defined as the "period of time in the software life cycle during which a software product is created from design documentation and debugged" [2], which also comprises bug fixing and therefore quality assurance activities. Nevertheless, quality assurance during implementation, which we also call integrated quality assurance, lacks a common body of knowledge and is often handled as a "black box" in the overall development process individually managed by developers. Given that a considerable large amount of the total project effort is spent on implementation [3], it is important to investigate the state-of-practice and to provide guidelines for respective quality assurance techniques and tools. This holds especially for software houses, i.e., companies whose primary products are software [4], for which quality assurance is essential to guarantee quality of their delivered software products.

The goal of this paper is to investigate the state-of-practice of quality assurance during the implementation phase in software houses. For this purpose, we present results of a survey conducted by the University of Innsbruck together with the Austrian consultancy company Software Quality Lab in software houses from Germany (D), Austria (A) and Switzerland (CH), the so called "DACH region". Overall 57 software houses from the DACH region responded to questions on software quality assurance techniques, tools, effort, and perceived quality after implementation. The results were complemented by interviews and results from related surveys. However, this is the first survey dedicated to software quality assurance during implementation in software houses, which provides due to central role of software development for the whole organization a valid source to investigate best practices. Furthermore, our survey does not only consider agile practices like other surveys (for instance, [5,6]) and especially also statistically investigates correlations between software quality assurance techniques and tools.

The results presented in this paper provide information on the state-of-practice and are equally relevant for research (by guiding it to relevant topics) and practice (by serving as a baseline for comparison).

This paper is structured as follows. Section 2 presents related work. Section 3 discusses the survey goal, design and execution. Section 4 presents results and discusses them. Finally, Sect. 5 concludes the paper.

2   Related Work

In this section, we summarize related results on software quality assurance during implementation from other surveys reporting respective results [3,5–8]. Relevant related results reported in these studies address the project effort spent on implementation, tool support during implementation as well as the usage of agile practices during implementation. In the following paragraphs we summarize these quantitative and qualitative results and later in Sect. 4 we relate them to our findings.

Regarding agile practices, Vonken et al. [5] found that the use of a coding standard correlates to the subjective satisfaction with the development process. 70 % of the participants responded to use coding standards regularly or extensively and only 4 % responded to never use any coding standard. In addition, Perez et al. [6] found that pair programming has a positive correlation with the perceived quality of the development process. Schindler [8] examined in a 2008 Austrian-wide survey that although the agile practice pair-programming is known by 71 % of all participants, it was only used by 46 %. Furthermore, all of the participants that claimed to use this practice, also admitted to not use pair-programming regularly but instead rarely or on demand [8]. Furthermore, a third of the 46 % also said to only use pair-programming in the case of complex tasks. Schindler [8] also noted that pair programming is important for knowledge exchange between senior and junior developers as well as to get new developers up to speed. Another observation made by Vonken et al. [5] is that pair programming correlates with unit testing and refactoring. A more unexpected observation made by the same authors is that unit testing and refactoring are unrelated, which is surprising as unit testing can be considered as safeguard during refactoring.

Regarding the effort spent, Garousi et al. [3] found that on average around 31 % of the total project effort was spent on implementation. This is more than two times the effort of the second most reported effort consuming activity, i.e., testing. Armbrust et al. [7] observed a higher amount of the total project effort allocated to implementation. According to their findings, on average around 48 % of the software development effort was assigned to development, the smallest amount assigned was 10 % and the highest 85 %.

Regarding tool support, Pérez et al. [6] found that version control (93 %) as well as bug notification and tracking (86 %) are commonly used tools. In contrast, tools that support the development process like continuous integration (45 %), testing (52 %) or configuration (45 %) are only used by about half of the respondents. Furthermore, Vonken et al. [5] found similar high usage ratios for version control systems (88 %). Also Garousi et al. [3] investigated the usage of tools [3] and found that static code analysis and automation tools are used by 64 % of all respondents. Whereas 24 % responded to never use and 12 % to seldom use this type of tools. Finally, Schindler [8] identified that the most frequently used tools to support agile development are unit tests (75 %), generators for documentation from source code (71 %) as well as continuous integration (39 %).

3   Survey Goal, Design, Distribution, and Analysis

This section provides the survey goal and research questions (Sect. 3.1), the survey design (Sect. 3.2), the survey distribution (Sect. 3.3), as well as the survey analysis (Sect. 3.4). Finally, Sect. 3.5 provides a summarizing timeline of the performed survey design, distribution and analysis activities.

3.1   Goal and Research Questions

The goal of this survey is to investigate the role of software quality assurance during the implementation phase in software houses from Germany, Austria and Switzerland. The target audience of the survey are therefore software houses that are located in Germany, Austria or Switzerland and do not operate in a domain that may impose restrictions on their software development, e.g., medical or automotive. Based on the goal and taking industrial relevance from experiences of the involved company Software Quality Lab into account, we raise the following four research questions (RQs):

RQ 1 *Which quality assurance techniques are used during development?*
RQ 2 *Which tool support is used for quality assurance during development?*
RQ 3 *How much effort is spent on implementation and integrated quality assurance?*
RQ 4 *How is the perceived software quality after implementation (including the integrated quality assurance)?*

3.2   Survey Design

In the survey design, we used and benefited from lessons learned and guidelines reported by other researchers in software engineering [9, 10]. We therefore present the sampling plan, the questionnaire design and the performed pilot test.

Sampling Plan. The sampling plan describes how the participants are representatively selected from the target population. The first decision, whether a probabilistic, non-probabilistic or census sample should be considered, was already made by selecting the target audience. Given that no list of all companies exists that have the characteristics of to target audience, a truly probabilistic or census sample is not feasible. The first (probabilistic) would require an enumeration of all members of the target audience to select randomly participants and the later (census) can as well only be conducted if all individuals of the target audience are known. As a result, non-probabilistic sampling was chosen.

As a method to draw the sample from the population quota sampling with the two strata geographical location of the software house (Germany, Austria or Switzerland) and number of employees (less or equal 10, 11 to 100 and more than 100) was applied.

Overall 57 software houses, 19 from each of the three countries, evenly distributed over the three company sizes were selected and could be consulted within the given time and resources. Based on the activities relevant for software houses from the OECD [11] industry categories, i.e., 62 – Computer programming, consultancy and related activities, as well as 631 – Data processing, hosting and related activities; web portals, the overall number of software houses in Germany, Austria and Switzerland could be estimated based on data from governmental statistical offices. For Germany, the "IKT-BRANCHE IN

DEUTSCHLAND" [12] report identified 61,029 companies in 2013 that are classified with one of the two categories[1]. For Austria, the governmental statistical office reported 13,281 companies in the respective categories[2] in 2012. Finally for Switzerland, the federal statistical office measured 2008 in the census of companies[3] 15,466 companies that have amongst their main activities programming, information technology consulting and data processing. As a result, the total number of software houses in the DACH region can be estimated with 90,000 $(61,029 + 15,466 + 13,281 = 89,776)$. Taking the population size of 90,000 into account, with the 57 participating companies a precision [9], which measures how close an estimate (resulting from the survey data) is to the actual characteristic in the population, of 87 % is achieved.

Questionnaire Design. The questionnaire was designed based on the experiences of Software Quality Lab and the involved researchers in conducting surveys as well as academic findings of related surveys (see Sect. 2) and the software engineering body of knowledge (SWEBOK) [13]. The knowledge and practical consultancy experience of Software Quality Lab was a valuable input to design the questionnaire. Furthermore, a technical report of a survey on software quality conducted by Winter et al. [14] in 2011 provided many useful insights for the questionnaire design. The questions included in the questionnaire were transformed into closed-ended questions and ordered by topic. The questionnaire was implemented and performed online with the survey tool LimeSurvey[4]. For software quality assurance during implementation five questions were raised, i.e., one question for RQ 1, one for RQ 2, two for RQ 3, and one for RQ 4, and embedded into a larger questionnaire on software quality processes. The questions of the questionnaire correspond to the research questions, where RQ 3 is split into two questions, one for the development and one for the bug fixing effort. The answer options for each of the five questions are shown in Figs. 2, 4, 6, 7, and 8, respectively. The complete questionnaire is available via the first author upon request.

Pilot Test. The questionnaire was validated *internally*, i.e., by the involved researchers and Software Quality Lab, as well as *externally* by six employees of software houses. Internally, there were several iterations and the involvement of researchers and industrialists guaranteed a high quality review from different perspectives. Externally, the reviewers provided valuable, written feedback to further improve the questionnaire.

3.3 Survey Distribution

The distribution of the questionnaires among the potential participants included a pre-notification, the invitation with the questionnaire, reminders and a thank-you letter. The survey distribution started on April 1, 2015. The participants

---

[1] http://bit.ly/1Sqfb3z.
[2] http://bit.ly/22IjjeS.
[3] http://bit.ly/22IkScL.
[4] http://www.limesurvey.org.

were selected by using Google Maps and searching for 'software company'. Searching for this term reveals all software companies at the related location. Furthermore, information about the number of employees for each found software house were determined. This allowed to come up with 450 participants – 50 small, 50 medium and 50 big software houses per country. Two weeks after the pre-notification emails were sent, the invitation emails with a link to the online survey were distributed. As a result, 13 participants responded to not wish to participate and 20 software houses participated. One reminder were sent in the middle of the survey (end of April 2015) to remember possible participants about the survey. Due to the low number of responses, additional 500 software companies were contacted via email. In addition, new participants were searched and contacted exclusively by phone to invite them to the survey. During three days within the last week, 200 potential software houses in Germany, Austria and Switzerland were called and asked for participation. In this three days 18 software houses could be convinced to participate. Thus, the response rate for the phone calls was 9 %, which is double the response rate of the email invitations (4 % for the first half of the survey and 3 % for the second). In the phone calls, also some of the reasons against the participation were mentioned. Amongst others, no time, no interest, already having participated in similar surveys and the absence of the respective decision maker were mentioned. The survey distribution ended on May 22, 2015.

3.4   Survey Analysis

The data was first analyzed *quantitatively* and then *qualitatively* by interviews with survey participants and evidence extracted from related work.

As the responses for each question were nominally scaled, the votes for each question were counted and then visualized in bar charts. Furthermore, Pearson correlation coefficients between answers were computed to find correlations within and between quality assurance techniques and tools to support implementation. The analysis was performed in IBM SPSS and the resulting correlation coefficients have been interpreted as suggest by Evans [15], i.e., in steps of 0.2 from very weak to very strong.

We performed 12 interviews with survey participants (i.e., 21 % of all participants) to triangulate the quantitative analysis and to identify the reasons behind some survey answers. The semi-structured interview type was chosen, because the structured interview limits the discussion freedom to enter unforeseen subtopics or ask questions that may arise during the interview. Another alternative would have been the unstructured interview. However, this form would have not allowed to ask prepared questions of interest that emerged during the analysis of the empirical survey. Telephone calls were used contact each participant in an economic and for the interviewee time- and place-flexible way. In the short interview one question on implementation was asked. In addition, the non-structured part of the interview followed subtopics of interest that were raised by the interviewee or that turned out as a result of previously conducted interviews to be of interest.

3.5   Survey Timeline

This section summarizes the survey design, distribution and analysis by providing the concrete timeline in which the respective activities were performed in 2015. Figure 1 shows the timeline for survey design, distribution and analysis activities. Activities with concrete dates in parentheses were performed in the given date range, the other activities were performed during the whole month.

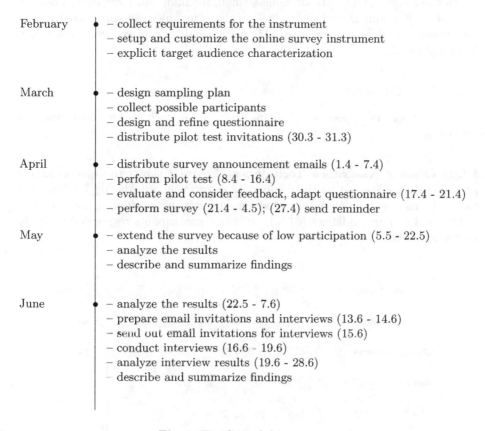

February
– collect requirements for the instrument
– setup and customize the online survey instrument
– explicit target audience characterization

March
– design sampling plan
– collect possible participants
– design and refine questionnaire
– distribute pilot test invitations (30.3 - 31.3)

April
– distribute survey announcement emails (1.4 - 7.4)
– perform pilot test (8.4 - 16.4)
– evaluate and consider feedback, adapt questionnaire (17.4 - 21.4)
– perform survey (21.4 - 4.5); (27.4) send reminder

May
– extend the survey because of low participation (5.5 - 22.5)
– analyze the results
– describe and summarize findings

June
– analyze the results (22.5 - 7.6)
– prepare email invitations and interviews (13.6 - 14.6)
– send out email invitations for interviews (15.6)
– conduct interviews (16.6 - 19.6)
– analyze interview results (19.6 - 28.6)
– describe and summarize findings

Fig. 1. Timeline of the survey.

4   Results and Discussion

In this section, we first present the demographics of our survey, then we present and discuss main findings for each of the four research questions, and finally we discuss threats to validity.

4.1 Demographics

Overall 57 software houses, 19 from Germany, 19 from Austria and 19 from Switzerland, participated in the survey. Most of the software houses (84 %) stated that they perform more than one type of software project. On average three types were stated. The three most common project types are development of web-applications (71 %), individual software (61 %), and standard software (56 %).

In the sample of 57 software houses small, medium and large companies are present with a similar frequency: 38 % of the companies are small-sized (up to 10 employees), 35 % medium-sized (11 to 100) and 26 % large-sized (more than 100 employees).

4.2 Main Findings

In this section we present the main findings for each of the four research questions.

RQ1: Quality Assurance Techniques. Figure. 2 shows the quality assurance techniques applied by the responding software houses during implementation. The most commonly used techniques are unit testing (68 %), code reviews (63 %) and coding guidelines (61 %). Only one participants responded to apply no technique at all.

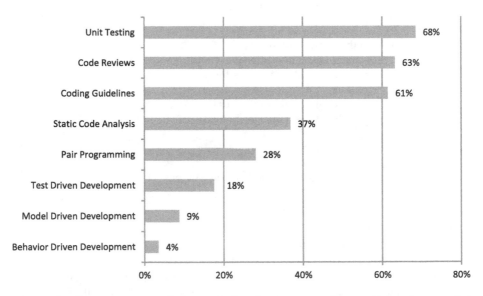

Fig. 2. Quality assurance techniques during development. One participant responded to apply no techniques at all.

So similar to Vonken et al. [5], we found a high ratio of people using coding guidelines. Furthermore, our results are also compliant with the finding of Schindler [8] that pair programming is only applied moderately.

Correlation analysis shown in Fig. 3 revealed six positive relationships between quality assurance techniques, i.e., using one technique increases the likelihood of using the related one. Static code analysis is related to coding guidelines, test-driven development (TDD) as well as unit testing. Furthermore, coding guidelines are related to TDD, unit testing to code reviews and model-driven development to behavior-driven development (BDD). Considering the relationships, it is surprising that static code analysis is not amongst the most commonly used techniques given its positive correlations to coding guidelines and unit testing which are both used by more than 60 % of the responding software houses. Another notable, relationship is between model-driven development and BDD that have only a significant positive correlation to each other, but not to other techniques.

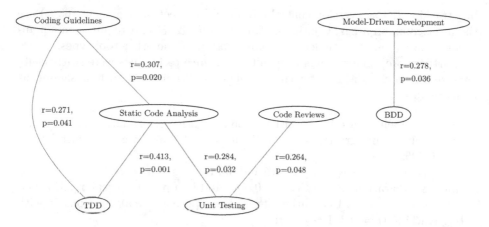

Fig. 3. Positive correlations between quality assurance techniques. Note that for all relationship $n = 57$, which is why it is not explicitly mentioned at every correlation.

Quality assurance techniques like unit testing, code reviews or the usage of coding guidelines are commonly practices according to the results of the empirical survey. In addition, reviews, tests during development, checklists and reviews at milestones are commonly used methods to control and support the software development process. Thus, it seems that implementation is well supported by respective quality assurance techniques. However, in the interviews with most participants the domain-specific side of the software, the rules and peculiarities of the domain, are seldom addressed explicitly, although they often lead to costly bugs.

RQ2: Tool Support. The participants were asked to indicate in which areas implementation is supported by tools. The results depicted in Fig. 4 show that

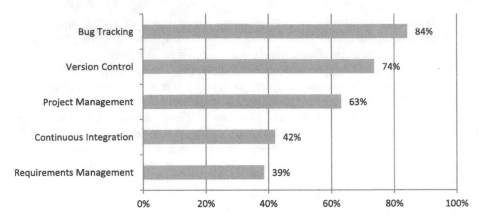

Fig. 4. Areas in which tools are used to support implementation.

bug tracking (84 %), version control (73 %) and project management (63 %) are
the most common areas. Continuous integration (42 %) and requirements management (38 %) are mentioned only half as often as the other tool types.

Furthermore, relationships to quality assurance techniques were statistically
analyzed. The calculation of each possible correlation revealed four significant
relationships:

- Coding guidelines are in a positive, moderate strong correlation with the use
  of continuous integration ($r = 0.457, p = 0.000$) and version control tools
  ($r = 0.426, p = 0.001$).
- Static code analysis is in a positive and moderate strong correlation with continuous integration ($r = 0.454, p = 0.000$) and in a positive, weak relationship
  with version control. In addition, it also has a positive, weak relationship with
  bug tracking ($r = 0.331, p = 0.012$).
- Code Reviews are in a weak, positive correlation with version control ($r = 0.287, p = 0.030$) and bug tracking ($r = 0.367, p = 0.005$).
- Unit testing is in a weak, positive correlation with project management ($r = 0.264, p = 0.048$) and in a strong, positive with bug tracking ($r = 0.430, p = 0.001$).

Thus, coding guidelines and static code analysis are often used in environments with continuous integration and version control. Bug tracking tools are
often used in environments in which also static code analysis, code reviews and
unit testing are performed.

Correlations between the tool types have also been analyzed and are shown in
Fig. 5: continuous integration tools are positively correlated with requirements
management and version control tools, and bug tracking tools are positively
correlated with version control and project management tools. One can observe
that all tools are related directly or indirectly (via other tools). Thus, it seems
that the introduction of one tool leads to the adoption of several others. This is

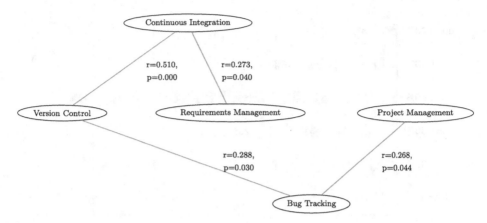

Fig. 5. Positive correlations between the tool types. Note that for all relationships hold that $n = 57$.

supported by the fact, that a high number of participants (64 %) stated to use three or more tools. Tools supporting implementation are therefore often used together.

Also several other surveys [3,5,6,8] found that different types of tools are commonly-used to support development. Our results confirm the findings of Perez et al. [6] who also found that version control and bug tracking tools are often used, but continuous integration only moderately. Furthermore, Vonken et al. [5] also found high usage rates of version control systems. Finally, Schindler [8] reported a similar usage rate of continuous integration (around 40 %) as we did.

RQ3: Effort. We asked for the ratio of the total project effort spent on implementation and integrated quality assurance. Figure 6 indicates a clear trend towards the range 41 % to 60 % of the total project effort, which was selected by 49 % of all participants. Thus, it seems that in practice most often a ratio between 41 % and 60 % of the total project effort is spent on implementation.

So in our case, the effort spent on programming is higher than reported in Garousi et al. [3] (i.e., 31 %) and compliant with the finding of Armbrust et al. [7] who reports a ratio of the overall effort spent on implementation of 48 % (and integrated quality assurance).

The most important integrated quality assurance technique during implementation is bug fixing. Figure 7 shows that with respect to the ratio of the total project effort developers spend on bug fixing, most participants (63 %) responded that up to 20 % of the total project effort is spent on bug fixing. Even higher efforts were stated by 25 % of the respondents. Moreover, 12 % could not estimate the effort for bug fixing, which may indicate that they are not aware of the effort that is used for bug fixing or do not measure it.

According to two interviewees, a reason for the relatively high bug fixing effort is that a small amount of bugs requires a large amount of time and effort

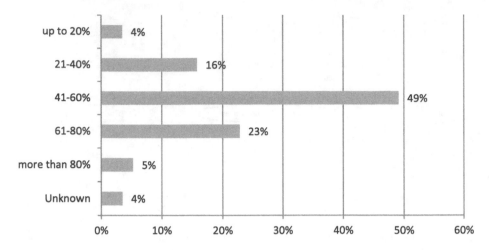

Fig. 6. Amount of total project effort dedicated to implementation.

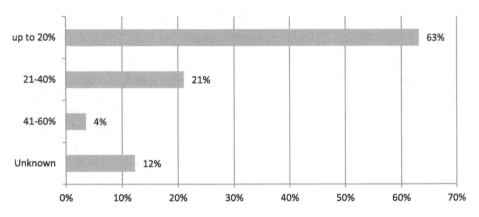

Fig. 7. Ratio of total project effort spent on bug fixing by developers.

to be fixed. An example stated by one interviewee was a wrong variable name caused by copying similar source code. Another reason that was commonly mentioned are incomplete requirements specifications that result in bugs that are not caused by wrong code, but by missing edge cases that were not properly specified. One interviewee explicitly highlighted that not technical aspects cause high bug fixing efforts, but domain aspects. Developers typically do not have the same deep understanding of the business domain of the software as for instance requirements engineers or customers have. This often results in bugs caused by missing or wrongly interpreted domain-specific aspects of requirements.

Given that more developers work on the same code, bugs may be introduced by other employees that have to fix them. As a result, it could be that a higher ratio of the total effort is spent on bug fixing with an increasing number of employees. This is also supported by the fact that with an increasing number of developers also the system complexity increases, which makes it more difficult to find and fix bugs. The statistical analysis confirmed this correlation and identified a strong positive correlation between the number of employees in software development and the effort for bug fixing ($r = 0.485, n = 56, p = 0.000$). Thus, the more developers a software company has, the more effort is spent on bug fixing.

RQ4: Perceived Quality. We asked for the perceived software quality after implementation (including the integrated quality assurance) at the handover to system testing. Figure 8 shows that 41 % responded to perceive the quality neither as good nor as bad, 56 %, more than half of all companies, rated the quality as rather good to good. Only one participant mentioned that the quality of the software at this point in development is rather bad. Thus, it seems that the quality of the software is considered to be in an at least rather good quality in most cases. This may indicate that the applied quality assurance measures during the development are working.

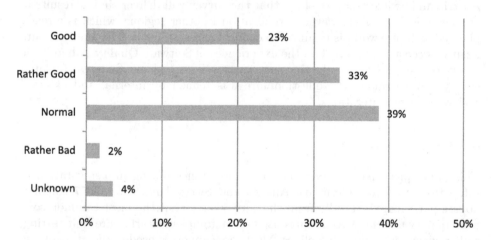

Fig. 8. Perceived software quality after implementation with integrated quality assurance.

The software quality in development may also depend on the number of developers. Thus, the correlation between the number of employees in total and the number of employees in software development, respectively, as well as the perceived software quality before testing was statistically analyzed. As a result, two weak, negative correlations were found:

- Perceived software quality is in a weak, negative correlation with the number of employees ($r = -0.334, n = 55, p = 0.013$).
- Perceived software quality is in a weak, negative correlation with the number of employees in software development ($r = -0.307, n = 55, p = 0.023$).

These two negative correlations indicate that the higher the number of employees, the lower the perceived software quality is.

4.3 Threats to Validity

In this section we discuss critical threats to validity and how we addressed them. One critical threat to validity is the limited number of participating software houses, i.e., 57. Nevertheless by estimating the overall number of software houses in the DACH region, a precision of 87 % of our results could be reached. To further increase validity of the results, the questionnaire was triangulated by interviews and evidence from related studies. Conclusions on correlation were drawn based on statistical significance.

Furthermore, it has to be mentioned that the study was only conducted in the DACH region and that the validity of the results is therefore limited to that region. But due to the facts that similar surveys were initially performed in the DACH region and then replicated in other regions with similar results [16, 17] and that we could not find significant differences between the results from Germany, Austria and Switzerland, we think that the survey will deliver similar results in other regions as well. However, a replication in other regions, which is already planned as future work, is required to confirm this statement. The questionnaire itself was constructed based on the experiences of Software Quality Lab and the involved researchers in conducting surveys as well as academic findings of related surveys. Furthermore, the questionnaire was refined by internal and external reviews in several iterations.

5   Conclusion

This paper presented a survey on quality assurance during implementation in software houses from Germany, Austria and Switzerland. Overall 57 software houses participated. Results from the survey show that the most common software quality assurance techniques used during implementation are unit testing, code reviews and coding guidelines. Most tool support is used in the areas of bug tracking, version control and project management. Due to relationships between the used tool types, it seems that the introduction of one tool leads to the adoption of several others. We also found that coding guidelines and static code analysis are often used in environments with continuous integration and version control. Bug tracking tools are often used in environments in which also static code analysis, code reviews and unit testing are performed. Bug fixing takes a significant ratio of the overall project effort assigned to implementation. Furthermore, we found that the more developers a software company has, the more effort is spent on bug fixing. Finally, more than half of all companies rated the quality after implementation as rather good to good and there seems to be a negative correlation between the number of employees and the perceived software quality.

In future, we plan to replicate the survey in other regions and to perform case studies to investigate in which context (for instance, with respect to the process model applied) specific quality assurance techniques during implementation are promising. Based on the results of these empirical studies we plan to derive practical guidelines to improve quality assurance during implementation.

Acknowledgments. The authors thank Software Quality Lab GmbH and especially its CEO Johannes Bergsmann for joint operation of this survey as well as all participating companies, interview partners and colleagues who helped to make this survey possible.

References

1. Venkitaraman, R.: Software quality assurance. Int. J. Res. Appl. Sci. Eng. Technol. (IJRASET) **2**, 261–264 (2014)
2. ISO, IEC, IEEE: Iso/iec/ieee 24765: 2010 - systems and software engineering - vocabulary. 418 (2010)
3. Garousi, V., Coşkunçay, A., Betin-Can, A., Demirörs, O.: A survey of software engineering practices in turkey. J. Syst. Soft. **108**, 148–177 (2015)
4. Roebuck, K.: Legacy Application Modernization: High-impact Strategies - What You Need to Know: Definitions, Adoptions, Impact, Benefits, Maturity, Vendors. Emereo Publishing, Aspley (2012)
5. Vonken, F., Brunekreef, J., Zaidman, A., Peeters, F.: Software engineering in the Netherlands: the state of the practice. Technical report, Delft University of Technology, Software Engineering Research Group (2012)
6. Pérez, J., Puissant, J.P., Mens, T., Kamseu, F., Habri, N.: Software quality practices in industry-a pilot study in wallonia. University of Mons, Technical report (2012)
7. Armbrust, O., Ochs, M., Snoek, B.: Stand der praxis von software-tests und deren automatisierung. Fraunhofer IESE-REPORT NR 93 (2004)
8. Schindler, C.: Agile software development methods and practices in austrian it-industry: results of an empirical study. In: 2008 International Conference on Computational Intelligence for Modelling Control and Automation, pp. 321–326. IEEE (2008)
9. Kasunic, M.: Designing an effective survey. Technical report, DTIC Document (2005)
10. Linaker, J., Sulaman, S.M., Maiani de Mello, R., Höst, M., Runeson, P.: Guidelines for conducting surveys in software engineering v. 1.0 (2015)
11. On Indicators for the Information Society, W.P: Information economy - sector definitions based on the internet standard industry classification (isic 4). DSTI/ICCP/IIS(2006)2/FINAL (2007)
12. Bundesamt, S.: Ikt-branche in deutschland - bericht zur wirtschaftlichen entwicklung (2013)
13. Society, I.C: Guide to the Software Engineering Body of Knowledge (SWEBOK(R)): Version 3.0. IEEE Computer Society Press (2014)
14. Winter, M., Vosseberg, K., Spillner, A., Haberl, P.: Softwaretest-umfrage 2011-erkenntnisziele, durchführung und ergebnisse. In: Software Engineering, pp. 157–168 (2012)

15. Evans, J.D.: Straightforward Statistics for the Behavioral Sciences. Brooks/Cole, Salt Lake City (1996)
16. Fernandez, D.M., Wagner, S., Kalinowski, M., Schekelmann, A., Tuzcu, A., Conte, T., Spinola, R., Prikladnicki, R.: Naming the pain in requirements engineering: comparing practices in Brazil and Germany. IEEE Soft. **5**, 16–23 (2015)
17. Kalinowski, M., Felderer, M., Conte, T., Spínola, R., Prikladnicki, R., Winkler, D., Fernández, D.M., Wagner, S.: Preventing incomplete/hidden requirements: reflections on survey data from Austria and Brazil. In: Winkler, D., Biffl, S., Bergsmann, J. (eds.) SWQD 2016. LNBIP, vol. 238, pp. 63–78. Springer, Heidelberg (2016). doi:10.1007/978-3-319-27033-3_5

Crowdsourcing in Software Engineering

Images of Enterprise Test Organizations: Factory, Center of Excellence, or Community?

Michal Doležel[1,2(✉)]

[1] Department of Information Technologies, University of Economics,
W. Churchill Sq. 4, 130 67 Prague, Czech Republic
michal.dolezel@vse.cz
[2] MSD IT Global Innovation Center,
Svornosti 2, 150 00 Prague, Czech Republic

Abstract. The organization of the testing process is an important part of any enterprise software quality management effort. However, little consensus exists how enterprise test organizations should be built up and structured, especially in connection with continuing penetration of recent trends such as enterprise agile development. This position paper is built upon our industry experience. During our transformation efforts connected with changing a test organization's sourcing arrangement and management approach in a large multinational firm, we noticed that people tend to prefer one distinct perspective to make sense of enterprise test organizations. But such a one-sided approach makes it difficult for them to talk to each other about the test organization. To illustrate this, we use Gareth Morgan's *Images of Organization* as an analytical lens to discuss three distinct images of test organizations we claim people typically carry in their minds. Our work increases understanding of design and transformation efforts related to management of enterprise software testing.

Keywords: Test organization · Test factory · Testing center of excellence · TCoE · Community of practice · Agile testing · Organization design · Transformation

1 Introduction

In a seminal paper published more than ten years ago, Nicholas Carr provocatively argued that *IT Doesn't Matter* [1]. In short, Carr said that information technologies (IT) had become a commodity which is accessible to everybody (like gas or electricity) and didn't make a big difference for company's success. It is not the point of the present article to discuss the general Carr's ideas. We want, however, ask a slightly different question: *Does software testing matter?*

Nowadays in the commoditized (read: outsourced and offshored) world of factory-like enterprise software testing, little space seems to remain for creativity and joy from the profession. In this world, big words such as "Testing Center of Excellence" are often used just for impression making instead of their original sense rooted in knowledge sharing practices and innovation. We think this is unfortunate. Interestingly, digital disruption has triggered some fundamental changes impacting also commoditized

© Springer International Publishing AG 2017
D. Winkler et al. (Eds.): SWQD 2017, LNBIP 269, pp. 105–116, 2017.
DOI: 10.1007/978-3-319-49421-0_8

enterprise IT. This shift will arguably change enterprise test organizations to a great extent. At present, however, very little is scientifically known not only about these transformation trends but also about current forms of enterprise test organizations. In this short position paper which stems from our industry experience, we thus want to take a step back and look at the topic.

Our work falls under the stream of relatively infrequent computing research focused on problems of organization of software testing (e.g., [2–4]). Consider the present paper as an enterprise Software Quality Management (SQM) contribution probing into test organizations at the macro level of analysis. That means, our analysis looks beyond the level of individual development teams. We understand test organizations as structural elements within software enterprises or within IT functions of non-software enterprises [5]. Our experience comes from the latter context. Note that we take the existence of formal or informal test organization for granted (as our own case demonstrates). We thus don't discuss some organizational alternatives like when testers are relatively isolated in respective project teams and there is little to no test knowledge sharing across the teams within the enterprise [2].

Primarily, our aim is to analyze here several basic types of enterprise test organization's structural patterns. To do so, we sketch some of their elementary attributes. We use Gareth Morgan's *Images of Organization* [6] *(Images)* as an analytical lens to present our findings. Our key thesis is the following. When one speaks about a test organization, she often uses a distinct term. By relating these terms to Morgan's metaphors, we are able to identify distinct characteristics and key assumptions that person holds about the test organization.

Our intention with this paper is threefold. First, to define the terms that are currently being used in a somewhat inconsistent way in the industry. Second, to help practitioners look beyond a single *Image* they might tacitly operate within. Third, to show that the *Images* are not necessarily mutually exclusive as some might argue, but that they can complement each other quite nicely. Moreover, the last point is quite a timely contribution because many experts see the transformation of enterprise test organizations as a striking issue for practitioners nowadays [7].

In what follows, we first discuss the context of the experience and used method. Then we review some key Morgan's ideas and apply them in order to describe three cardinal images of test organization we encountered. Next, we share a more tangible piece of our experience and some recommendations. We conclude by highlighting implications of our work.

2 Context and Method

In the past year and a half, we have had an opportunity to observe (and later also shape) organization design of a test organization in a large, multinational company listed in Fortune 500 (http://fortune.com/fortune500/). This has been part of a broader IT transformation effort [8]. Specifically, in this paper, we want to take an initial step and form conceptual basis for sharing more tangible aspects of our experience later on. In order to do so, we use the concept of reflective IT management practice [9].

Apparently, this is not intended as a rigorous case study. Rather, we position the paper as a descriptive account grounded in our industrial experience. As such, one might consider it as a form of alternative research genre, often perceived as quite an opposite to evidence-based research practices. Importantly, this shouldn't evoke that reflective discourse is not a valid knowledge generating mechanism [10]. Our main aim was to capture an interesting "story" and provide a rich insight, rather than rigorously measure theoretical constructs. Methodologically speaking, we shared some common interest with ethnographers. Trying to capture highly subjective "lived experience" as their top priority, they characterize themselves as the ones conducting "the art and science of describing a group or culture" [11].

In our analysis, we use just three images from Morgan's work as explained below. It is important to note the following. The perspective and background motives that influenced our reasoning process and choice of these *Images* are highly subjective. They stem from our own experience and the unique organizational context we were part of. This might be interpreted as "biased" and "unscientific" by some, but note Morgan's (and Einstein's) thoughts on this: "Whoever we are, it is impossible to obtain a complete point of view. Our perspectives always have horizons and limits dictated by the factors that we implicitly or explicitly value and deem important. ... [O]ur observations are always shaped by the 'theory' through which we see". Morgan further explains that choice of *Images* relevant for one's analysis of organization reality is highly influenced by his professional background and motivation. For example, management consultants see organization reality differently from social critics. And practicing IT managers might follow different interpretations than computer scientists.

The reason we chose the concrete *Images* we use further was thus formed by our own "lived experience". In the middle of the battleground of a huge, IT-driven organization change, we were stuck between the old and new, i.e. "test factory thinking" and "software revolution of agile gurus". We were trying to make sense of our organization world and bridge the observed gap. We were effectively forced to understand many versions (and visions) of organization reality and explain these conflicting versions to our peers, team members, and executives to fill the mentioned gap and "make the change happen". We also had the luxury to reflect on our own actions from time to time. As Schön argues, this is quite infrequent in the industry reality: "Managers do reflect-in-action, but they seldom reflect on their reflection-in-action" [9].

3   Images of Organization

Thirty years ago (1986), Gareth Morgan published the first edition of his work *Images of Organization* that is now available in the third edition [6]. This book has gained exceptional attention in both scholarly and practitioner communities, counting some 15,000 Google Scholar citations up to date. Morgan, an organizational theorist and management consultant, used the concept of metaphor to describe and conceptualize different approaches to studying as well as managing organizations. Metaphors are essentially stylistic means, "ways of seeing things as if they were something else" [12]. These stylistic means are powerful tools but require imagination. When using the lens of a metaphor, one has to focus on commonalities and disregard obvious discrepancies.

That means, metaphor always provide "kind of one-sided insight" [6] and cannot be taken literally. As Morgan explains, if we say "The man is a lion", we find him "brave, strong, and ferocious". But we don't mean that "he is ... covered in fur and ... [has] four legs, sharp teeth, and a tail".

The fundamental Morgan's idea is intriguing: By adjusting the viewing angle one looks at the same organization, new realities, sceneries and patterns suddenly emerge. The interesting thing is that all these images of organization (observable from different viewing angles) are complementary and interconnected. Just by knowing what viewing angles are worthy, we can see much more than we would see using just the one single angle one might typically prefer.

The three archetypal metaphors we use in this paper of total eight Morgan introduced in his work are the following [13].

  I. *"The machine metaphor encompasses such theories as Taylor's scientific management, Weber's bureaucracy and views of organizations that emphasize closed systems, efficiency and mechanical features of organizations."*

  II. *"The brain metaphor focuses on the cognitive features of organizations and encompasses learning theories and cybernetics."*

  III. *"The culture metaphor emphasizes symbolic and informal aspects of organizations as well as the creation of shared meanings among actors."*

One can consider Morgan's book as a sort of *catalog* of organization theories. All theories of organization implicitly work with an image; they look at organization with a specific set of premises. While organization theorists might want to use Morgan's book primarily as a way how to categorize these theories, in this paper we want to focus on IT management practice. The central argument we make in-line with Morgan's thoughts is that founders and managers tend to look at their own organizations using one of the lenses; doing it either implicitly or explicitly. The lens which they take on typically depends on many factors, for example, their beliefs, core values, and assumptions. When managers, nevertheless, stay fixed just on a single metaphor in their professional work, their respective management actions might become one-sided and imbalanced.

4   Test Organization Designing as Image Painting

4.1   Motivation

Consider the following dialogue in which the author of this paper personally participated in. The dialogue captures a "demand management" conversation. This conversation was related to specific administrative tasks connected with a late-formalization of an ongoing allocation of few agile test engineers in an agile development initiative (A – author, SM – service manager).

> SM: *What IT client is this?*
> A: *It's not an IT client, it's a [self-organizing] agile team.*
> SM: *What project is it then?*

A: It's not a [time-boxed] project, it's a product development of [application name].
SM: How many test resources are we talking about?
A: Two. But they are not "resources", they are members of a cross-functional
agile team.
SM: [silence] OK. How many months you need them for?
A: Uh... forever?

This example clearly demonstrates a clash occurred between two distinct approaches to the organization of the test process. The first one is rooted in the traditional enterprise model of resources pooling and time-boxed allocations for waterfall-like development projects. The second one is influenced by the new paradigm of "agile testing" [14] which calls for whole team responsibility, long-term relationships and treating people as people again, not merely "resources". Although being far away from counting himself as one of "agile purists", the author still remembers the level of personal frustration and hopelessness which remained long after this dialogue. On the other hand, he can imagine that his replies caused at least a strong confusion on the other side.

Taking this as the point of departure for our paper, we want to show our findings involving some fundamental qualities of images of enterprise test organizations. In this section, we will analyze three distinct patterns of enterprise test organizations: test factory, the testing center of excellence, and agile testing community of practice.

4.2 Test Factory: Test Organization as Machine

Morgan's Message. The *test factory* metaphor leads us to understand the test organization as a machine. Machines are designed by engineers and their design reflects engineering approach. Machines are precise, predictable and accurate. They transform inputs to outputs in a defined and expectable logic. One doesn't have to understand machinery and inner components as long as he remains just an operator. Machines are reliable; they don't exhibit mankind's weaknesses whereas people do.

The term machine also implies effectivity and efficiency. This is the prevailing perspective of management as advocated by Frederick Winslow Taylor (1856–1915), an American mechanical engineer and father of "scientific management". He is probably most famous for his stopwatch motion studies, perceived by him as a panacea against inefficiencies of factory workers. Albeit effective, from today's perspective, the similar view of management is perceived as highly reductionist and dehumanizing. Applied on modern societies, Morgan calls similar approaches to organizing as "McDonaldization". This is to emphasize "ruthless efficiency, quantification, predictability, control, and deskilled jobs" [6].

That said, Morgan argues that a large number of similar principals had become deeply rooted in our minds. Even more than 100 years after formulation of these principles, people tend to look at organizations using the "classical management theory" lens primarily. Also, numerous managers use this paradigm as the prevailing one.

Application on Test Organizations. Understanding a test organization as a machine might bring some advantages. Putting effectivity and efficiency in the spotlight seems to be very attractive for a corporate environment where these two factors naturally play a crucial role. Similarly, emphasis on quality is a cornerstone of all modern factories. Translation into a similar context thus seems appropriate.

The legacy of this metaphor lies in routinization. Likewise, the main goal declared as "to provide consistent testing services to engagements in a standardized, managed and industrialized fashion"[1] sends a clear message. This message must be interpreted in a broader context of efforts which aims to transform various IT areas (analysis, development, operations, testing) of the corporate IT function: from the original "immature" craftsmanship tier we have reached higher tiers of commodity and utility [15]. The problem of such messaging is that "less mature" (= non-commoditized) levels are automatically perceived as a suboptimal solution by many members of the corporate world. But is this really the case? We don't think so. Also, notice a critique from a practitioner who sees a typical test factory as full of "'brain dead' people" [16].

To briefly sum, some key attributes of enterprise test factory model might include: (1) centralized administration and decision-making, (2) test process standardization and process manuals, (3) extensive administrative procedures connected with test engagements, (4) overemphasis on test planning and control, (5) perception of change as an undesired test management factor, (6) impersonalized, substitutable "test resources", (7) emphasis on manual testing connected with absence of innovation and improvement thinking.

4.3   Testing Center of Excellence: Test Organization as Brain

Morgan's Message. Basic qualities frequently attributed to the brain include the complexity of its functions and high mental potential enabled by processes of learning and creativity. The concept of *learning organization* is a vital fundament on which this metaphor builds. Many organizations apply some of its elements very well in the form of so-called "single-loop learning". These organizations are quite fluent in setting up high-level goals, cascading them down, picking appropriate management controls and acting respectively. Sometimes, however, also "double-loop learning" is necessary. This process of learning is able to question some fundamental assumptions and is capable of causing modification of the goals and controls consequently. At times, this may even temporarily result into kind of "creative chaos".

In reality, the somewhat fuzzy concept of learning organization is often supported by more tangible knowledge management (KM) efforts. But it would be too mechanistic to reduce KM efforts just on creation and maintenance of a common knowledge base. It's necessary to understand the KM efforts quite broadly [17].

Application on Test Organizations. Test Center of Excellence (TCoE) is probably the most ambiguous image in our analysis. While there is a lot of research on (general) centers of excellence in the domain of knowledge management, the TCoE term is, at the same time, usurped by numerous management consultants and vendors to describe a different reality (typically a sourcing arrangement). This is visible also in the

---

[1] A non-published vendor presentation. Quite paradoxically, the vendor uses this formulation to define a key quality of Testing Center of Excellence, not Test Factory.

well-known *World Quality Report 2015–16* (WQR) [7] prepared by some big names in the IT outsourcing industry. By defining "a fully operational TCoE" (capitalization ours) as "similar to the application development factories currently driving efficiency in this area", the report does a disservice to the knowledge management oriented concept of TCoE in favor of commoditization and economies of scale.

Interestingly, the report argues that organizational dispersion of test resources contributes to the lack of maturity of the testing profession in organizations. Based on the WQR survey sample, only 37 % organizations take centralized, i.e. "TCoE", approach. It is unclear, however, what the "centralized approach" essentially means and why it can't be replaced by some modern KM mechanisms. Test Center of Excellence remains a fuzzy term, although management consultants and vendors often try to suggest otherwise. We perceive it as an image of both formal or informal test organization, rather than a concrete sourcing strategy.

So differently from many vendors, we understand the term in the original sense in-line with its roots in KM. We envision a center of excellence as a relatively "small group of individuals recognized for their leading-edge, strategically-valuable knowledge, and mandated to leverage and/or make that knowledge available throughout the global firm" [17]. Centers of excellence are primarily created to drive innovation and knowledge sharing, not productivity and cost savings [5]. Another aspect of test excellence resonates in the mythical story of IBM Black Team established in the 1960's by putting alike quality experts together [18]. Through team's expertise, shared vision and unique identity, the Black Team earned high respect and impacted software quality within IBM considerably. Regarding the size of TCoE, we point to Mark Summers: "TCoE doesn't mean you have to dedicate an army!" [19] (capitalization ours). That means that building of a TCoE might have a sense even for a mid-size company with no outsourcing ambitions.

To sum our understanding of the term, some key characteristics of this model in test space might include: (1) TCoE people are given space and encouraged to come with new ideas even it might conflict with the current test management approach, (2) new test tools, processes, practices and industry trends are being evaluated, (3) the original ones are being questioned in a participative atmosphere, (4) TCoE members are encouraged to work across organizational boundaries to help others (i.e. non-members) to achieve "test excellence", (5) "test excellence" is not an empty promise, but a strong commitment and everyday operating philosophy, (6) role of immediate cost-effectiveness is reduced in favor of long-term organization goals.

4.4 Agile Testing Community of Practice: Test Organization as Culture

Morgan's Message. Culture can be defined as an integrated system of core values, beliefs, and underlying assumptions. In the managerial literature, culture is sometimes portrayed as an independent organization variable capable of extensive manipulation by managers and executives. In fact, the pragmatic definition "How we do things around here" (coined by McKinsey) captures some aspects of this approach. But Morgan and many others clearly see culture as more than just a variable, and thus find the pragmatic definition as inadequate and just surface scratching. Morgan says that culture is an "active, living phenomenon through which people jointly create and re-create the worlds in which they live" [6]. Social scientists have always realized an enormous power of culture. Managers and computing researchers have been traditionally more reserved.

Application on Test Organizations. Apparently, many people perceive agile software development (Agile) as a brand new philosophy for application creation. In his book about Extreme Programming, for example, Kent Beck says that Agile "is about social change" [20]. Also, an empirical study found that for software professionals Agile was much "more than a software development methodology" [21]. This suggests that we should perceive Agile rather as a specific culture-forming mechanism than a simple process prescription how to develop software. Moreover, the mentioned mechanism influences not only technical personnel responsible for application development but broader enterprise context, co-forming a new social reality in the sense of Morgan's thoughts. Ideally, this reality should be non-hierarchical and thus not contaminated by "vertical ideology of control" [22].

There are many agile flavors, i.e. levels of agile orthodoxy vary across organizations and among proponents. But one of the key characteristics of Agile is that – in its purest form – all software development processes are considered as empirical, instead of defined. That means that process can be tailored as the team goes [23]. Moreover, the *Manifesto of Agile Software Development* (http://www.agilemanifesto.org/) doesn't mention the world "testing" anywhere. Scrum (http://www.scrum.org), a well-known agile framework, similarly doesn't distinguish between the role of programmer and tester. All of the team members are considered as *developers*.

This clearly has some challenging implications on the organization of software testing. While many had called for the elimination of separated "test team" in Agile, some already realized that complete and radical elimination of dedicated test roles would be unfortunate. In fact, it would call for a huge cultural change of its own. This also represents a potentially challenging mental shift for many programmers socialized in more traditional models who typically treat testing as an inferior activity. Similarly, many decision makers in regulated fields will hardly accept the *whole-development-team-is-responsible* logic; they believe in segregation of IT roles as a form of control.

From today's perspective, it is quite hard to say how an "agile test organization of the future" will exactly look like in the new agile world which demands quite specific test culture. Thus we cannot simply list some key attributes here. Maybe test organizations will really become a "thing of the past" as some management consultants argue. Possibly they will transform themselves into informal *agile testing communities of practice (CoP)* [14]. But we rather think of them as hybrid and somewhat fuzzy structures compatible with ideas of the agile movement but also reflecting the particular context of every enterprise. We don't think that a universal prescription works here. We are, however, strongly convinced that one has to stop looking at test organizations just from the "default", i.e. the test factory perspective. It is necessary to accept that key assumptions of Agile are very different. New values, beliefs, and ideals must be *imported* into factory-like test organizations if they are to survive in the new world. This is, obviously, a huge cultural change, not a minor tweaking of their current design.

5 Short Discussion of Our Experience

The starting point of our transformation effort was an outsourced, offshored test factory model with few hundred of "test resources". Our past year and a half transformation journey that encompasses organization design of the two remaining *Images* offers some interesting discoveries. Unfortunately, the short paper format doesn't allow to share many details about these initiatives in the present contribution which has rather aimed to develop solid theoretical/practical conceptual basis. Thus in this section, our intention is to present just a few fundamental discoveries.

Test Factory. Firstly, our test organization is very different than it used to be a year and a half ago; definitely not a pure test factory anymore. Still, we don't think that the test factory concept itself is dead. Importantly, we are strongly convinced that it needs to be repositioned carefully and find the right segment where it is still fit for purpose. This segment might be represented, for example, by large enterprise IT initiatives. It is clear to us, however, that test factory is not the universal enterprise test panacea anymore.

Testing Center of Excellence. Based on the claim above, we think that enterprise test managers need to broaden their management horizons in the changing world of enterprise software testing. If they are in a similar situation as we were, we encourage them to go back to the roots of the Center of Excellence's meaning and think about bringing *the core* of test excellence back in. We did this by hiring several experienced test engineers while the majority of test capacity remains outsourced and commoditized. It could be quite convenient to fully rely on vendors but we can confirm many pain points similar to the ones captured in [24] for "independent test agencies".

Agile Testing Community of Practice (CoP). Speaking about agile development initiatives at present, we rather think of our organization design as *Agile TCoE* than a pure *Agile Testing CoP*. We use the former label to emphasize the learning element of TCoE but also to say that Agile forms a very specific cultural context for this learning. Still, we keep Agile TCoE largely under the tent of our formal test organization built in the past. In general, we strive to design our Agile TCoE to (1) become a formal home-base for test engineers embedded into agile development teams; the home-base enables effective knowledge-sharing and career planning for them, (2) act as a protective shell in "hostile" enterprise environment of a hierarchy-driven organization, (3) as an important organization player, contribute to co-forming the right "agile testing culture", and (4) live in harmony with "softer" concepts such as informal agile testing CoPs.

In sum, we see the above three *Images* of test organization as complementary rather than mutually exclusive in our IT organization-in-transition. This is briefly summarized in Table 1 which captures the essence of our management approach. All of the described images might fit particular needs in one enterprise because one size doesn't fit all. Looking from these three different angles gives us, at the end, a folded image rather than just one distinct. It makes a perfect sense to us to allow co-existence of these three diverse images under one tent. In the end, it is like using different tools from the home toolbox. We will hardly use a screwdriver or drill to hit nails because a hammer is a better fit. But to complete a more extensive home repair, we might need all the three tools.

Table 1. Key qualities of three images of test organization

	Test factory	Testing center of excellence	Agile testing community of practice
		(~ Agile Test Center of Excellence)	
Metaphor	Machine	Brain	Culture
Rhetoric	Commoditization	Innovation	Shared norms, ideals, and values
D. methodology	Waterfall	Methodologically neutral	Agile
Organization form	Centralized, formal organization offering test services (often outsourced, offshored)	Formal or informal group of individuals holding, spreading and further advancing strategically important test know-how	Informal network of test professionals driven by interest of its members often empowered to take particular decisions
Mission	Provide standardized test services	Keep pace with recent trends in the software testing industry, focus on real excellence	Support informal and voluntary test knowledge sharing across agile teams, coordinate decision-making
Key contribution	Cost-effective for designed purpose	Support organization learning and evolution in changing environment	Support values and ideals of agile development

Also, note that modern organization theory teaches us there is "no one best way" to organize [25]. Our experience shows support for this claim. On the one hand, the (outsourced, off-shored) test factory model has been promoted as the ideal set-up by many (vendor) experts [7]. On the other hand, Agile has triggered the exactly opposite thinking that frequently declares similar "test commoditization" models as obsolete and argues for just another "best way", that is testing community of practice. Moreover, some organizational mechanisms focused on expertise, learning, and innovation seems to be crucial irrespectively of which of these options is chosen.

Our experience indicates that instead of blindly following latest enterprise test management fashions and ill-judged replacing "old" with "new", enterprise test people should consider taking a more pluralist approach represented by the possible intro- duction of additional *Images* to the existing ones, similarly as we did. Some factors to consider when choosing the fitting *Images* are business agility and requirements volatility, the size of development teams, the complexity of developed solutions, cost pressures vs. expected benefits of co-location, level of expertise of test organization's members, and level of novelty of programming and test tools used.

6 Conclusion

This position paper has provided three distinct images of enterprise test organization and analyzed their key qualities. The interdisciplinary perspective given in this paper is obviously highly subjective and based on a single case only. We consider ourselves as reflective practitioners and our view is rooted in our enterprise SQM industrial experience and work responsibilities in a large, multinational company with very high proportion of outsourced, offshored IT services. In this paper, little empirical evidence in a purely scientific sense is presented to back up our findings at this moment. Nevertheless, we believe that the paper still provides important ideas and timely insights useful both for the practitioner and scholarly audience.

For practicing software quality/IT managers, the ideas can be useful and applicable in their professional work. Building upon these ideas, they should be able to broaden their thinking and consequently improve their design efforts concerning enterprise test organizations. In general, relevant "corporate newspeak" currently lacks unity in the usage of the key terms we have sketchily conceptualized. Our paper thus laid some foundations; either for agreement or for critique. Concerning our own test factory transformation efforts, we plan to publish a subsequent paper with a full summary of the actions taken and elaborated lessons learned. We also plan to focus more on the relation of the presented *Images* and so-called contingency approaches in organization theory and design [25]. We suspect that some prescriptions presented in the practitioner literature nowadays are a bit over-simplistic and often ignore the vital role of context.

For the scholarly audience, the present paper can primarily serve as an impulse for future research. As far as we are aware of, there is no scientific research study in the field of software engineering or information systems which explores this important area of IT management practice from a similar angle. Studying more enterprise test organizations and interviewing their managers using qualitative, interpretative case study approach would shed more light on this area.

Clearly, the reality of test organizations is more complicated than the metaphorical perspective presented in this paper. That also means that our paper doesn't suggest that every manager or test engineer might entirely influence the design of her test organization. On the other hand, many test organization can be shaped and we think that there is a lot of opportunities to do so. We are also convinced that, in the future, test professionals will increasingly often ask during job interviews what sort of test organization they are actually considering to join. We fully understand the reasons why they will query. There is a great difference between working in a *test factory*, and a *testing community of practice*, as examples. Hence, in a reply to the paraphrased Carr's question presented in the introduction, we are certain: *Software testing does matter.*

Acknowledgements. I would like to thank Theresa Pullen for her insightful comments on an earlier version of this manuscript and sharing my passion for reflective IT management practice. Some ideas presented in this work emerged from our previous discussions of the topic and our shared management effort.

References

1. Carr, N.G.: IT doesn't matter. Harv. Bus. Rev. **81**(41–9), 128 (2003)
2. Ahonen, J.J., Junttila, T., Sakkinen, M.: Impacts of the organizational model on testing: three industrial cases. Empir. Softw. Eng. **9**, 275–296 (2004)

3. Mäntylä, M.V., Itkonen, J., Iivonen, J.: Who tested my software? Testing as an organizationally cross-cutting activity. Softw. Qual. J. **20**, 145–172 (2012)
4. Prechelt, L.: Quality experience : a grounded theory of successful agile projects without dedicated testers. In: International Conference on Software Engineering (2016)
5. Sia, S.K., Soh, C., Weill, P.: Global IT management structure for scale, responsiveness, and innovation. Commun. ACM **53**, 59–64 (2010)
6. Morgan, G.: Images of Organization. Sage, London (2006)
7. Capgemini, Sogeti, HPE: World Quality Report 2015–16 (2015). https://www.capgemini.com/thought-leadership/world-quality-report-2015-16
8. Masters of disruption. http://www.computerworld.com/article/3036168/
9. Schön, D.A.: The Reflective Practitioner: How Professionals Think in Action. Basic Books, New York (1983)
10. Mantzoukas, S., Watkinson, S.: Redescribing reflective practice and evidence-based practice discourses. Int. J. Nurs. Pract. **14**, 129–134 (2008)
11. Given, L.M.: The Sage Encyclopedia of Qualitative Research Methods. SAGE Publications Ltd, London (2008)
12. Manning, P.K.: Metaphors of the field: varieties of organizational discourse. Adm. Sci. Q. **24**, 660–671 (1979)
13. Örtenblad, A., Putnam, L.L., Trehan, K.: Beyond Morgan's eight metaphors: adding to and developing organization theory. Hum. Relat. **69**, 875–889 (2016)
14. Crispin, L., Gregory, J.: Agile Testing: A Practical Guide for Testers and Agile Teams. Addison-Wesley, Upper Saddle River (2009)
15. McKeen, J.D., Smith, H.A.: Developments in practice XXVII: delivering IT functions: a decision framework. Commun. Assoc. Inf. Syst. **19**, 725–739 (2007)
16. A bizarre idea called Software testing factory. http://shrinik.blogspot.cz/2012/11/a-bizzare-idea-called-software-testing.html
17. Moore, K., Birkinshaw, J.: Managing knowledge in global service firms: centers of excellence. Acad. Manag. Exec. **12**, 81–92 (1998)
18. The Black Team. http://www.t3.org/tangledwebs/07/tw0706.html
19. Creating a Testing Center of Excellence. http://www.cio.com/article/3019419/
20. Beck, K., Andres, C.: Extreme Programming Explained: Embrace Change. Addison Wesley, Boston (2004)
21. Whitworth, E., Biddle, R.: The social nature of agile teams. In: AGILE, pp. 26–36 (2007)
22. Denning, S.: Agile: it's time to put it to use to manage business complexity. Strateg. Leadersh. **43**, 10–17 (2015)
23. Williams, L., Cockburn, A.: Agile software development: it's all about feedback and change. Computer **36**, 39–43 (2003)
24. Kaner, C., Falk, J., Nguyen, H.Q.: Testing Computer Software. Wiley, New York (2000)
25. Daft, R.L., Murphy, J., Willmott, H.: Organization Theory and Design. Cengage Learning, Cheriton House, Boston (2010)

Analysing the Quality Evolution of Open Source Software Projects

Lerina Aversano[⊠], Daniela Guardabascio, and Maria Tortorella

Department of Engineering, University of Sannio,
Via Traiano, 82100 Benevento, Italy
{aversano,guardabascio,tortorella}@unisannio.it

Abstract. Reuse of software components depends on different aspects of software artifacts. In particular, software quality should be taken into account before considering an open source software for being adopted in an operative context. In this direction, this paper presents a study aimed at assessing the quality of open source software projects along the software project history. The study entails the gathering and analysis of relevant information of some open source projects. The analysis of the considered software projects required the evaluation of the quality of the software products, their attractiveness and community trustworthiness. The related trends are presented as results.

1 Introduction

The way organizations develop, acquire, use and commercialize software is deeply influenced by the availability of Open Source Software (OSS) [5]. Actually, the accessibility of large repositories of open source software projects makes possible the exploitation of existing pieces of software for facing new or emerging requirements. In fact, the adoption of Free libre Open Source Software – FlOSS – can support any business, whatever the size, and can be very advantageous for enterprises [6, 10], as it permits to quickly obtain customized solutions. Some of the advantages of adopting a FlOSS project regards the possibility of really trying the system, reducing vendor lock-in, having low license cost and the opportunity of personalizing a software system.

Nevertheless, while adopting a FlOSS represents a competitive advantage for a company, it could be useless or even harmful if the system does not achieve the required quality level and/or adequately fit the organization needs. Then, the selection and adoption of such a kind of system cannot be faced in a superficial way, and it is important to obtain quantitative information regarding its evolution and quality for effectively helping software engineers in the execution of this complex task.

This paper aims to present a study analyzing how the quality of OSS projects evolves during their life. The analyzed quality characteristics are: Product Quality, Community Trustworthiness and Product Attractiveness [15]. They are evaluated for different releases of a set of OSS projects. The evaluation is performed by using the EFFORT – Evaluation Framework for Free/Open souRce projects – quality framework [1, 2]. The analysis is based on the historical data regarding the considered OSS

© Springer International Publishing AG 2017
D. Winkler et al. (Eds.): SWQD 2017, LNBIP 269, pp. 117–129, 2017.
DOI: 10.1007/978-3-319-49421-0_9

software projects across multiple releases. It considers the software systems developed by using different paradigms, with different evolution trends and concerning different application domains. Due to the large availability of FlOSS projects and related releases, the study analyses just a set of such a kind of projects.

The remainder of this paper is organized as follows: Sect. 2 reports the main related works; Sect. 3 describes the performed study and identification of the software projects; Sect. 4 analyses the achieved results; and Sect. 5 discusses concluding remarks.

2   Related Works

The literature has proposed approaches regarding the evolution of OSS projects. These approaches analyse the OSS projects for gaining an understanding of their evolutionary aspects. A systematic review regarding this aspect is presented in [13].

Besides the evolution aspects, the analysis presented in this paper required the study of the approaches proposed for characterizing and evaluating the quality of a FlOSS project. Various models have been proposed with this aim. Kamseu and Habra proposed in [8] an approach for analyzing the different factors that potentially influence the adoption of an OSS system. The quality of a FlOSS product evaluated on the basis of standard ISO/IEC 9126 was analysed by Sung, Kim and Rhew in [12]. IRCA – Identify, Read reviews, Compare, and Analyze – is a FlOSS selection process, based on a side by side comparison of different software [14]. QSOS – Qualification and Selection of Open Source software – proposes a 5-steps methodology for assessing FlOSS projects [11]. The OpenBRR project – Business Readiness Rating for Open Source – was proposed with the same aim of QSOS [10]. One of the biggest initiatives concerning the OSS and realized by the European Union is QualiPSo – Quality Platform for Open Source Software described in [4].

This paper analyses different kind of characteristics during the evolution of a FlOSS project. They can be both product intrinsic, such as Product Quality, and specific FlOSS dimensions, such as Community Trustworthiness and Product Attractiveness. The models cited above only partially address these aspects and very often face just one or two of them and offer a reduced coverage to the other characteristics. Their comparison showed that the most complete model with reference the product quality is IRCA, but it does not provide an adequate operational tool for its application [1].

The EFFORT – Evaluation Framework for Free/Open souRce projects – framework, described in [2], was selected for performing the evaluation considered in this paper, as it analyses all the cited quality characteristics and provides a working support for applying the framework.

3   Organization of the Study

This section discusses the main aspects of analysis presented in this paper. The next two subsections describe the selection process of the analysed OSS projects and the EFFORT framework applied for their evaluation.

3.1   The OSS Projects Analysis and Selection

The main source of information for the proposed study were the source code repositories, necessary for downloading the artefacts of OSS projects. The chosen ones were Google Code and SourceForge. In particular, the latter one was considered the primary source of the data required for the execution of the performed study.

To perform the initial selection of the projects to be analyzed, the belonging to multiple categories was considered. This analysis brought to the identification of the Internet and Software Development sub-categories of the Development category, as the most significant ones. Thus some projects of these sub-categories were selected. In addition, it was decided to analyze just the projects using the Java programming language because of the availability of tools analyzing Java software.

Another aspect that influenced the choice of the projects was their status. In fact, the projects hosted in SourceForge can have different status, classified as: Active, Inactive, Planning, Pre-Alpha, Alpha, Beta, Production/Stable and Mature. Actually, only the Active and Stable projects were primarily considered. This decision was taken for not influencing the results by considering projects that are immature. Finally, for obtaining a more significant analysis, it was decided to consider projects registered before 2009, so to analyse software projects with a lifetime of at least 7 years. The execution of these steps permitted to select 30 software projects. Three of them were chosen for discussing in this paper the achieved results in a major details. They are ProGuard, Open-SearchServer and Phex, belonging to the Software Development and Internet categories. Then, the gathering of the needed data could start, by analyzing the identified data sources, such as the commits on the SVN and CVS project repositories. The analysis of each project focused on the releases of three temporal points of the timeline: Initial Point (IP), Middle Point (MP) and the Final Point (FP). Specifically, IP was referred to the effective start of the project. It was assumed that the 20 % of the timeline could be considered as an effective starting point, as it was observed that in numerous cases the first point in the timeline corresponds to the first commit regarding the creation of the empty repository. Similarly, the MP point was associated to the 50 % of the timeline; while the FP point to the last available release. Therefore the evaluation of the quality was performed by applying the EFFORT framework [1, 2] to the three selected release of each chosen project.

3.2   The EFFORT Framework

EFFORT is a framework defined for evaluating the quality of FlOSS systems [2]. It can be considered as a base framework to be specialized to a specific working context. EFFORT was defined on the basis of the GQM – Goal, Question, Metrics – paradigm [3]. It considers the quality of a FlOSS project as synergy of three main elements: quality of the product developed within the project; trustworthiness of the community of developers and contributors; and product attractiveness to its specified area. Then, one Goal is defined for each of these elements. Questions, consequentially, map the second-level characteristics, even if, considering its complexity and the amount of aspects to be considered, Goal 1 is broken up into sub-goals.

The following subsections summarily describe each goal, with its formalization, definitions of specific terms and list of questions. The listed questions are answered through the evaluation of a set of associated metrics. A complete description of the framework, with all the considered metrics can be found in [1, 2].

Product Quality. One of the main aspects that denotes the quality of a project is the product quality. It is unlikely that a product of high and durable quality has been developed in a poor quality project. All the aspects of the software product quality have been considered in the framework, as defined by the standards ISO 9126 and ISO/IEC 25000 [7].

Goal 1 is defined as follows: *analyze the software product with the aim of evaluating its quality, from the software engineer's point of view.*

This goal is analyzed by considering six different sub-goals concerning: portability, maintainability, reliability, functionality, usability, and efficiency. For reasons of space, Table 1 just shows the questions of the first sub-goal.

Table 1. Some sub-goals of the product quality

Sub-goal 1a: Analyze the software product with the aim of evaluating it as regards the portability, from a software engineering's point of view	
Q 1a.1	What degree of adaptability does the product offer?
Q 1a.2	What degree of installability does the product offer?
Q 1a.3	What degree of replaceability does the product offer?
Q 1a.4	What degree of coesistence does the product offer?

Community Trustworthiness. Community Trustworthiness indicates the degree of trust that a user can give to a community with reference to the offered support. Support can be provided by communities by means of: use of tools, such as wiki, forum, trackers; and provision of services, such as maintenance, consulting and outsourcing, and documentation.

Goal 2 is defined as follows: *Analyze the offered support with the aim of evaluating the community with reference to the trustworthiness, from the (user/organization) adopter's point of view.*

Table 2 shows the set of questions related to Goal 2.

Table 2. Questions regarding community trustworthiness

Q 2.1	How many developers does the community involve?
Q 2.2	What degree of activity has the community?
Q 2.3	Support tools are available and effective?
Q 2.4	Are support services provided?
Q 2.5	Is the documentation exhaustive and easily consultable?

Product Attractiveness. The third goal has the purpose of evaluating the attractiveness of the product toward its catchment area. The term attractiveness indicates all the factors that influence the adoption of a product by a potential user, who perceives convenience and usefulness to achieve his scopes.

Goal 3 is formalized as follows: *Analyze software product with the aim of evaluating it as regards the attractiveness from the (user/organization) adopter's point of view.* Table 3 includes the related questions.

Table 3. Questions regarding product attractiveness

Q 3.1	What degree of functional adequacy does the product offer?
Q 3.2	What degree of diffusion does the product achieved?
Q 3.3	What level of cost effectiveness is estimated?
Q 3.4	What degree of reusability and redistribution is left by the license?

The goal considers: the function adequacy; the diffusion, intended as a marker of how the product is valued and recognized as useful and effective; the cost effectiveness, an estimation of the TCO (Total Cost of Ownership) [9], and the type of license.

Once data have been collected the metrics cannot be directly aggregated and compared as they have different scales. Then, they have been normalized and mapped to the values of a discrete scale defined on the basis of the experience and information coming from the literature. Moreover, questions do not have the same relevance in the evaluation of a goal. A relevance marker is associated to each metric in the form of a numeric value in the [1–5] interval. The markers are selected on the basis of the relevance that the current literature gives to the each quality attribute. Then the metric values are aggregated to obtain an evaluation of each question and Goal [1].

4 Evaluation of the Open Source Software Projects

In the following a discussion of the results of the chosen three open source software projects are analyzed. Then, a quick evaluation of thirty projects is given.

4.1 The Proguard System

ProGuard is a free Java class file optimizer, obfuscator, and verifier, that detects and removes unused classes, fields, methods, and attributes, optimizes bytecode and removes unused instructions. It was registered on the SourceForge site on 31 May 2002. 36 versions were available at the time of the analysis. The three analyzed versions are the following: ProGuard 1.7.2 (IP), ProGuard 3.7 (MP) and ProGuard 5.2.1 (FP).

Table 4 includes the evaluation of Goal 1 regarding the quality of the ProGuard project. It can be noticed that the values of many parameters improve going from the IP to FP version. Actually, the Portability improves. The analysis of the values of the

Table 4. Values of the software product quality (GOAL 1)

Subgoal	Metric	ProGuard			OpenSerachServer			Phex		
		1.7.2	3.7	5.2.1	1.1.3	1.5.1	1.5.13	0.7.3	2.8.10	3.4.2
		Avarage value			Avarage value			Avarage value		
1.a Portability	Adaptability	5.00	5.00	5.00	5.00	5.00	5.00	3.00	3.00	3.00
	Installability	3.36	3.45	3.73	3.55	3.55	3.55	3.55	3.91	4.00
	Replaceability	1.00	1.00	1.00	1.00	1.00	1.00	1.00	1.00	1.00
1.b Maintenability	Analizzability	3.71	3.71	3.86	3.57	3.71	3.86	3.86	3.71	3.71
	Changeability	4.20	4.20	4.00	4.00	3.80	3.80	4.00	4.40	4.00
	Testability	3.625	3.00	3.00	3.88	4.13	3.88	3.75	3.38	3.63
	Tecnological concentration	4.00	4.00	4.00	3.00	3.00	3.00	3.00	3.00	3.00
1.c Reliability	Robustness	2.00	3.33	3.83	4.33	4.50	4.17	3.67	3.67	4.83
	Recoverability	1.00	1.00	1.00	5.00	5.00	5.00	1.00	1.00	1.00
1.d Functionality	Fuctional adequacy	3.00	3.00	3.00	5.00	5.00	5.00	3.00	3.00	3.00
	Interaperobility	1.00	1.00	1.00	5.00	5.00	5.00	2.00	2.00	2.00
1.e Usability	Pleasantness	3.00	3.00	4.00	4.00	4.00	4.00	3.00	3.00	4.00
	Operability	4.50	4.75	5.00	4.00	4.25	4.25	4.25	4.25	4.75
	Understandability	2.89	2.89	3.78	3.33	3.44	3.56	3.11	3.11	3.56
	Learnability	1.50	1.50	1.75	2.75	3.00	3.25	1.25	1.25	1.25

related metrics showed that the improvement is due to the Installability for the increased availability of automatic installation scripts and efficacy of the guide in the third analysed version. On the other hand, the value of other evaluated metrics, such as Adaptability and Replaceability, are equal in the three analysed versions.

Regarding the Maintainability, Table 4 shows that all the evaluated parameters either improve or decrease in the three analyzed versions, but the Technological Concentration that reaches one of the highest value, due to a decrease of the overloaded methods and improvement of the average of number of Parameters per method in the last two analyzed versions. Analyzability increases thanks to the increment of the Density of Comments metric. The Reliability also increases in the three versions, with particular reference to the Robustness as the number of bugs decreases from 3000 in the first version to 598 in the third one. As a consequence, the Average Defect Number and Defect Density decrease. Table 4 shows also that Functionality parameters keeps the same values in the three versions.

Finally, the table highlights that the Usability increases in all the parameters. In particular, the improvements are the following: Pleasantness increases in the last version for a higher number of icons to execute programs; Understandability improves thanks to the increased code understandability and on-line help; the improvement of the consultation facility level impacts the Learnability value.

Analyzing the three ProGuard columns of Table 4, it is possible to observe the trend of its product quality metrics from the first to the third analyzed version.

Table 5 includes the results obtained by analyzing the Community Trustworthiness of ProGuard in the three considered versions. The table shows the trend of the five

Table 5. Values of the community trustworthiness (GOAL 2)

	ProGuard			OpenSerachServer			Phex		
	1.7.2	3.7	5.2.1	1.1.3	1.5.1	1.5.13	0.7.3	2.8.10	3.4.2
Metric	Average value			Average value			Average value		
Community dimension	1.00	1.00	1.00	2.00	2.00	4.00	1.00	1.00	1.00
Community activity	1.60	1.80	2.00	2.60	2.40	2.40	2.40	2.20	2.60
Support tools	1.67	1.67	2.00	1.78	1.78	1.78	1.11	1.11	1.22
Support services	1.00	1.11	1.00	1.00	1.00	1.00	1.00	1.22	1.33
Documentation	2.00	2.50	2.00	1.67	1.83	2.27	1.33	1.67	2.00

parameters considered within Goal 2. The data indicate that the Community Dimension are equal from the first to the third considered version. The positive trend can also be found in parameter Community Activity and this is mainly due to the increase of commit number. In addition, the analysis of the analytical data indicates that the number of the solved bugs increases thanks to the community activity and all this activity also brought to an increase of the number of FAQs. A slight improvement can be also observed in the Support Services parameter for second considered release. This is mainly due to the inclusion of training and maintenance services in the second considered version. Finally, the Documentation quality improves in the same release and the number of covered topics increases from version IP to version MP, for decreasing going from version MP to version IP.

Table 6 shows the evaluation of the Goal 3 metrics, regarding Attractiveness of the project ProGuard. The table shows that the Product Attractiveness increases through the three considered versions. In particular, the Diffusion is the only parameters having a really positive trend. The most relevant aspect of this increasing is the increment of the number of performed downloads among the different considered versions; in fact, the collected data indicate that the IP and MP versions have been downloaded just twice, while the FP version has been downloaded 908823 times.

Table 6. Values of product attractiveness (GOAL 3)

	ProGuard			OpenSerachServer			Phex		
	1.7.2	3.7	5.2.1	1.1.3	1.5.1	1.5.13	0.7.3	2.8.10	3.4.2
Metric	Avarage value			Avarage value			Avarage value		
Functional adequacy	3.00	3.00	3.00	5.00	5.00	5.00	3.00	3.00	3.00
Diffusion	1.45	1.82	3.45	2.45	2.45	2.45	3.55	3.91	4.00
Economic convenience	3.20	4.00	4.00	4.00	4.00	4.00	1.00	1.00	1.00
Legal reusability	2.00	2.00	2.00	1.00	1.00	1.00	3.86	3.71	3.71

In addition, there has been a great increment with reference to the published documents concerning ProGuard, and the Google visibility tripled in the three versions.

Figure 1 shows the overall trend of the considered goals for ProGuard. It is worthwhile noticing that all the goals improved their values going from the first to the

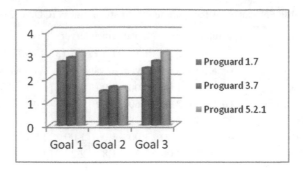

Fig. 1. Comparison among Goal1 Goal2 and Goal3 – ProGuard.

third considered version, just Goal2 slightly decreases its value in the last considered version. Figure 1 permits to relate the values achieved in three goals. It can be evicted that the Product Quality increase slightly contributes to increase the Community Trustworthiness, while it contributes to improve the Product Attractiveness.

4.2   The OpenSearchServer System

OpenSearchServer is an open source search with RESTFul API and crawlers. It allows the development of index-based applications such as search engines. It is developed in Java and works with operative systems Windows, Linux, Mac OS X and BSD. It belongs to the Development category and was recorded on SourceForge on june 11th, 2009. Twenty-four versions were available at the time of the analysis and the three considered versions are: OpenSearchServer 1.1.3 (IP); OpenSearchServer 1.5.1 (MP); and OpenSearchServer 1.5.13 (FP).

Table 4 includes the evaluation of the Product Quality of the OpenSearchServer project. It can be noticed that the values of many parameters improve going from the IP to MP version, and remain stable going from MP to FP version.

In particular, Portability and Functionality remain stable going from the IP to FP versions. Maintainability improves only for the Analyzability, while the other characteristics worsen going to the first to the last version. The worst trend concerns the Testability. The analysis of the analytical data indicates that this is due to two factors: the increasing of the number of children for each class and the function of built in test. This factor does not contribute to increase the Testability of the system. Regarding Reliability, the values are stable with the exception of Robustness that reaches the worst value in the third analyzed version. This is mainly due to the increasing of the index of the number of unresolved bug. Finally, the only characteristic that improves in the three considered releases is Usability. Just Pleasantness is equal among the three releases. Regarding the other factors, each of them increase from IP to FP version. The increasing of Operability is due to the increasing of the use of icons for launching commands (from 8 to 18). Regarding Understandability and Learnability, they increase thanks to the improvement of the on-line documentation.

Table 5 includes the evaluation of the Community Trustworthiness. The data indicate that the Community Dimension increases from the first to the third considered releases. The community activity decreases in the last two considered versions. In particular, the total number of major releases for year decrease from 3 in the first version to 1 in the third considered one. At the same time, also the number of commits per committer increases going from 239 to 591. The product documentation, increases from the first to the third version, thanks to two factors: the increase of web pages for users and ease of access to them. The parameters regarding Support Tool and Support Service remain equal in the three version.

Finally, Table 6 shows the results of the evaluation of the Product Attractiveness. The data report that all characteristic are equal in the three releases. Figure 2 shows the overall trend of the considered goals for OpenSearchServer. It is worthwhile noticing that the second goal improves his values going from the first to the third considered release. The other goals remain equal in the three considered version.

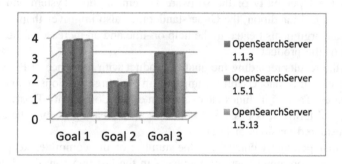

Fig. 2. Comparison among Goal1 Goal2 and Goal3 – OpenSearchServer

Definitively, regarding OpenSearchService, there is not a significant relation among the results achieved for the three goals.

4.3 The Phex System

Phex is an open source peer-to-peer file sharing client for the Gnutella network. It is developed in Java and works with Windows, Linux, Mac OS X e Solaris operative systems. It belongs to the Communications category and was on SourceForge on may 10th, 2001. Twenty-five versions were available at the time of the analysis and the three considered versions are: Phex 0.7.3 (IP); Phex 2.8.10 (MP); and Phex 3.4.2 (FP).

The results of the evaluation of GOAL1, regarding the Product Quality of the Phex versions, can be observed in the last three columns of Table 4. The table shows that the results of sub-goal 1.a, concerning the Portability, indicate its improvement in the three version, due mainly to the Installability. The analysis of the analytical data indicated that the improvement is due to three factors: the automation level of the installing procedure, increased from the 50 % to 75 %; the number macro-steps included in the guide; and the improved efficacy of the guide.

The analysis of sub-goal 1.b, regarding Maintainability, shows that the Analyzability decreased in the three versions. This is due to a strong increment of the package number that was 35 in the first version and reached 119 in the third one. Concerning Changeability, the best value has been achieved in the second version, thanks to the increasing of the method cohesion and the decreasing of the efferent coupling. Testability decreased for the overloaded methods whose number is higher in the last two considered versions. In addition, the LOC of the system almost doubled going from the first to the last version, and this did not contribute to increase the testability.

Regarding the Reliability, Table 4 shows that the Recoverability remains unchanged in the three versions, while the Robustness increases in the third version. This is mainly due to the number of unsolved defects that decreases in the last version.

The value of the Functionality parameter is unchanged in the three versions.

With reference to sub-goal 1.e, Table 4 indicates that almost all the Usability parameters improve in the three versions. The analysis of the project showed that the Pleasantness improved thanks to the higher user interface friendliness. This improvement affects the Operability of the software system, as both system and operations visibility increase. In addition, the Understandability also improves thanks to a bigger coverage of the arguments treated in the help on-line and an increase of the easiness of consultation of the product.

Overall, the results regarding the quality product with reference to Phex show that Portability, Reliability and Usability, improve in the three versions, while Maintainability decreases. Table 5 includes the evaluation of the Community Trustworthiness of Phex. In general terms, it is possible to observe an increasing of this characteristic in the three considered versions of Phex.

Just the first parameter concerning the number of the committer keeps its value. Nevertheless, the community activity increases in the last two considered versions. In particular, the total number of commits increases from 324 (IP) to 789 (FP) and the number of commits per committer increases going from 44 to 348.

Also the parameters regarding both Tool Support and Service Support increase. The former parameters improves due to the increase of the answered threads and FAQ number. In the latter case, the improvement is due to the introduction of training services in the last considered versions. Figure 3 shows the overall trend of the considered goals for Phex. It is worthwhile noticing that the first and the third goal

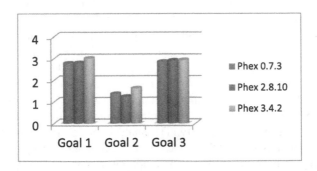

Fig. 3. Comparison among Goal1 Goal2 and Goal3 – Phex

improved their values going from the first to the third considered release. Only the second goal grows from first to third release, except for the second release which decreases. Analyzing Fig. 3, it is possible to observe that the increasing of the Product Quality positively impacts on both Community Trustworthiness and Product Attractiveness, that increase too. In the same way, with the increasing of the Community Trustworthiness, there is also an improvement of the Product Attractiveness.

4.4   Results from the Thirty Project Analysis

The analysis previously discussed has also been executed on thirty OSS systems and the complete results are shown in Fig. 4. The analysis confirmed the results obtained for the three projects analysed above and shows that there is a general improvement of the three considered goals in the three versions of each software system. In particular, the Product Quality improved for the 94 % of the projects, and those ones that worsened their quality are Saxon e Judo, both belonging to the Software development category. Both Product Attractiveness and Community Trustworthiness improved for the 87 % of the analyzed projects. The software projects that decreased the Community Trustworthiness are: the software system Simple of the WWW/http category, and Xdoc, Judo, EasyMock and Saxon for the Software development category. The Product Attractiveness decreased for software systems Cmod e HttpUnit of the WWW/http category, and Jasmine, Judo and Saxon of the Software development category.

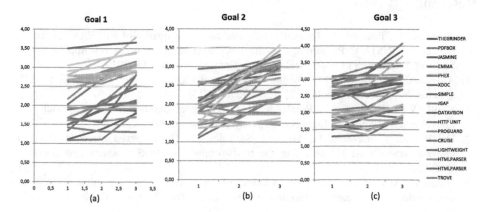

Fig. 4. Trends of Goals 1, 2 and 3 for all the projects

5   Conclusions

This paper reports a study on the evolution of the quality of OSS projects. In particular, Product Quality, Community Trustworthiness and Product Attractiveness of the considered OSS projects is evaluated. The analysis is based on the EFFORT quality framework and required its application to different versions of the selected software projects. Therefore, the performed analysis focused on historical data concerning the evolution of software systems, with the aim of analysing how the quality of the software projects evolves across multiple releases. The paper discusses with more details the evolution trends observed for the quality parameters of three software projects, ProGuard, OpenSearchServer and Phex, and, then, presents the results.

In the case of ProGuard the results shows that the improvement of the Product Quality contributes to improve the Product Attractiveness. The Product Attractiveness also improves with the improvement of the Community Trustworthiness. Overall, the results regarding the Quality Product with reference to Phex indicates that Portability, Reliability and Usability improve in the three versions, while Maintainability decreases. Regarding OpenSearchServer, Product Quality and Attractiveness are stable, while a growth can be observed in the Community Trustworthiness among the three releases. This is mainly due to three factors: increase of the number of developers and improved documentation.

Future investigation will regard the application of the framework with questionnaires and other tools for evaluating the customer satisfaction. This obviously includes a more complex analysis. In particular, methods and techniques specialized for exploiting this aspect will be explored and defined. In addition, with reference to the ISO standard, further investigations will be performed with reference to the in-use quality characteristic. Furthermore, the authors will continue to search for additional evidence of the usefulness and applicability of EFFORT.

References

1. Aversano, L., Pennino, I., Tortorella, M.: Evaluating the quality of FREE/OPEN source project. In: INSTICC Proceedings of the ENASE (Evaluation of Novel Approaches to Software Engineering) Conferences, Athens, Greece, pp. 119–134 (2010)
2. Aversano, L., Tortorella, M.: Quality evaluation of FlOSS projects: application to ERP systems. Inf. Softw. Technol. 55(7), 1260–1276 (2013)
3. Basili, V.R., Caldiera, G., Rombach, H.D.: The goal question metric approach. In: Encyclopedia of Software Engineering. Wiley Publishers (1994)
4. Del Bianco, V., Lavazza, L., Morasca, S., Taibi, D.: The observed characteristics and relevant factors used for assessing the trustworthiness of OSS products and artefacts. QualiPSo (2008)
5. Hauge, Ø., Ayala, C.P., Conradi, R.: Adoption of open source software in software-intensive organizations - a systematic literature review. Inf. Softw. Technol. 52(11), 1133–1154 (2010)
6. Hyoseob, K., Boldyreff, C.: Open source ERP for SMEs. In: ICMR 2005. Cranfield University, U.K (2005)
7. International Organization for Standardization: The ISO/IEC 25000 series of standards, also known as SQuaRE (System and Software Quality Requirements and Evaluation)
8. Kamseu, F., Habra, N.: Adoption of open source software: is it the matter of quality? In: PReCISE. Computer Science Faculty, University of Namur, Belgium (2009)
9. Kan, S.H., Basili, V.R., Shapiro, L.N.: Software quality: an overview from the perspective of total quality management. IBM Syst. J. 33(1), 4–19 (1994)
10. OpenBRR 2005: Business Readiness for Open Source. Intel (2005)

11. QSOS, 2006: Method for Qualification and Selection of Open Source software. Atos Origin (2006)
12. Sung, W.J., Kim, J.H., Rhew, S.Y.: A quality model for open source selection. In: Proceedings of the IEEE Sixth International Conference on Advanced Language Processing and Web Information Technology, China, pp. 515–519 (2007)
13. Syeed, M., Hammouda, I., Syatä, T.: Evolution of open source software projects: a systematic literature review. J. Softw. **11**(8), 2815–2829 (2013)
14. Wheeler, D.A.: How to evaluate open source software/free software (OSS/FS) programs (2009). http://www.dwheeler.com/oss_fs_eval.html#support
15. Del Bianco, V., Lavazza, L., Morasca, S., Taibi, D.: A survey on open source software trustworthiness. IEEE Softw. **28**(5), 67–75 (2011)

Software Testing and Traceability

Tool Support for Change-Based Regression Testing: An Industry Experience Report

Rudolf Ramler[1(✉)], Christian Salomon[1], Georg Buchgeher[1],
and Michael Lusser[2]

[1] Software Competence Center Hagenberg,
Softwarepark 21, 4232 Hagenberg, Austria
{rudolf.ramler, christian.salomon,
georg.buchgeher}@scch.at
[2] OMICRON Electronics GmbH, Oberes Ried 1, 6833 Klaus, Austria
michael.lusser@omicron.at

Abstract. Changes may cause unexpected side effects and inconsistencies. Regression testing is the process of re-testing a software system after changes have been made to ensure that the new version of the system has retained the capabilities of the old version and that no new defects have been introduced. Regression testing is an essential activity, but it is also time-consuming and costly. Thus, regression testing should concentrate on those parts of the system that have been modified or which are affected by changes. Regression test selection has been proposed over three decades ago and, since then, it has been frequently in the focus of empirical studies. However, regression test selection is still not widely adopted in practice. Together with the test team of an industrial software company we have developed a tool-based approach that assists software testers in selecting regression test cases based on change information and test coverage data. This paper describes the main usage scenario of the approach, illustrates the implemented solution, and reports on its evaluation in a large industry project. The evaluation showed that the tool support reduces the time required for compiling regression test suites and fosters an accurate selection of regression test cases. The paper concludes with our lessons learned from implementing the tool support in a real-world setting.

Keywords: Regression testing · Test case selection · Change-based testing

1 Introduction

"Change is continual" is the first of the five laws by Lehman and Belady [1] that characterize the dynamics of program evolution. Changes to the software often cause unexpected side effects and inconsistencies with other parts of the software. Regression testing is the process of re-testing a software system after changes have been made to ensure that the new version of the system has retained the capabilities of the old version and that no new defects have been introduced [2]. While regression testing is an essential and valuable quality assurance measure, it is also a time-consuming and costly activity [3]. The required efforts and costs can be reduced by concentrating primarily on those tests, which exercise the parts of the system that have been changed or that are

© Springer International Publishing AG 2017
D. Winkler et al. (Eds.): SWQD 2017, LNBIP 269, pp. 133–152, 2017.
DOI: 10.1007/978-3-319-49421-0_10

affected by changes. However, selecting a minimal relevant set of regression test cases is challenging as it requires in-depth knowledge about the system's implementation to spot all direct and indirect dependencies between the changes made in development and the related test cases.

The idea of regression test selection has been proposed over three decades ago [4–6]. Since then many different approaches for selecting test cases to compile an optimal regression test suite have been proposed [5, 6]. However, regression test selection has not been widely adopted in practice [7] and reports about successful applications in real-world projects are still rare [3, 8].

In this paper we describe an approach for change-based regression testing that has been implemented in a large industry project. The approach is supported by a tool named *Sherlock* that assists testers in selecting regression test cases based on changes made to the software system. The tool integrates information about test cases, changes and dependencies from different sources of the development lifecycle. The information is used to support testers in making decisions which test cases to select when compiling a regression test suite.

The industry context and motivation for our work are described in Sect. 2. Section 3 provides an overview of the approach for change-based regression testing and the implemented tool-support. The tool has been evaluated together with the company's test team. Section 4 describes the evaluation approach, and Sect. 5 discusses the results. The paper concludes with sharing our lessons learned and an outlook on future work in Sect. 6.

2 Industry Context and Motivation

This section describes the background of the studied company and the software system subject to testing. It illustrates the challenges experienced by the testers when selecting regression test cases in this context. Finally, it describes the derived goals and practical requirements for implementing tool support for regression testing.

2.1 Company Background and Software System

The tool support for regression test case selection has been developed together with test engineers of OMICRON electronics GmbH[1], an international software company in the electrical engineering domain. The company offers hardware and software products. One of these is a large software solution which has a development history of about 20 years. Over these years the system has grown tremendously in size as well as in complexity. The current version consists of over 2.5 million lines of code (MLOC) containing different programming languages and a mix of different software technologies. The system is structured into more than 40 functional modules. The modules interact with each other and share a common framework as well as various base libraries and hardware drivers. The system has grown to its current size due to

---

[1] https://www.omicronenergy.com/.

numerous contributions made by many different people in the role of developers, architects, product owners and testers. With the continuous growth of the system also the amount of dependencies between the different modules, libraries and layers has increased. Thus, today, one of the foremost challenges of effective and efficient regression testing lies in acquiring and managing the knowledge about the huge amount of dependencies in the software system.

The system is still under active development and new versions extending the rich set of features are released on a regular basis. We followed the development for about 1.5 years (20 months). In this time approximately 1.300 work items (features, change requests, and bug fixes) were implemented by 36 different people resulting in changes to 115.000 methods part of 3.600 source code files.

A team of five testers has to ensure that newly implemented functionality performs as expected and – by running regression tests – that these changes do not adversely affect the existing, unchanged functionality. For each of the functional modules the testers maintain up to several hundred test cases. Overall, more than 5,000 test cases exist for the whole system. The software system is primarily tested manually. Automated tests are only available for a small part of the system, mainly on the level of technical interfaces. Most test cases require manual interaction because the functional modules are user interface centered and, furthermore, they also have strong dependencies on hardware equipment that has to be setup and operated manually.

For a large, complex system like the one described in this paper, executing all available tests in regression testing is impossible due to time and resource constraints. Therefore, a relevant subset of all available test cases has to be selected. The problem, however, lies in knowing which test cases are relevant. The testers select regression tests based on the textual description of the implemented feature or fixed bug and their detailed knowledge of the system which they acquired over years of testing. For less experienced testers, e.g., those who are new to the team, it is particularly hard to select all relevant test cases due to the complexity of the system and due to the many dependencies that can only be traced on code level. In order to avoid missing relevant test cases, less experienced testers often tend to select unnecessarily large sets of regression test cases. These sets contain unrelated test cases that increase the testing effort but not the chance of spotting side-effects induced by the changes.

2.2   Challenges of Experience-Based Regression Testing

Figure 1 illustrates different situations a tester may face in regression testing after the developers have made changes to the system, e.g., due to a bug fix. In each of the six examples (*a - f*) three methods have been changed (shown as dark gray blocks). The ellipses show the coverage footprint of the available test cases (*test case A* to *test case G*), i.e., the methods covered when the test case is executed.

In the following examples *test case A* (shown as gray filled ellipse) represents the error-revealing test case that has initially been executed by the tester when the bug was found. This test case is usually linked to the bug report. It will be re-executed when the bug has been resolved by the developers to make sure the change works as expected

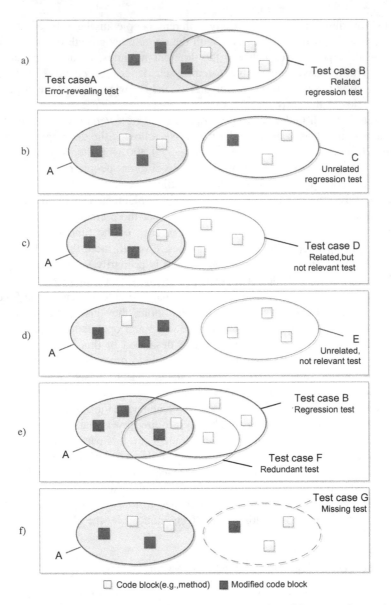

Fig. 1. Examples illustrating scenarios where test cases are selected for regression testing (bold ellipse), are not considered relevant (thin ellipse) or are missing (dashed ellipse).

and the bug report can be closed. In addition, the testers run regression tests to make sure the fix did not lead to unintended side effects.

The selection of regression test cases is based on the testers' personal knowledge and intuition. Different testers may therefore propose different sets of regression test cases. Generally the testers try to be as inclusive as possible, but they also try to keep the regression test set as small as possible to warrant efficiency. The examples illustrate the different situations the testers may face.

Example (a). The tester usually knows the usage scenario that initially revealed the bug. It is depicted as *test case A* (gray filled ellipse). In re-testing the tester runs this test case to make sure the bug has actually been fixed. One of the changed methods is also relevant for another usage scenario, shown as *test case B* (bold ellipse). Test case B has to be selected for regression testing. It makes sure that this alternative usage scenario still works in the same way as before and that it is not negatively affected by the change. Testers are usually able to identify suitable regression test cases when the usage scenarios of the initially error-revealing test and the regression test are overlapping or closely related, e.g., when they affect the same functional module.

Example (b). When changes are spread out across the system they often have "unexpected" side-effects occurring in different functional modules. This situation makes selecting relevant test cases (*test case C*) particularly hard. It requires detailed knowledge of the system which is often possessed only by experienced testers.

Example (c). Testing further, unrelated usage scenarios that do not depend on any of the changed methods such as *test case D* (thin ellipse) will not be able to spot side-effects and can therefore be omitted from regression testing. This is usually the case for most of the test cases. Usually all test cases relating to modules other than the one directly affected by the change can be excluded.

Example (d). However, test cases for usage scenarios similar to the error-revealing scenario are sometimes selected for regression testing, even when they do not cover any of the changed methods (*test case E*). Without knowledge of the changed code it can be very hard or even impossible for the testers to decide which of the test cases are relevant for regression testing and which are not.

Example (e). Sometimes test cases exercise almost the same usage scenarios but observe the system's behavior from a different viewpoint, e.g., functional correctness versus performance or results displayed on the user interface versus stored in the database. Similarly, larger test cases (*test case B*) sometimes subsume other tests (*test case F*), which focus on a small, specific aspect of the system. Such a relationship between test cases can usually be observed by comparing their coverage footprints. A tester may consider test cases that have the same or a smaller coverage footprint as redundant, depending on whether the tests' particular viewpoints or specialization is relevant in context of regression testing.

Example (f). Finally, despite the comprehensive set of test cases that exists in the test management system, it may still be possible that some of the changed methods are not covered by any of the existing test cases in the test management system. Thus, the tester has to come up with a new test case (*test case G*, shown as dashed ellipse) to be able to fully cover the change. Since testers are often not aware of the coverage footprints of the existing test cases, such uncovered changes may easily slip through regression testing. Thus, the testers are also performing exploratory testing in addition to running regression tests based on the test cases specified in the test management system.

2.3   Goals and Requirements

The goal of developing tool support for regression testing was to aid the testers in selecting a set of relevant test cases. Regression testing is considered to be safe [4] if all test cases are selected that may reveal a fault, i.e., a negative side-effect resulting from a change. Accordingly, all test cases may be selected that cover any of the changed parts of the system. However, the set of selected test cases should also be minimal ("small") in order to keep the required effort and time involved in regression testing as low as possible.

It is worth noting that the goal was not to cut testing costs or to reduce the length of testing cycles, but to increase the defect detection capability of regression testing. In the time-frame available for testing the testers should focus on the most relevant test cases covering the critical and the changed functionality to minimize risk of defects slipping through to production. Hence, on the long run, this approach is expected to reduce effort and costs by avoiding the usually expensive hotfixes and service release.

Following requirements were derived from these overall goals.

(1) Find all test cases that cover the changes. In order to reveal a fault, a test case has to be able to trigger the fault by executing the faulty part of the code. Thus, a test case should be selected for the initial set of regression tests if it fully or at least partially covers the changed code. Since changes were related to methods, the measure *method coverage* was proposed to select relevant test cases.

(2) Exclude unrelated test cases. Test cases that do not contribute to the coverage should be excluded from the initially proposed set of tests to keep the regression test suite small. Nevertheless, exceptions should be possible and testers should still be able to add "unrelated" test cases, for example, critical and high priority tests that have to be part of every regression test run.

(3) Identify redundant test cases. Changed parts may be covered by several similar test cases. Including all these test cases may lead to a highly redundant regression test suite. Testers should therefore be able to skip redundant test cases by deselecting them from the regression test suite.

(4) Interactive decision support. The tool should support human testers by automatically proposing a set of relevant test cases that are compiled into a regression test suite with minimal redundancy. However, the aim is not to replace the human tester and his knowledge, but to compile the relevant information, provide a comfortable overview, and support making quick yet sound decisions.

(5) Integration with existing tools. Regression testing relies on information that is maintained in tools currently used in testing and development. The regression tests are selected from the test cases stored in the company's test management system. Overall, it contains several thousand test cases. The test management system is also used to define and manage the test runs and to document test execution results. Additional tools exist for profiling and measuring test coverage. Change information has to be retrieved from the versioning system of the Microsoft Team Foundation Server used by the development team.

3   Approach and Tool Support

Numerous approaches for regression test case selection and prioritization have been investigated in empirical research. A comprehensive overview of the related work can be found in the literature reviews published by Engström, Runeson and Skoglund [5] and by Yoo and Harman [6]. An overview of code-based change impact analysis techniques has been provided by Li et al. [9]. The approach described in this paper assists testers in the selection of test cases related to changes made to the software system. Thus, it can be classified as test case selection approach, which deals with the selection of a subset of tests that check system modifications [6]. The approach has been implemented in form of the tool *Sherlock*. Its implementation is related to the graph-walk technique [10] and the modification-based technique [11]. Potentially relevant test cases are identified based on their coverage footprint, which is determined by recorded code coverage information from previous test runs. The coverage footprint provides the dependency information necessary to link test cases to the modified code.

In the following subsections we give an overview of Sherlock's integration with other tools and its high-level architecture, and we describe the steps how the tool support is used for compiling a regression test suite.

3.1   Data Sources and Tool Architecture

Figure 2 shows the overall architecture of the tool Sherlock – split into a client and a server part – and its interfaces to the testing tools serving as data sources.

Data Sources. For identifying and selecting the relevant regression test cases, Sherlock incorporates information from three data sources: (1) information about changes is retrieved from the *version control system* of Microsoft's Team Foundation Server (TFS)[2], (2) the list of available test cases and their properties are retrieved from the *test management system* SilkCentral Test Manager[3], and (3) information about which test cases are related to the source code changes is extracted from *code coverage analysis* results produced in previous test runs for the individual test case with the profiler SmartBear AQtime Pro[4].

Adapter. Dedicated adapters have been implemented for each of the three data sources. The adapters are used to extract, transform and load (ETL) the data into Sherlock's central data store. For data extraction the typically proprietary interfaces of the different tools are used. For example, Microsoft's TFS provides a REST API to retrieve a wide range of information including information about changed code in form of change sets attached to work items, the test management system's export interface is used to gain the list of available test cases, and the coverage information is extracted from coverage result files in XML format. These data sets are transformed into a tool-agnostic graph format consisting of nodes and edges. Nodes represent check-ins,

---

[2] https://www.visualstudio.com/en-us/products/tfs-overview-vs.aspx.

[3] http://www.borland.com/en-GB/Products/Software-Testing/Test-Management/Silk-Central.

[4] https://smartbear.com/product/aqtime-pro/overview/.

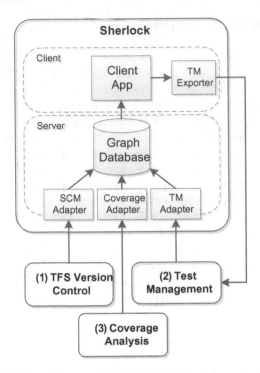

Fig. 2. High-level architecture of Sherlock and its interfaces to other test tools.

files, methods, test cases, etc. Edges represent dependencies such as those between check-ins and files, files and methods, as well as dependencies between methods and test cases. An example for one of the more complex transformations in the ETL process is computing the list of methods of a class that have been changed, based on the information of which lines in a source code file have been changed, added or removed. While the lines can be easily retrieved on file level from TFS, there is no support for linking this information to source code entities such as methods [12]. Finally, the nodes and edges are stored into a graph database.

Graph Database. Sherlock uses Neo4j[5], a NoSQL database optimized for storing and retrieving data structured in form of a graph. The database supports the creation of a simple graph-oriented data model and provides an intuitive query language. Different types of nodes can be defined, which can be combined by edges representing different types of relationships. Since optimized for scalability, the database is able to handle a huge number of nodes and dependencies. Figure 3 shows a basic data structure containing four different types of nodes and three types of relationships. Besides work items, change sets, methods and test cases, the database also contains nodes for source code files, source folders, branches and developers. The graph database runs as server and allows several testers working on regression test suits in parallel.

---

[5] https://neo4j.com/.

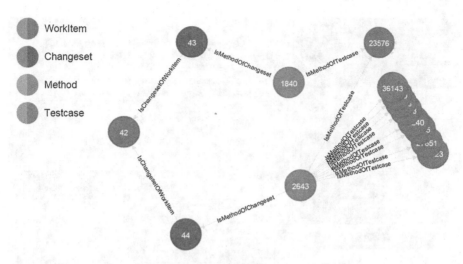

Fig. 3. Nodes and dependencies part of the basic structure of the graph database.

Client App and Export. The tester access the information stored in the graph database via a dedicated client application that guides the user through the different steps of interactively composing regression test suites. Initially the tool retrieves the test cases from the graph database that cover the investigated changes. These test cases are candidates for regression testing. The tester can sort and explore the list according to different criteria and exclude redundant or irrelevant test cases. Finally, a selected subset of the test cases is exported to the test management system where the test run is started and managed. Figure 4 depicts the Sherlock's client application displaying a list of regression test candidates to be selected.

3.2   Steps in Compiling a Regression Test Suite

Sherlock supports testers in regression testing when bug fixes and enhancements have been made to the software system. The testers use the tool for identifying test cases related to an individual change (e.g., a bug fix), for all changes within a specified date range (e.g., all fixes and enhancements combined in a maintenance release), or all changes made on a branch before it is merged back into the trunk (e.g., all changes made while implementing a new feature). The main focus of Sherlock lies in automatically proposing a list of relevant test cases that should be considered when compiling a regression test suite. The resulting test suite is the basis for subsequent regression test runs executed via the test management system. In addition, Sherlock also indicates coverage gaps, i.e., all parts of the source code that have been changed but are not covered by the selected test cases.

The following steps are typically carried out when compiling a regression test suit with Sherlock.

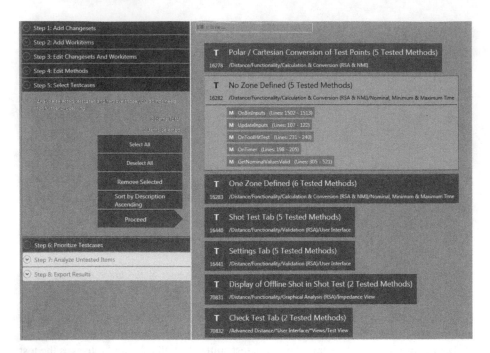

Fig. 4. User interface of the Sherlock client application. Tester interactively compile a regression test suite by selecting test cases and analyzing test gaps.

(1) Select Changes. The version control system of TFS keeps track of any modifications to the source code. Each modification is linked to a change set associated to a work item, e.g., a bug, a task or a requirement. Change sets group together all changes to one or several files as well as any new files created in the course of completing a work item such as resolving a bug or implementing a requirement. The tester starts with selecting the change sets for testing and/or by choosing work items, which refer to change sets relevant for testing. The selection depends on what should be tested, for example, a single bug fix, the tasks completed by a particular developer, or all changes that will be included in an upcoming release.

(2) Determine Affected Code. Based on the links between change sets and source code maintained by the TFS, the relevant code changes can be determined for the selected work items. Technically, the maintained information identifies the particular revision of a source code file in the versioning system and, thus, allows retrieving the lines that have been modified, added or removed. Using this information allows computing the list of modified methods (functions) per source code file. Resolving changes to the level of individual methods has been found to be a useful level of granularity in order to avoid large test sets [12].

(3) Query Related Tests. More than 5,000 test cases are stored in the SilkCentral test management system. The test cases are organized according to the modules of the software system. Each test case is specified by a list of steps for manual execution and a set of meta-data including, for example, the estimated execution time of the test or the test priority indicating how important the test is for testing the associated module.

In addition, optionally, coverage information is associated to each of the test cases. The coverage footprint is defined in terms of the list of files and methods executed when the test is run. For some modules the coverage information has been collected throughout full regression test runs using a coverage analysis tool. The coverage information can be used to retrieve all test cases that are able to contribute to the coverage of a changed file or method.

(4) **Interactive Selection of Tests**. In the previous step a list of all possibly relevant test cases is provided. Hence a test case may cover one or more changed methods, and a method may be covered by zero to many test cases. The Sherlock client allows sorting and filtering the suggested test cases according to various different criteria such as their total coverage contribution or their unique coverage contribution as well as their priority and other meta-data from the test management system. The tester can interactively select or deselect test cases and observe the impact on the overall coverage, the number of selected test cases, the overall estimated execution time, and possibly uncovered methods. Furthermore, Sherlock implements an optimization algorithm to compute test suits with minimum redundancy, which can serve as starting point for further manual adjustments.

(5) **Report Test Gaps**. Despite the huge number of existing test cases in the test management system, some parts of the software system are not covered by tests. For these parts, either no test cases are available or the code has recently been added and is not yet fully covered by tests. The testers are constantly extending the set of tests and aim to increase code coverage also for these parts. The goal is to close any test gaps [13] resulting from recently changed code that is lacking sufficient tests to achieve full coverage. To support the work of the testers, detected gaps are reported.

(6) **Export Test Suite**. Sherlock aggregates information from a broad range of sources and offers mechanisms to automatically sort and select test cases. Once the tester has made the decision which test cases to select, the selection is used to create a test suite in the test management system. There the test suite can still be adjusted before it is run. Typically, additional test cases are added, e.g., test cases that are not covering the changed code but which are mandatory or considered relevant for some reason based on the tester's experience, and the test execution order can be redefined.

4 Evaluation Design

The approach and the tool prototype have been developed in close cooperation with the company partner. Throughout development the approach and the tool support were reviewed and discussed with the testers on a regular basis. In addition, the usefulness of the tool support was assessed together with the team of testers in an *informal experiment* conducted as part of a regular workshop.

4.1 Goal and Research Questions

The goal of the evaluation was to compare *(a) regression test selection with tool support* to *(b) manual regression test selection based on personal experience* in order to explore following "research questions":

RQ1:   How does the use of the tool support *impact the strategy* applied for selecting regression test cases?

RQ2:   How does the use of the tool support *impact the time required* for selecting regression test cases?

RQ3:   How does the use of the tool support *impact the number of selected test cases*?

RQ4:   Does the use of the tool lead to a *different selection of test cases* than the manual approach?

4.2   Evaluation Setup

The evaluation of the tool support was conducted by comparing the selection of regression test cases (a) by a tester using the support of the tool Sherlock and (b) by testers manually selecting relevant test cases based on their personal knowledge and experience, i.e., the control group.

All five testers of the test team took part in the workshop. Table 1 shows the experience in number of years involved in testing at the company and the knowledge of the participants in testing the selected software system for the evaluation. *Tester A* was a senior member of the test team. He had been involved in the development of the tool and therefore performed regression test selection with Sherlock. *Tester B* was one of the most experienced testers who also had most knowledge about the modules selected for the evaluation. B's selection of test cases was considered the "gold standard" for the discussed examples. *Tester C* had medium experience and medium knowledge about the tested modules. *Tester D* was the less experienced member of the test team with only about one year. Therefore, D and *Tester E* decided to team up and to conduct the evaluation together.

Table 1. Knowledge and experience of the workshop participants.

Participant	A	B	C	D+E
Experience in years	> 10	> 10	> 5	< 1 (D) > 5 (E)
Knowledge about tested modules	some	high	some	some
Test selection approach	tool-based	manual	manual	manual

The evaluation was performed based on two major modules of the analyzed software system with an overall set of 392 specified regression test cases in the test management system. The participants were asked to select a suitable set of regression tests from this pool of test cases for different work items (bug fixes and small features) that had been resolved in the past. For each work item a textual description (e.g., initial bug report or requirement rationale, clarifying comments, details about the resolution) was available. Furthermore, the change history of each work item showed the list of

Table 2. Changes related to the example work items used in the evaluation.

Work Item	Type	Number of Check-ins	Changed Files	Changed Methods	Affected Module
WI-1	bug fix	1	1	1	M1
WI-2	bug fix	2	1	1	M1+M2
WI-3	bug fix	1	1	1	M2
WI-4	feature	5	12	28	M2
WI-5	bug fix	1	5	8	M2
WI-6	bug fix	1	1	2	M1

changes the developers made to the source code. We prepared a list of eight work items for the evaluation. Two work items were discarded in the workshop as not directly related to the two selected modules. Table 2 shows the six remaining work items that were analyzed and discussed further.

4.3 Limitations and Validity Threats

The blueprint of the evaluation is similar to an experiment design. However, it has not been conducted in a controlled environment since it was embedded in a workshop with the goal to discuss usage scenarios and envisioned benefits of the tool support.

The investigated usage scenario and the selected examples are specific for the project and company context, and they were deliberately chosen in order to foster the discussion with the members of the test team. The evaluation has been performed in an informal, interactive setting that promoted feedback and new insights rather than producing generalizable results. The participants were eager to produce accurate and representative results. However, the workshop setting also led to occasional disruptions such as participants leaving the room or taking phone calls.

We addressed these limitations by documenting all workshop activities, discussions as well as interruptions in a detailed protocol and by conducting an ex-post analysis of the results with one of the participants to confirm our observations before drawing conclusions. Due to the small number of analyzed cases and participants the findings were not tested for statistical significance.

5 Results and Discussion

In the workshop the testers (*A*, *B*, *C* and *D* + *E*) were given the task to select regression test cases for each of the previously chosen work items (*WI-1*, *WI-2* etc.). Each work item was processed as follows. First, the unique ID of the work items was announced and the starting time was recorded. The testers looked up the work item in TFS, read the work item description, and selected the test cases they considered relevant for regression testing. They specified their selection in a predefined Excel sheet by listing the test case name and ID of the test cases specified in the SilkCentral test managment system. Finally they sent their list by email to the workshop moderator. The time stamp of the email was defined as completion time. Once all testers had sent their selections, the individual results were presented side by side and discussed by the whole team. Questions that were typically asked included, for example, why a particular test case was selected or not selected by a tester, whether a particular test case could be considered equivalent to another with respect to a certain test objective, or what additional test cases may have to be designed. We asked further questions about how the testers performed test case selection, what information source they consulted, etc. and documented the discussion and feedback, which was used to discuss and answer our research questions.

5.1   Strategies Used for Test Case Selection (RQ1)

The first research question investigates the way the testers perform the task of regression test selection with or without tool support. In both cases the testers have to make decisions that require experience and knowledge. The rationale of this question is to explore which kinds of experience and knowledge are required when different strategies for test case selection are applied.

(a) **Regression test selection using tool support.** When using Sherlock, tester *A* studied the description of the work item and queried the associated changes stored in the Sherlock database. The tool presented a list of all candidate test cases covering the changed methods from which the final regression test suite was derived by deselecting the tests considered redundant or irrelevant. The decision which test cases to select or deselect was mainly based on the short description of the test cases shown in Sherlock. Tester *A* did not add any test cases to the regression test suite other than those initially proposed by the tool.

(b) **Manual regression test selection.** The testers *B*, *C*, and *D + E* performing manual selection also started by studying the description of the work item. Then they browsed the hierarchically structured set of existing test cases in the test management system and built up their regression test suite by adding the relevant tests to the initially empty list. The most experienced tester *B* occasionally also looked at the list of changed files associated to the work items and usually selected individual test cases based on his detailed knowledge of the modules. In contrast, the other testers tended to selected all test cases related to a specific function (e.g., all test cases concerned with "Reporting"). For selecting a specific test case out of all related test cases the less experienced tester usually had to check the detailed test case description and the list of specified test steps.

Our observations and the feedback from the testers show that **the tool support leads to a test case selection strategy** (*initial proposal and deselection*) **that is different from the manual selection approach** (*bottom-up selection*).

The discussion of the effect the two different strategies have on the produced regression test suites constitutes the answers to the following research questions.

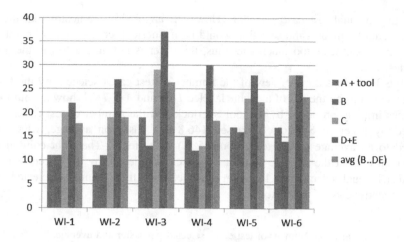

Fig. 5. Time required for regression test selection by work item and tester. (Color figure online)

5.2 Time Required for Regression Test Selection (RQ2)

The second research question investigates if the tool support impacts the time that is necessary for selecting regression test cases. The purpose of this question lies in identifying possible usability issues related to the handling of the tool, which may result in an observable holdup when Sherlock is used.

Figure 5 shows the time required (by testers, in minutes) to select the regression tests for each of the work items. The first bar (dark blue) is the time of tester *A* using the tool Sherlock. For all work items, tester *A* required less time than the *average of the other testers* (last bar, shown in light blue) selecting the regression tests manually. In most cases tester *A* performed the test selection in about the same time as the most experienced tester *B* (second bar, shown in red).

The total of test case selection for all 6 work items, the time required by tester *A* was 1:28 h, the minimum overall time was 1:17 h (tester *B*), the maximum time was 2:52 h (team of testers *D* + *E*), and the average overall time of the testers performing manual selection was 2:07 h.

The results indicate that **the usage of the tool does not have a noticeable adverse effect on the time required for selecting regression test cases.**

5.3 Number of Selected Test Cases (RQ3)

The third research question aims to investigate how the tool support impacts the number of test cases selected for regression testing. The actual number of selected test cases is likely depending on the tester's personal experience and the knowledge he or she has about the tested modules. Therefore, we do not expect that the number of test cases selected by the tester using Sherlock differs much from those of the other testers performing manual test case selection. However, an obvious indicator that the tool support actually impacts the selection would be if Sherlock constraints the number of initially proposed tests too much and, thus, the tester is not able to select the appropriate test cases.

Table 3 provides an overview of the number of test cases selected by the testers. The two columns on the left of the table labeled *Tool* and *A + Tool* show the number of test cases initially proposed by the tool Sherlock and the number of test cases finally selected by tester *A*. Sherlock proposed 146.8 test cases on average, which were reduced to an average of 7.3 tests (about 5 %) by tester *A*. The right column (*Avg BCDE*) shows that the average number of test cases selected by the testers who performed a manual selection is 13.3. On average, thus, they manually selected about twice as many tests as tester *A*.

Table 3. Number of test cases selected per tester and average.

Work Item	Tool	A+Tool	B	C	D+E	Avg BCDE
WI-1	14	9	5	6	16	9.0
WI-2	48	3	1	11	14	8.7
WI-3	200	4	10	16	19	15.0
WI-4	222	15	30	-	34	32.0
WI-5	222	6	6	5	2	4.3
WI-6	175	7	1	15	17	11.0
Average	146.8	7.3	8.8	10.6	17.0	13.3

Moreover, tester *A* using the tool support selected roughly the same number of test cases as tester *B*. In those cases where tester *A* selected less tests than tester *B* (*WI-3* and *WI-4*), the reason is obviously not a confined preselection by Sherlock. For four of the work items (including *WI-3* and *WI-4*) Sherlock found a very large number of test cases since all of them covered one or more of the changed methods. For these cases Sherlock was not able to make an appropriate preselection and, thus, almost all test cases for the particular module were returned.

It can be observed from these results that **the tool support did not lead to a specifically high or low number of selected test cases.**

5.4   Differences in Selected Test Cases (RQ4)

The fourth research question investigates if the use of the tool produces a different set of regression test cases than the manual selection approach. The purpose of this question is to identify the need for a further analysis of the applied selection strategies and the resulting test cases in order to adjust and improve the tool support.

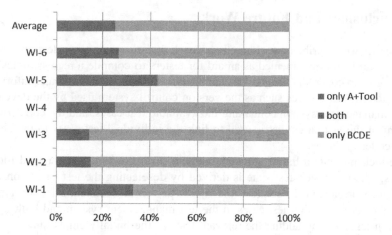

Fig. 6. Test cases selected uniquely by tester *A*, by the group of the testers *BCDE*, or by both.

Figure 6 shows the number of test cases that were only selected by tester *A* using Sherlock (blue portion), only by the group of testers performing manual selection (testers *BCDE*, green portion), or by both (red portion). The top bar shows the average shares: 11 % of the test cases were uniquely selected by tester *A* and 75 % uniquely by the testers *BCDE*. 14 % of the test cases were selected by both.

On the first glance the agreement in terms of the 14 % test cases shared by tester *A* and the testers *BCDE* seems small. However, the relatively low share is not surprising since tester *A* generally selected a low number of test cases, 44 in total for all six work items (or 7.3 tests on average as shown above). In contrast, *BCDE* together selected 155 unique test cases in total.

We also compared the selection made by tester *A* with tool support to the "gold standard" provided by tester *B*. The intersection *A* ∩ *B* shows a 23 % overlap between the test cases selected by *A* and those selected by *B*. In the follow-up discussion the testers explained the differences by the presence of redundant test cases of which only one or a few are selected. Since these tests are considered equivalent, it is merely a personal choice which test case out of the several redundant ones is eventually selected by a tester.

> **The regression test suited produced with the tool support differs from the regression test suited produced manually to about the same extent as the test suites produced with manual selection by different testers.**

Finally, when computing the agreement between the testers *B*, *C* and *D* + *E* in terms of the intersection *B* ∩ *C* ∩ *DE* one can observe that on average only 6 % of the manually selected test cases were selected by all three of them. The relatively small overlap between the tester *A* and the group of testers *BCDE* can therefore not be attributed to the tool support.

6   Conclusions and Future Work

In this paper we described a tool-based approach for regression test selection. The tool Sherlock had been implemented as an aid for testers to compile a regression test suite with the goal to cover all changed files and methods. Sherlock incorporates information from different data sources such as the version control system used by the developers, the test management system containing the available test cases, and the code coverage footprint of the test cases that is used to link the individual test cases to the changed source code.

Sherlock presents a list of all candidate test cases covering the changed files and methods. The regression test suite is derived by deselecting the test cases considered redundant or irrelevant. In contrast, the testers performing manual selection typically browse the set of existing test cases in the test management system and built up their regression test suite by adding the relevant tests to the initially empty suite.

An evaluation conducted together with the members of the test team showed that the tester who used Sherlock was able produce test suites with less or equal effort and at the same level of accuracy as the testers in the control group who selected the test cases manually. The performance of the tester using Sherlock was about the same as the one showed by a highly experienced tester who had detailed knowledge about the changes to be tested.

For junior testers, who lack the necessary background and experience, Sherlock can be considered a valuable aid providing guidance in selecting appropriate regression test cases. Experienced testers find the tool support useful to double-check and enhance a manually compiled test suite with the automatically proposed list of tests. Furthermore, the tool also allows identifying coverage gaps in the set of available test cases.

In developing the tool support for change-based regression testing we encountered several challenges and open issues, which we consider of general importance when establishing test case selection in practice. The key lessons we derived from these challenges and issues are also the topics that drive our future work.

Lack of details provided by version control systems. Modern tools for task management and version control are able link work items such as bug fixes and features to changes in the source code shown in form of the list of changed, added and deleted lines in the affected source files. The source files are treated as standard text files. Their internal structure defined by the implementation is ignored by the tools. However, the semantic of the change is different whether a changed line maps to a class, method, comment, blank line, etc. Restoring this information is a complex task that requires parsing the changed files and, thus, dealing with different programming languages and technologies.

Selecting from redundant test cases. The code coverage footprint of a test case reveals what parts of the code are executed by the particular test. When two different test cases have the exactly same coverage footprint they may be considered redundant in change-based regression testing. However, these tests may still differ in the way they assert the results and in what properties and aspects of the system's functionality they verify. For example, one test checks only the results shown on the user interface while the other also verifies the values stored in the database. Code coverage information alone is not sufficient to determine the relevant test cases for regression testing. In Sherlock, thus, the tester currently has to decide which test cases to select in case there are several "redundant" tests proposed for a change.

Large and polluted coverage footprints. The execution of a test case comprises many different steps such as starting the tested module, logging in as a test user, opening network connections and files to setup the test scenario, exercising the functionality under test, and checking the outcome and possible side-effects. Therefore, many different parts of the system are exercised throughout test execution, including parts that are not actually subject to testing. Nevertheless, these parts may still be included in coverage measurement. In consequence they pollute the coverage footprint of the test and inflate it with irrelevant entries. Test cases with such coverage footprints often show up as false positives in the initially list of test cases proposed by the tool support. Furthermore, classes and methods required for the module startup or which are frequently used in the test setup are included in the coverage footprint of many test cases. If a change set contains such a method, a huge set of test cases is proposed. Sherlock deals with this problem by excluding coverage information collected in the setup phase and by considering the hit count in determining the relevant tests, i.e., the number of times a method or class has been executed in testing.

Creating and maintaining coverage footprints. The availability of up-to-date coverage footprints is essential for the described change-based regression testing approach [14]. Collecting these footprints from test execution is often the only way to obtain the information necessary for establishing the connection between changes and tests. In the studied project, similar information could not be retrieved via static analysis due to the size of the software system and the various different technologies used in its implementation. For a project that already has a large base of test cases it is a major challenge to establish the critical mass of coverage information that is necessary to make the tool support useful for the testers as part of their daily work. The testers will only start using the tool if they trust that the information it provides is accurate and complete. Furthermore, keeping code coverage information up-to-date requires frequent re-execution of the tests, which is particularly costly for manual test cases. Organizational measures are necessary to keep the effort required for maintaining the coverage footprints in balance with the benefits of a change-based regression testing approach.

Acknowledgments. The research reported in this paper has been supported by the Austrian Ministry for Transport, Innovation and Technology, the Federal Ministry of Science, Research and Economy, and the Province of Upper Austria in the frame of the COMET center SCCH. Furthermore, the authors also thank the industry partner and the members of test team for their valuable time, support and feedback.

References

1. Lehman, M.M., Belady, L.A. (eds.): Program Evolution: Processes of Software Change. Academic Press Prof., London (1985)
2. Ammann, P., Offutt, J.: Introduction to Software Testing, 1st edn. Cambridge University Press, Cambridge (2008)
3. Juergens, E., Hummel, B., Deissenboeck, F., Feilkas, M., Schlogel C., Wubbeke, A.: Regression test selection of manual system tests in practice. In: 15th European Conference on Software Maintenance and Reengineering (CSMR), pp. 309–312 (2011)
4. Rothermel, G., Harrold, M.J.: Analyzing regression test selection techniques. IEEE Trans. Softw. Eng. **22**(8), 529–551 (1996)
5. Engström, E., Runeson, P., Skoglund, M.: A systematic review on regression test selection techniques. Inf. Softw. Technol. **52**(1), 14–30 (2010)
6. Yoo, S., Harmann, M.: Regression testing minimisation, selection, and prioritisation: a survey. Softw. Test Verif. Reliab. **22**(2), 67–120 (2012)
7. Gligoric, M., Eloussi, L., Marinov, D.: Practical regression test selection with dynamic file dependencies. In: Proceedings of the 2015 International Symposium on Software Testing and Analysis (ISSTA 2015), pp. 211–222 (2015)
8. Elbaum, S., Rothermel, G., Penix, J.: Techniques for improving regression testing in continuous integration development environments. In: Proceedings of the 22nd ACM SIGSOFT International Symposium on Foundations of Software Engineering (FSE 2014), pp. 235–245 (2014)
9. Li, B., Sun, X., Leung, H., Zhang, S.: A survey of code-based change impact analysis techniques. Softw. Test Verif. Reliab. **23**(8), 613–646 (2012)
10. Rothermel, G., Harrold, M.J.: A safe, efficient regression test selection technique. ACM Trans. Softw. Eng. Methodol. **6**(2), 173–210 (1997)
11. Chen, Y.-F., Rosenblum, D.S., Vo, K.-P.: TestTube: a system for selective regression testing. In: Proceedings of the 16th International Conference on Software Engineering (ICSE 1994) (1994)
12. Buchgeher, G., Ernstbrunner, C., Ramler, R., Lusser, M.: Towards tool-support for test case selection in manual regression testing. In: Proceedings of the 2013 IEEE Sixth International Conference on Software Testing, Verification and Validation Workshops (ICSTW), pp. 74–79 (2013)
13. Eder, S., Hauptmann, B., Junker, M., Juergens, E., Vaas, R., Prommer, K.H.: Did we test our changes? Assessing alignment between tests and development in practice. In: Proceedings of the 8th International Workshop on Automation of Software Test (AST), pp. 107–110 (2013)
14. Beszedes, A., Gergely, T., Schrettner, L., Jasz, J., Lango, L., Gyimothy, T.: Code coverage-based regression test selection and prioritization in WebKit. In: Proceedings of the 28th IEEE International Conference on Software Maintenance (ICSM), pp. 46–55 (2012)

Challenges of Establishing Traceability in the Automotive Domain

Salome Maro$^{(\boxtimes)}$, Miroslaw Staron, and Jan-Philipp Steghöfer

Chalmers Institute of Technology and University of Gothenburg, Gothenburg, Sweden
{salome.maro,miroslaw.staron,jan-philipp.steghofer}@cse.gu.se

Abstract. Traceability, i.e., relationships between artifacts in software development, is prescribed by quality standards such as ISO 26262 and therefore mandatory for automotive companies that develop safety-critical systems. However, establishing traceability is a challenge for many automotive companies. The objective of this study is to identify traceability challenges and solutions in this domain and compare these challenges and solutions with the ones in literature. To achieve this, we conducted a case study with a large automotive supplier to discover their traceability challenges and a tertiary literature review on existing traceability literature surveys to identify reported challenges and their solutions. We found 13 challenges from the literature study, of which ten were also found at the company. Three challenges are solved at the company with solutions that correlate with those proposed in literature, three are partially solved while four are still unsolved even though there are solutions in literature.

Keywords: Traceability · Software processes · Distributed software development · Tools · Human factors · Software development organisation

1 Introduction

More and more software is being developed and embedded in today's modern cars. This software is not only increasingly complex but even used to control safety-critical functions such as speeding up and braking [1]. It is therefore important to make sure such software is well specified, designed, implemented and tested. Due to the complexity of software being developed and the organizational structure (e.g., OEM and supplier relationships), the amount of artifacts produced in this process is high, artifacts are of diverse formats, and distributed between various organizations [2]. To ensure that the developed systems are of high quality, traceability plays a major factor. Traceability is defined as "the degree to which a relationship can be established between two or more products of the development process, especially products having a predecessor-successor or master-subordinate relationship to one another" [3]. It directly contributes

© Springer International Publishing AG 2017
D. Winkler et al. (Eds.): SWQD 2017, LNBIP 269, pp. 153–172, 2017.
DOI: 10.1007/978-3-319-49421-0_11

to quality attributes of a system such as maintainability [4]. It also helps stakeholders to understand how different artifacts are related, the rationale behind the artifacts and, most importantly, if the whole software has been verified and validated before delivery to the end user.

Due to the complexity of the systems and the distributed nature of development, achieving traceability is a difficult and costly activity. It requires both monetary investment in tools and trainings as well as time investment for creating and maintaining traceability links [5]. On the one hand, there exists a large body of knowledge on traceability. For example, the systematic literature review by Nair et. al found 70 studies on traceability published between 1993 and 2012, only in the Requirements Engineering conference [6]. On the other hand, the practicalities of traceability are still a problem in many companies. This led us to our main research question:

How are the proposed solutions in traceability literature relevant for solving the challenges found in practice in the automotive domain?

To answer this question, we conducted a case study at an automotive supplier company and reviewed 15 secondary publications on traceability. Our reason for investigating an automotive supplier is that these companies are required to establish traceability by safety standards such as ISO 26262 [7] and ASPICE [8]. Moreover, our reason for reviewing secondary studies is based on the fact that recent systematic literature reviews on traceability already exist [9]. We wanted to leverage this previous work and validate it in an industrial context rather than replicating existing studies. Our study found 13 challenges from the literature study and ten of these challenges were also found at the company. Three challenges are solved at the company with solutions that correlate with those proposed in literature, three are partially solved while four are still unsolved even though there are proposed solutions in literature.

The rest of the paper is structured as follows; Sect. 2 describes our research method and research questions in detail, Sect. 3 presents the results and provides a discussion of the results. This is followed by Sect. 4 which discusses previous similar work. Limitations of the study are discussed in Sect. 5 and Sect. 6 concludes the paper and outlines future work.

2   Research Method

The study aims to answer the following research question:

– *RQ: How are the proposed solutions in traceability literature relevant for solving the challenges found in practice in the automotive domain?*

To answer this research question, we applied two types of research methods: a case study and a tertiary literature review. The case study provided data on which challenges exist in practice and their solutions if any and followed the guidelines laid out in [10]. The tertiary literature review provided data on the challenges and solutions in the literature. Before conducting these two studies, we defined the scope that is important to us and which both studies will cover.

In [11], the authors have a defined a traceability process model, which contains the important activities that are needed to establish traceability. The activities defined by the researchers are: planning and managing a traceability strategy, creating, maintaining, and using traceability.

Based on our initial contact with the case company, we are aware that the major problems lie in the activities of creation and maintenance of traceability links. In our study, a traceability link is a connection between two or more artifacts that are in a relevant relation to each other. It is *created* when a relation is identified. For instance, acceptance test cases are often related to the requirements whose fulfillment they are supposed to test. If a new requirement has been elicited from the customer and the developer programs the necessary acceptance test, these two artifacts (the requirement and the acceptance test) are then related by a newly created traceability link. Often, design artifacts such as models are also related to requirements, code, or test cases through traceability links. Likewise, maintenance of a traceability link describes all activities that pertain to keeping the links up-to-date. If a design model changes, e.g., due to an architectural refactoring, existing traceability links might have become obsolete and should be *updated*. If the traceability links connect more than two artifacts, additional artifacts might have to be added or existing ones removed.

Thus for this study, we narrowed our scope to focus on these two activities. Moreover, due to the OEM-Supplier relationship that exists in the automotive domain, traceability information also needs to be exchanged. Therefore, we added a third activity to the scope of our study on the exchange of traceability. Our resulting scope is thus divided into three categories: *Creation, Maintenance and Exchange of Traceability*. The remaining activities, namely planning and managing a traceability strategy and using traceability, will be studied in our future work as discussed in Sect. 6.

For the *Creation* category we studied how traceability links are usually created, for the *Maintenance* category, how they are updated when the artifacts they connect evolve, and for the *Exchange of traceability* category, how traceability information is exchanged between different teams in the same company and between different companies. For all the categories we studied the challenges that are associated with them and their solutions if any. The details of the case study and tertiary literature review are described in the following subsections.

2.1   Case Study Design

Case and Subject Selection. The study was conducted at a large company whose core business is to supply automotive software and equipment to automotive Original Equipment Suppliers (OEMs). Two departments developing embedded systems were involved. We selected these two departments because they already implement traceability in their projects and develop safety-critical systems for which traceability is a requirement. The two departments are also interested in improving their traceability practices, thus the topic is relevant and of interest to them. To be able to understand how traceability is implemented through out the development life cycle, we conducted the study with seven participants of the following roles: two senior experts working on traceability, four software system architects and one functional developer.

Data Collection Procedure. For this study we collected data through observations and semi-structured interviews. The model describing the scope of our study and interview questions were sent to the participants a week before the study took place. For each participant, we started with the participant giving a demonstration on how they implement traceability and using the scope as a guide. This was followed by a semi-structured interview. The interviewer only asked questions which were not answered by the demonstration part. Due to legal issues, the interviews were not recorded but the interviewer took notes. The interviews and observation for each person lasted between 90 min to four hours with breaks in between. The longer sessions were with senior experts who explained and demonstrated the traceability process in detail. The interview guide for these interviews are available online[1].

Analysis Procedure. The data analysis started immediately after the observations and interviews were completed. This was to make sure that we avoid forgetting important information that was mentioned since the interviews were not recorded. The interviewer drafted a summary of the sessions and what was learned from the study and presented it to one of the senior experts for confirmation purposes. After this, the challenges identified from the study were mapped to the phases in the model describing the scope of the study.

2.2   Tertiary Literature Review

Our tertiary literature review followed the guidelines for conducting a systematic mapping study as proposed by [12].

Definition of Research Questions. The literature study aimed to answer the following sub research questions:

1. What traceability challenges are reported in literature?
2. What are the proposed solutions of these challenges?

Conducting the Search. Since this is a tertiary literature review, our aim was to find literature reviews published on traceability in the domain of computer science. We searched the databases Scopus, ACM Digital Library and IEEE Xplore. The search string used was "Traceability AND (Literature Review OR Review OR Literature Survey OR Survey)" or a variant thereof to fit the search syntax of the database. Since a search of the meta-data yielded a large number of irrelevant literature, the search was limited to paper titles. This led us to an initial set of 21 publications, from which one could be excluded as a duplicate.

---

[1] http://tinyurl.com/j7dlco3.

Screening of Papers. We went through all the papers by first reading the title and abstract. Here we excluded papers that were not relevant to our study using the following inclusion criteria.

1. The paper is in English.
2. The paper is published in a peer-reviewed venue.
3. The paper is in the field of computer science.
4. The paper is reviewing literature on traceability.

Exclusion criteria are negations of the inclusion criteria. The screening process left us with 15 relevant papers.

2.3   Data Extraction and Classification

We went through all the 15 papers and extracted the challenges and solutions they report and listed them in a spreadsheet. After this process, we read all the challenges in the list and devised a classification scheme. Initially, we intended to use the conceptual model used to define the scope as the classification scheme. However, we realized that challenges for the *Creation* and *Maintenance* categories were overlapping a lot. We therefore merged the challenges of these categories. After merging we went through the challenges in this category once again and discovered that some challenges were more on the technical side while some were due to the employees and others related to the organization setting. We therefore came up with three sub-categories to represent these three perspectives which we called Tool Support, Human Factors and Organizations and Processes as shown in Fig. 1.

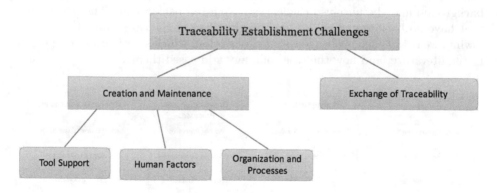

Fig. 1. Categories of traceability challenges

3   Results

In this section, we report the results both from the literature review and the case study. Our results are divided into four subsections which are the different categories of the challenges as depicted in the classification scheme in Fig. 1. For each category, we first describe the challenge, then describe the solutions from literature and finally compare these with what was found at the company. As a summary, our main findings are as follows:

Tool support. There are five challenges identified from the literature: *diversity of artefacts and tools, manual link creation and maintenance, lack of flexible tools, cost,* and *inaccessibility of artefacts.* All five of these can be found at the case company. The challenges of *manual link creation and maintenance* as well as of *cost* have not been solved yet.

Human factors. The two challenges in this category are *misuse of traceability data* and *traceability perceived as an overhead.* Only the latter is found at the case company, but no solution exists as of now.

Organization and Processes. The literature reports on three challenges in this category: *ad-hoc process for establishment of traceability, distributed software development,* and *lack of understanding of traceability.* The first two are found at the case company, where the first has only been partially solved and the second has been fully solved. *Lack of understanding of traceability* is not an issue for the case company.

Exchange of traceability. A total of three challenges was identified: *lack of universal standards, access to artefacts,* and *conflicting objectives.* The first two challenges were also found at the case company, but only the first one was partially solved.

Overall, the solutions found at the case company always matched those reported in the literature. Figure 2 shows the challenges, where the solved challenges have a green background, the partially solved challenges have a yellow background and the unsolved challenges have a red background. The challenges that have no background color were not identified in the case study. In the following, we detail each challenge with a description, which solutions are proposed in the literature, and how the case company addressed them.

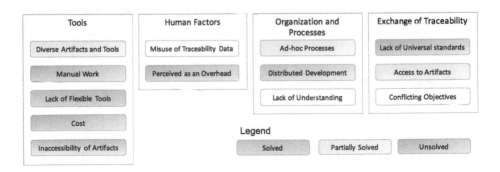

Fig. 2. Challenges of establishing traceability (Color figure online)

3.1 Tool Support

We found five major challenges from literature which were reported in this category. Four of these challenges were also found at the case company. On further analysis (as shown in Table 1) only two of these challenges have been solved, one has a workaround solution, while two of them still remain unsolved.

Table 1. Challenges associated with tools

Challenge from literature	Papers	Found at company	Challenge solved?	Solutions match?
Diversity of artifacts and tools	[13–19]	Yes	Partially	Yes
Manual link creation and maintenance	[6, 9, 13–16, 19–22]	Yes	No	
Lack of flexible tools	[15]	Yes	Yes	Yes
Cost	[9, 14–16, 19, 20, 26]	Yes	No	
Inaccessibility of artifacts	[26]	Yes	Yes	Yes

Diversity of Artifacts and Tools

Description: In the software development life cycle there are a number of activities such as requirements engineering, system design and so on. In many cases each of these activities utilizes a different tool and produces artifacts in different formats. Most traceability tools either do not support linking to artifacts located outside the tool or only support linking to specific tools and a specific format [13, 14].

Solutions in Literature: Eight of our reviewed studies report this challenge [13–19]. From the studies, there are two different solutions for this challenge. The first option is to use one tool that supports all the development activities. The advantage of such a *holistic* tool is that since all the artifacts are stored in one database they can be accessed for traceability link creation. The second solution is to integrate all the existing tools so that it is possible to create traceability links between them. This is however not a trivial task and requires a considerable effort especially if there are many tools that need to be integrated.

Comparison to Case Company: In the case company, there are a total of eight tools that are used for the different development activities. Tool integration is a technically challenging task. Therefore currently to link to artifacts in different tools, the company uses implicit links which are created by copying IDs from one tool to another. This is not only time consuming but also error prone and does not allow for any analysis to be done on the links. To overcome this problem, the company is planning to acquire a holistic tool that will be able to store all of their artifacts and thus make them accessible for creating traceability links. The main drawback of this solution is that existing tools that claim to be holistic tools only support some commonly known parts of the development life cycle. Currently, there are no tools supporting activities like simulations which means that even with the holistic tool in place, other tools will still be used as well. Therefore this challenge is partially solved as linking to tools outside the holistic tool requires implementation of special plugins which is costly in terms of time and might require rework as the involved tools evolve.

Manual Link Creation and Maintenance

Description: The task of creating traceability links is one that is time consuming especially when it is done manually. Moreover, traceability links immediately become outdated when the artifacts they connect evolve. This means that they also need to be updated in order to remain correct. Updating them is also time consuming and most of the time error prone.

Solutions in Literature: This is one of the most reported challenges in the literature. In our review it has been reported by ten out of 15 papers [6,9, 13–16,19–22]. To overcome this challenge, the literature proposes the use of automated techniques to generate and update the traceability links. Examples of these techniques are machine learning [23], information retrieval [24], event based techniques [14] or model-driven techniques [25].

Comparison to Case Company: Interestingly, none of these solutions was viable for the company. Generally machine learning, information retrieval and event-based techniques have a low precision and therefore the chance that false traceability links are generated is high. Given that the company produces safety-critical systems and the traceability links are also used for the certification process, false links are not tolerable. Model-driven techniques on the other hand require that all the artifacts being linked to and from are represented as models which is not the case for the company, where only some of the artifacts are models.

Lack of Flexible Tools

Description: Since traceability link types can greatly differ from company to company or even project to project, it is crucial for the tools to allow for custom traceability link types to be defined. Providing a tool that can only be used in a specific context is a limiting factor, tools need to allow for customization of which links can be created depending on the users' needs.

Solutions in Literature: This challenge was only reported by one study in our review [15]. The solution described is quite straightforward urging developers of traceability tools to take in into account how flexible the tool should be. The more flexible the tool, the better as companies can tailor it to fit their project needs.

Comparison to Case Company: This is one of the challenges that the company has solved. For Requirements Management, they have adopted DOORS[2], a

---

[2] http://www-03.ibm.com/software/products/en/ratidoor.

tool that is flexible and allows for definition of custom traceability links. Out of the box, the tool allows definition to different types of links to link to and from requirements. Linking to other artifacts that are stored outside the tool can be done through OSLC[3] or for artifacts that do not have OSLC representations, special attributes in the requirements can be defined to store IDs or names of artifacts that are outside the tool.

Cost

Description: Establishing traceability links of a high quality requires the company's investment both in terms of money for the tools and in terms of time. The cost of this is significant while the benefits of it cannot be easily measured.

Solutions in Literature: Seven out of 15 papers report that traceability establishment is an expensive process [9, 14–16, 19, 20, 26]. This is because developers need to spend extra time to create and maintain traceability links. Most managers think that a project that implements traceability is more expensive than one which does not [15]. This is because currently there are no measurements that can provide evidence of these direct benefits of traceability. Research proposes cost-benefit models that can be used to show how much traceability has contributed to activities such as maintenance and understandability [16], but these still need to be validated in practice. This is not a trivial task as such benefits are mostly visible at the end of the project. To minimize the effort spent on traceability creation and maintenance, researchers have proposed Value-Based Traceability, which means tracing to only high priority requirements as compared to full traceability [15].

Comparison to Case Company: From the case study, all of the interviewees including the managers confirmed that they think traceability is expensive. However, since it is a mandated task, they have to do it. Value-Based Traceability is also not a feasible solution for them as *full* traceability is a mandatory requirement in this safety-critical domain. It is also hard to maintain an exclusive list of high priority requirements that need traceability as priorities can rapidly change over time.

Inaccessibility of Artifacts

Description: When creating or updating a traceability link, it is crucial to have access to the artifacts that need to be connected by the traceability link. In a situation where a project contains a large number of artifacts, tool support is needed to assist locating the different artifacts. It is very cumbersome if one has to search through hundreds or even thousands of elements manually.

Solutions in Literature: Only one of the reviewed papers mentioned this challenge [26]. The solutions proposed is that the company, through tools, should ensure that users have all the necessary information and access to the artifacts needed to create traceability links. Tools should provide features such as search by ID or keywords, to make it easy for the users to find the artifacts they need.

---

[3] http://open-services.net.

Comparison to Case Company: For the case company, this is not a challenge as the tools they use have the ability to search for and locate specific artifacts in an easy way. For traceability links involving artifacts stored in different tools the user still needs to copy the ID from one tool to another but every tool has a search functionality.

3.2   Human Factors

In this category we found two main challenges that have been reported in the studied literature. As shown in Table 2, only one of these challenges was found at the case company.

Table 2. Challenges associated with human factors

Challenge from literature	Papers	Found at company	Challenge solved?	Solutions match?
Misuse of traceability data	[15, 18, 19]	No		
Perceived as an overhead	[14, 18, 22, 26]	Yes	No	

Misuse of Traceability Data

Description: This challenge refers to the fact that in some situations, people responsible for creating and maintaining the traceability links have a fear that this data may used against them, e.g., during performance appraisals.

Solutions in Literature: This challenge has been reported by three of our reviewed literature [15, 18, 19]. The authors describe that employees have a fear that traceability data can be used against them and threaten their job security. This is an inappropriate use of traceability data as the data is supposed to be used for quality assurance of the system rather than used for judging employees' expertise. The studies propose that both management and employees need to be educated on what traceability is and what the potential benefits are.

Comparison to Case Company: At the case company, this was not part of the challenges that we identified. However, they have a system that already logs user activities with respect to creating and modifying development artifacts. If there is a problem in the system it is easy to identify who was working on the artifact and contact them about the problem. This is an indication that the development environment is already very transparent and that is why employees do not have this fear of misuse of traceability links.

Perceived as an Overhead

Description: In situations where traceability links are created manually, developers usually perceive this as an extra activity that they need to do on top of their daily work. Since the people creating the links are also not the ones that end up using them, they see it as doing a job that only benefits other people.

This is a problem as they become demotivated and assign a low priority to this task, which can lead to either wrong or missing links.

Solutions in Literature: Four of our reviewed studies report this challenge [14,18,22,26]. Proposed solutions for this problem are to ensure that the traceability links created provide immediate benefit to the user who is creating the links. This can be done with tools that enable quick navigation from one artifact to another or visualization techniques that give users an overview of the connection between different artifacts.

Comparison to Case Company: At the case company this is a challenge, due to the break between tools and the fact that implicit links are created between artifacts in different tools. It is hard for developers to get an overview of the traces. Across tools they still have to find artifacts by searching for ID thus do not see the immediate benefits of traceability. All of the interviewees pointed out that being able to navigate easily using the traceability links and having graphical representations of how everything is connected would be a feature that will encourage them to create more correct and complete traceability links. Allowing for easy navigation across tools requires integrating the tools which is also not a trivial task as discussed in Sect. 3.1.

3.3   Organization and Processes

In this category, we found three challenges and out of these three challenges, two were found at the company. At the company, only one challenge has been solved while the other is partially solved (see Table 3).

Table 3. Challenges associated with organization and processes

Challenge from literature	Papers	Found at company	Challenge solved?	Solutions match?
Ad-hoc processes for establishment of traceability	[17,18,22,26]	Yes	Partially	Yes
Distributed software development	[19,26]	Yes	Yes	Yes
Lack of understanding of traceability	[6,13–15,18,19,22]	No		

Ad-Hoc Processes for Establishment of Traceability

Description: In order to achieve correct and complete traceability links, a well defined process for how traceability links should be created and maintained is required. This process needs to be defined, communicated to people in the company, and also integrated into the existing development process. If such a defined process does not exist, traceability links are created in an ad-hoc manner by the different people working on the system which can lead to low link quality.

Solutions in Literature: From the literature, most companies lack this kind of defined process and instead traceability links are created and maintained in an ad-hoc manner [17,18,22,26]. The solution for this challenge is to have a well defined process for traceability creation, maintenance as well as analysis. Such a process will define which links need to be created, when, and by whom. It is also recommended that such a process include a guideline for how the captured traceability links can be used in various scenarios [17].

Comparison to Case Company: In the case company, this challenge is solved by putting in place requirements for which artifacts should be traced. For instance, testers are aware that their tests should be linked to the code being tested, while developers are aware that every development should be linked to a requirement or an issue. The decisions on which artifacts to trace to are mainly based on the ASPICE [8] safety standard that the company needs to follow. However, the challenge with such standards is that they do not define concrete processes but only suggest what should be linked [14]. This means that the company will have to define and refine their process as they move along based on their experiences. With regards to evaluation, the company does not have a proper solution as well. Simple metrics such as completeness of traceability between requirements and tests can be achieved but these are not feasible for traceability links across tool boundaries with their current technology. By switching to a *holistic* tool they hope to reduce this challenge since most traceability links will be in one tool. Some tools, such as simulation tools, will however not be part of the holistic solution. A bigger challenge for analysis of traceability links is checking for correctness. This has to be done manually as there is no way to be sure that the links are correct. Existing literature does not provide any methods for correctness checking that can be used to automatically check *manually* created links.

Distributed Software Development

Description: In large organizations, it is a common phenomenon that development activities are carried out at multiple sites. This adds complexity to traceability especially when the different sites need to share the development artifacts. If the development infrastructure is not well set up, it can be very hard to create traceability links between artifacts that are produced in different locations.

Solutions in Literature: The surveyed literature proposes a centralized repository for storage of all the development artifacts [19,26]. This way the location of the developers will not matter as everything is centrally stored and shared. Such a repository also needs to be guarded by an access control system to make sure that the right people have access to the artifacts they need.

Comparison to Case Company: Essentially, this is not only a traceability problem, but a distributed software development problem in general. The company has solved this challenge by having centralized repositories where the artifacts can be stored and different developers are given access rights accordingly. This is in line with what the literature proposes.

Lack of Understanding of traceability

Description: For effective establishment of traceability, one first needs to understand what traceability is and the intentions of traceability. For a company, if this is not clear to begin with then the chances of failure are high.

Solutions in Literature: This challenge has been reported by seven papers from our review [6,13–15,18,19,22]. In [22], for instance, the authors report that some companies especially those not working in safety-critical domain have no notion of the term traceability. The solution for this challenge is for organizations who want to establish traceability to set up their own traceability policies and conduct training on the concept to make people aware of these policies and their importance.

Comparison to Case Company: Given that the company operates in a safety-critical domain, employees are already aware of the concept of traceability. They base their understanding of traceability on the requirements defined by the safety standard they need to comply to. They even have expert roles whose job is to understand what the standards require, form a strategy on what they need to do to comply, and communicate this to the rest of the company.

3.4   Exchange of Traceability

In this category we found three challenges from the surveyed literature. Two of these challenges were also found at the company where one is partially solved and one is unsolved as shown in Table 4.

Table 4. Challenges associated with exchange of traceability

Challenge from literature	Papers	Found at company	Challenge solved?	Solutions match?
Access to artifacts	[27,28]	Yes	No	
Lack of Universal standards	[16]	Yes	Partially	Yes
Conflicting objectives	[27]	No		

Access to Artifacts

Description: As mentioned before, in the automotive industry, development activities are distributed between the OEM and different suppliers. This implies that the different artifacts produced are also distributed. Establishing traceability links that cross the organizational boundaries is a challenging task due to two main reasons. The first is legal and privacy implications. Some artifacts can be inaccessible to the supplier because they are confidential. The second reason are tool boundaries as organizations may use different tools to manipulate the various artifacts.

Solutions in Literature: In the reviewed literature, two of the papers [27, 28] mention this challenge but there are no proposals for how to establish traceability when the artifacts are restricted due to legal reasons. In case of tool boundaries, the papers propose having a universal standard or policy that can be used for exchanging traceability links. This is further discussed below and in Sect. 3.5.

Comparison to Case Company: The company also faces this challenge when some of the artifacts they want to trace to cannot be shared by the OEMs. Currently they do not have a solution for this. For the artifacts that are shared with them but from different tools, they rely on import and export mechanisms. This is not ideal but is a workaround that works for them. For instance, requirements can be exported in various formats, e.g., Word, PDF, or DOORS modules from the OEMs and manually imported into the suppliers' requirements management system. For some OEMs, the company shares an XML file which has fields that can only be visible to them and fields that can be visible to both the supplier and OEM. This is the company's initiative towards a standard for sharing data. However, the traceability links are still not visible in such files.

Lack of Universal Standards

Description: To facilitate the sharing and transfer of traceability information from one company to another, there is a need for a common standard. Currently this does not exist and traceability information exists in various formats ranging from implicit links established through copying IDs from one artifact to another, to well defined traceability links that utilize formal notations such as models.

Solutions in Literature: The literature proposes the need for one standard that can be applied by various companies in order to facilitate this sharing and exchange of traceability information [16].

Comparison to Case Company: This is a challenge that the company faces. For instance, OEMs can send requirements which could have traceability links as well. But if the tools at the company cannot identify these links then that information is lost and has to be created from scratch.

Conflicting Objectives

Description: When more than one company is involved in the development of a system, it is important to align objectives. This is true also for traceability, if the objectives for traceability in one company contradict the ones in another, there might be a conflict.

Solutions in Literature: Only one of our reviewed literature [27] report this challenge and they propose that at the beginning of the project, all the stakeholders need to align their objectives, including traceability objectives. It is important to define early on what each stakeholder requires and is expected to deliver in terms of traceability.

Comparison to Case Company: This challenge did not come up in the study at the company. Since the company is a supplier, the demand for traceability actually comes from their clients, the OEMs. The OEMs specifically ask them to be compliant to the ASPICE standard in which traceability is one of the requirements.

3.5 Discussion

In this section, we discuss our results in relation to the research question. To recap, our research question is: *How are the proposed solutions in traceability literature relevant for solving the challenges found in practice in the automotive domain?*

From the findings discussed in the results with respect to the proposed solutions in literature, the challenges fall into three different categories. Solved challenges, where the proposed solutions do solve the challenges, partially solved challenges, where the proposed solutions only partially solve the challenges and unsolved challenges where the proposed solutions do not solve the challenges. An overview of this is given in Fig. 2 in Sect. 3. In our discussion, we focus on the unsolved challenges.

In the Tools category the unsolved challenges are *Manual work* of establishing and maintaining the traceability links and the *Cost* of it. There are several studies (e.g., [23, 29]) focusing on a solution approach based on automating the creation and maintenance of traceability links. However, the chance that incorrect links are generated or links are missing is still high which is a hindering factor for applications of such techniques in a safety-critical domain, like automotive. For this reason, automated techniques have not yet been adopted in this domain. Complementing automatic techniques with manual techniques for checking if the links are correct has thus been proposed. This is a good technique for eliminating incorrect links. However this is not guaranteed, as in [30] the authors show that giving a set of generated links to humans to sort out incorrect links actually led to a worse set of traceability links in some cases. This technique also does not deal with missing links that the generating algorithm missed to begin with. A more promising solution is to have the links created manually and provide tool support for maintenance. Such support can be warnings when artifacts connected by a traceability link have changed and automatic fixes such as deleting a traceability link when the artifacts it connects have changed. This line of research has been investigated by [31, 32], but more case studies are needed to show its application in an industrial context.

In the Human Factors category, the unsolved challenge is that traceability is *perceived as an overhead*. This challenge has two aspects: an organisational and a technical one. The organisational issue is that the people creating and maintaining the traceability links are not the ones who use them. A relation to the challenge of understanding of traceability thus exists and sufficient training as well as the realisation of the immediate benefits of traceability links can help in this regard. The technical aspect is related to the tools that are in use and that offer little support in terms of visualisation, navigation, and analysis. If, based on traceability links, the tools used in the industry can offer features such as easy navigation, visualization, customized reports or even recommendation for artifacts that can be re-used, then the developers creating the links will see their benefits. It should be possible to customize the tools in a way that benefits the creators of the links as well [33]. Other ideas could be complimenting traceability tools with aspects of gamification to make the task of creating and maintaining the traceability links more motivating and engaging. This has been shown to work with other software engineering tasks such as requirements analysis and testing [34].

In the Exchange of Traceability category, the unsolved challenge is that there is *no common standard for exchanging of traceability links*. To solve such a challenge, both practitioners and researchers need to work together to establish the standard. For requirements, there is already a Requirements Interchange Format (ReqIF)[4], which is being adopted and provided as exports from several requirements management tools. Extending such a standard or creating a similar standard for traceability exchange will resolve this challenge.

4   Related Work

In this section, we discuss previous research that is similar to ours.

Regan and colleagues [19], conducted a literature review to identify the barriers of traceability and their solutions from literature. In their work, they propose a framework which consists of the categories of the challenges and their solutions. Their framework is quite similar to the categories of challenges that we have proposed. However, their work does not investigate if these proposed solutions work in practice, which is something that our research does by complimenting the literature review with an industrial case study.

More related studies are those by Torkar et al. [20] and Cleland et al. [22]. In [20], the authors performed a systematic literature review, with the aim of identifying requirements traceability definitions, tools, practices and challenges. They also compliment their work with a case study in two companies. In their results, they give a list of challenges and how they are relevant for the two companies. Their study is similar to ours but their literature review only includes papers of up to 2007 while ours includes studies of up to 2014. Also in their research the companies they study are not in the automotive domain but in the telecommunication domain and mobile applications domain. In [22], the authors reviewed four recent industrial studies and interviewed eight practitioners on traceability practices. The authors propose seven areas for further research based in their study. They also conclude that there is a need for more collaboration with industrial practitioners in order to ensure that the solutions from research are actually applicable in practice. Our study is an example of the research proposed here.

Another study is by Kannenberg & Saiedian [15] where the authors study why software requirements traceability still remains a challenge and conclude that manual traceability methods and existing tools are inadequate for the needs of the software development companies.

---

[4] http://www.omg.org/spec/ReqIF/1.1/.

5   Threats to Validity

In this section we discuss the threats to the validity of our study and ways in which we minimized these threats. We use the categories described in [10] but do not discuss internal validity as our study was not not examining a causal relation.

5.1   External Validity

This threat refers to how generalizable the results of the study are. In our case study, we applied data triangulation and interviewed seven employees of three different roles, to get data from different sources. However, since we conducted the study in only one company, we cannot generalize the obtained results without further replication of the study which is discussed as future work in Sect. 6.

With regards to the literature review, the most recent publication was published 2014, which reviewed papers of up to 2013. There is a chance that papers that propose newer solutions to our identified challenges have been published since then.

5.2   Construct Validity

To minimize this threat we had to make sure that what we wanted to study (Challenges of establishing traceability), was understood by our participants of the study. To achieve this we first had a meeting with the two experts from the two departments where we explained our intentions of study. In return, they also explained what their departments do. We also sent the interview guide and scope to the participants one week before the study. As mentioned in Sect. 2, the interviews we conducted were not recorded due to legal matters but the interviewer took notes. To make sure that we did not misinterpret our findings, we showed our initial analysis to one of the senior experts for confirmation. This is known as member checking [35].

5.3   Reliability

To ensure that the results of a study are reliable it is important to make sure that the study can be repeated by other researchers and get the same results. While the settings of the interview cannot be replicated, the artifacts used such as the definition of the scope of the study and the interview guide were well documented and can be used for replication of the study.

6   Conclusions and Future Work

In this paper, we have presented the challenges of establishing traceability in the automotive domain. We compared these challenges and their solutions to what has been reported in literature. Our results show that there are four major challenges which are largely unsolved even though some proposals for solutions exist in theory. These challenges are: (1) manual creation and maintenance of traceability links is error prone and time consuming, (2) the overall cost of traceability is too high and the benefits are not measurable, (3) traceability is considered an overhead and of low priority with people who have to establish it since they are not the ones who use the links and (4) there is a lack of uniform standard for exchange of traceability links between companies. This leads us to conclude that for such problems that are more practical, conducting research involving academia only is not sufficient. The created solutions and tools in research need to be validated in an industrial context where they can be integrated with the existing development processes and work flows that exist in companies. This way, researchers will be able to determine which parts of the solutions are not practically viable and improve or come up with new solutions accordingly.

As part of future work, we plan to carry out such research with companies in the automotive domain. Our first action will be to replicate the case study in more companies in order to check if our list of unsolved challenges is sufficient. This will also include expanding the scope to contain earlier phases involved before establishing traceability links, for instance planning and managing a traceability strategy, and later phases such as how is traceability used or measured after it has been established. Next will be to come up with new solutions and integrate these solutions in existing development processes in order to determine their applicability.

References

1. Broy, M.: Challenges in automotive software engineering. In: Proceedings of the 28th International Conference on Software Engineering, pp. 33–42. ACM (2006)
2. Pretschner, A., Broy, M., Kruger, I.H., Stauner, T.: Software engineering for automotive systems: a roadmap. In: 2007 Future of Software Engineering, pp. 55–71. IEEE Computer Society (2007)
3. IEEE: Standard glossary of software engineering terminology. IEEE Std 610.12-1990, pp. 1–84, December 1990
4. Salem, A.M.: Improving software quality through requirements traceability models. In: IEEE International Conference on Computer Systems and Applications, pp. 1159–1162. IEEE (2006)
5. Egyed, A., Biffl, S., Heindl, M., Grünbacher, P.: A value-based approach for understanding cost-benefit trade-offs during automated software traceability. In: Proceedings of the 3rd International Workshop on Traceability in Emerging Forms of Software Engineering, pp. 2–7. ACM (2005)
6. Nair, S., de la Vara, J.L., Sen, S.: A review of traceability research at the requirements engineering conference re@ 21. In: 2013 21st IEEE International Requirements Engineering Conference (RE), pp. 222–229. IEEE (2013)
7. International Organization for Standardization: Road Vehicles - Functional Safety. ISO26262:2011, November 2011
8. VDA QMC Working Group 13/Automotive SIG: Automotive SPICE Process Assessment/Reference Model. Technical report, Automotive Special Interest, Group (2015)

9. Javed, M.A., Zdun, U.: A systematic literature review of traceability approaches between software architecture and source code. In: Proceedings of the 18th International Conference on Evaluation and Assessment in Software Engineering, p. 16. ACM (2014)
10. Runeson, P., Höst, M.: Guidelines for conducting and reporting case study research in software engineering. Empirical Softw. Eng. **14**(2), 131–164 (2009)
11. Gotel, O., et al.: Traceability fundamentals. In: Cleland-Huang, J., Gotel, O., Zisman, A. (eds.) Software and Systems Traceability, pp. 3–22. Springer, Heidelberg (2012)
12. Petersen, K., Feldt, R., Mujtaba, S., Mattsson, M.: Systematic mapping studies in software engineering. In: 12th International Conference on Evaluation and Assessment in Software Engineering, vol. 17, pp. 1–10 (2008)
13. Spanoudakis, G., Zisman, A.: Software traceability: a roadmap. Handb. Softw. Eng. Knowl. Eng. **3**, 395–428 (2005)
14. Winkler, S., Pilgrim, J.: A survey of traceability in requirements engineering and model-driven development. Softw. Syst. Model. (SoSyM) **9**(4), 529–565 (2010)
15. Kannenberg, A., Saiedian, H.: Why software requirements traceability remains a challenge. CrossTalk J. Def. Softw. Eng. **22**(5), 14–19 (2009)
16. Gotel, O., Cleland-Huang, J., Hayes, J.H., Zisman, A., Egyed, A., Grünbacher, P., Antoniol, G.: The quest for ubiquity: a roadmap for software and systems traceability research. In: 2012 20th IEEE International Requirements Engineering Conference (RE), pp. 71–80. IEEE (2012)
17. Von Knethen, A., Paech, B.: A survey on tracing approaches in practice and research. Frauenhofer Institut Experimentelles Software Engineering, IESE-Report No. 95 (2002)
18. Ramesh, B.: Factors influencing requirements traceability practice. Commun. ACM **41**(12), 37–44 (1998)
19. Regan, G., McCaffery, F., McDaid, K., Flood, D.: The barriers to traceability and their potential solutions: towards a reference framework. In: 2012 38th EUROMICRO Conference on Software Engineering and Advanced Applications (SEAA), pp. 319–322. IEEE (2012)
20. Torkar, R., Gorschek, T., Feldt, R., Svahnberg, M., Raja, U.A., Kamran, K.: Requirements traceability: a systematic review and industry case study. Int. J. Softw. Eng. Knowl. Eng. **22**(03), 385–433 (2012)
21. De Lucia, A., Fasano, F., Oliveto, R.: Traceability management for impact analysis. In: Frontiers of Software Maintenance, FoSM 2008, pp. 21–30. IEEE (2008)
22. Cleland-Huang, J., Gotel, O.C., Huffman Hayes, J., Mäder, P., Zisman, A.: Software traceability: trends and future directions. In: Proceedings of the on Future of Software Engineering, pp. 55–69. ACM (2014)
23. Cleland-Huang, J., Czauderna, A., Gibiec, M., Emenecker, J.: A machine learning approach for tracing regulatory codes to product specific requirements. In: Proceedings of the 32nd ACM/IEEE International Conference on Software Engineering, vol. 1, pp. 155–164. ACM (2010)
24. Borg, M., Runeson, P., Ardö, A.: Recovering from a decade: a systematic mapping of information retrieval approaches to software traceability. Empirical Softw. Eng. **19**(6), 1565–1616 (2014)
25. Galvão, I., Goknil, A.: Survey of traceability approaches in model-driven engineering. In: Proceedings - IEEE International Enterprise Distributed Object Computing Workshop, pp. 313–324. EDOC (2007)

26. Gotel, O.C., Finkelstein, A.C.: An analysis of the requirements traceability problem. In: Proceedings of the First International Conference on Requirements Engineering, pp. 94-101. IEEE (1994)
27. Rempel, P., Mäder, P., Kuschke, T., Philippow, I.: Requirements traceability across organizational boundaries - a survey and taxonomy. In: Doerr, J., Opdahl, A.L. (eds.) REFSQ 2013. LNCS, vol. 7830, pp. 125–140. Springer, Heidelberg (2013). doi:10.1007/978-3-642-37422-7_10
28. Königs, S.F., Beier, G., Figge, A., Stark, R.: Traceability in systems engineering-review of industrial practices, state-of-the-art technologies and new research solutions. Adv. Eng. Inf. **26**(4), 924–940 (2012)
29. Asuncion, H.U., Asuncion, A.U., Taylor, R.N.: Software traceability with topic modeling. In: Proceedings of the 32nd ACM/IEEE International Conference on Software Engineering, vol. 1, pp. 95–104. ACM (2010)
30. Cuddeback, D., Dekhtyar, A., Hayes, J.H.: Automated requirements traceability: the study of human analysts. In: 2010 18th IEEE International Requirements Engineering Conference (RE), pp. 231–240. IEEE (2010)
31. Mäder, P., Gotel, O., Philippow, I.: Enabling automated traceability maintenance through the upkeep of traceability relations. In: Paige, R.F., Hartman, A., Rensink, A. (eds.) ECMDA-FA 2009. LNCS, vol. 5562, pp. 174–189. Springer, Heidelberg (2009). doi:10.1007/978-3-642-02674-4_13
32. Drivalos-Matragkas, N., Kolovos, D.S., Paige, R.F., Fernandes, K.J.: A state-based approach to traceability maintenance. In: Proceedings of the 6th ECMFA Traceability Workshop, pp. 23–30. ACM (2010)
33. Arkley, P., Riddle, S.: Overcoming the traceability benefit problem. In: Proceedings of the 13th IEEE International Conference on Requirements Engineering, pp. 385–389. IEEE (2005)
34. Pedreira, O., García, F., Brisaboa, N., Piattini, M.: Gamification in software engineering-a systematic mapping. Inf. Softw. Technol. **57**, 157–168 (2015)
35. Seaman, C.B.: Qualitative methods in empirical studies of software engineering. IEEE Trans. Softw. Eng. **25**(4), 557–572 (1999)

Process Improvement

Towards the Automation of the Travel Management Procedure of an Italian Public Administration

Antonello Calabró[1]([✉]), Eda Marchetti[1], Giorgio Oronzo Spagnolo[1],
Pierangela Cempini[2], Luca Mancini[2], and Serena Paoletti[2]

[1] Software Engineering Area, Istituto di Scienza e Tecnologie dell'Informazione
"A. Faedo" Consiglio Nazionale delle Ricerche (CNR),
via G. Moruzzi, 1 - 56124 Pisa, Italy
{antonello.calabro,eda.marchetti,giorgiooronzo.spagnolo}@isti.cnr.it
[2] Administrative Staff, Istituto di Scienza e Tecnologie dell'Informazione
"A. Faedo" Consiglio Nazionale delle Ricerche (CNR),
via G. Moruzzi, 1 - 56124 Pisa, Italy
{pierangela.cempini,luca.mancini,serena.paoletti}@isti.cnr.it

Abstract. Recently the Public Administrations pay a lot of attention to decreases the time required for document production and validation specifically in case of travel management. In this paper we describe the procedural steps followed to implement a first prototype framework for automating the travel management process adopted inside an Italian PA. To achieve this goal, we represent the process through Business Models specified into a formal notations. The experience highlighted important challenges in the application of automatic facilities for the travel management and let the detection of inconsistencies and improvements of the process itself.

Keywords: Business process · Monitoring · Learning assessment

1 Introduction

Recently a lot of attention has been dedicated by the (Italian) Public Administrations (PA) to reduce/optimize the management costs, and to improve the quality of services provided to users (citizen or employees). Indeed the automation in documents production is recognized as an important means to decrease the time and effort of the PA personnel in administrative activities and to speed up the overall PA management [1].

In this paper we focus on the travel management, which has been recognized as one of the hot topics for the Italian PAs according to a recent research of the School of Management in collaboration with AirPlus [2].

Currently, most of the times the single employees are forced to organize their travels only with the help of on-line travel services. They have also to collect hard copies of travel documentations and manually fill the required modules for travel

© Springer International Publishing AG 2017
D. Winkler et al. (Eds.): SWQD 2017, LNBIP 269, pp. 175–187, 2017.
DOI: 10.1007/978-3-319-49421-0_12

authorization and expenses refund. On the other side administrative personnel has to deal with a lot of inaccurate, incomplete or erroneous documentations, causing an increasing in the time and the effort necessary for their validation.

This is forcing the different Italian Public Administration towards the "digital maturity", i.e. massive adoption of ITC facilities to increase the quality and efficiency of travel management and refund.

In this paper we would like to move one step in this direction presenting a facility for the automation of the travel management process of the Istituto di Scienza e Tecnologie dell'Informazione "A. Faedo" (ISTI) of the Consiglio Nazionale delle Ricerche (CNR) in Pisa. In collaboration with the administrative staff of such institute, we analysed the possible quality improvements starting from three points of view: the technical position, related to the quality of the systems itself; the view of the user, which is more related to the usability experienced and the quality level obtained in the fulfilment of his/her tasks; and finally, the view of the PA personnel, which is interested in the maximization of the revenues in management.

To achieve this goal, we followed the basic guidelines of the Business Process Management [3] and we developed a Business Process Model (BPM) using one of the available Business Process Modeling Notation (BPMN) [4]. The defined BPM represents the steps that have to be performed by the different participants (people, teams distributed organizations or IT systems) during the execution of the travel management process. This approach provided us the possibility to easily model travel refunding process, to develop concise definitions and taxonomies useful for discussion with the ISTI administration, and to have a detailed reference guideline for the implementation of an executable framework. We also exploited the BPM representation for controlling the on-line execution of the travel management process. Specifically monitoring capabilities have been included in the developed framework, called COSO (COmpilazione miSsiOni), to keep track of the activities evolution and information exchange, as well as to perform a posterior statistical analysis of collected travel data.

The work presented in this article integrates different previous experiences in business management and monitoring discussed in [5–9]. In particular a detailed analysis of the ISTI regulations as well as a storytelling approach have been used to create the business process model for this PA. The application of monitoring facilities lets the collection of a set of useful parameters for subsequent business process statistics and improvements.

In the rest of the paper we first briefly introduce some background concepts (Sect. 2), then in Sect. 3 we explain the procedure followed for deriving the Business Process Models. We present the set of quality attributes to be included in the proposed framework in Sect. 4, while the main framework components are schematized in Sect. 5. A preliminary assessment of the framework is presented in Sect. 6. Finally, in Sect. 7 presents related works and discussion and conclusion are finally depicted Sect. 8.

2   Background

In this section we briefly provide some basic concepts about the Business Process Management and the CNR travel management procedure considered for the development of the proposed framework.

Business Process Management. Usually Business Process (BP) refers to any structured collection of related activities or tasks that are carried out to accomplish the intended objectives of an organization.

The main focus is therefore in creating an abstract but meaningful representation of the real business domains and sharing a formalized definition so to improve expressiveness and make easier tools development. [3]. Usually in the industrial context the process followed during the analysis and design phases of the Business Process Model, that is known as externalization [10], involves direct requirements elicitation from employees by means of meetings where the participants develop group stories [11]. Successively the collected information are translated into Business Model by using one of the available Business Process Modeling Languages (BPML) [12]. In this paper we refer to The Business Process Model and Notation (BPMN) [4] to represent the derived business models, which is the de facto standard for process modeling.

CNR Travel Management Procedure. As any other PA, ISTI and more in general the CNR, has a well-defined collection of travel policies and procedures. According to CNR rules the travel expenses have to be previously authorized using specific authorization module. Once travel has been completed, the expenses have to be reported into a specific module, supported by appropriate documentation and legitimated by the administrative staff. Variations from the established policies represent exceptional cases and have to be approved by the authorized department approver (Director). One of the main traveler's responsibility is to be familiar with, and strictly follow, the policies and procedures specified in the manual. It is out of the scope of this paper to provide detailed rules list; in the following we only mention the most important ones. Additional information regarding travel and reimbursement process is available on [13].

Authorization: The travel should be authorized by the Director, and authorization module should be produced at least five working days before departure. Travelers should provide their personal details, the motivation of the travel, the location, and an estimated amount of the total travel cost. Authorization for the use of own car or taxi should also preventively requested.

Advances: Advances are limited to transportation, accommodations, and meeting/conference fees. Travelers should complete specific authorization module and provide original documentation supporting travel cost.

Transportation: Class depends on the category of travelers and varies from national to international transportation.

Accommodation: Type of allowed accommodation depends on the category of travelers.

Reimbursing Travel Related Expenses: Rules varies in case of national or international travels. Travelers should fill a specific module in which they provide their personal details, the motivation of the travel, the location, the chronological list of all the travel expenses. Opportune justifications in case of exceptional events, not included in the travel manual, are needed.

Meal expenses: Only two meals are allowed and the total meal expenses for day are limited by specific boundaries depending from the country and the category of travelers.

Documentation: Original receipts for all expenses must be submitted to administrative staff and optionally a PDF copy can be provided. In case the traveler has chosen a per diem meal reimbursement, receipts are not required.

Mileage Reimbursement Rate: Reimbursements for mileage are made following specific mileage reimbursement rate in effect at the time of the trip.

Reimbursable Expenses: Reimbursable travel expenses include also: airline baggage fees, automobile rentals and meeting/conference fees.

However the Italian legislation about PA travel management is continuously modifying and due to its natural language specification, it often rises misunderstandings and misinterpretations. Being informed and knowledge about the travelers management evolution is one of the most difficult point for the travelers. Therefore often the documentations provided both for travel authorization and travel refund are full of errors and inconsistencies.

3   Create the Model

In this section we explain the method used to derive the Business Process Models of the ISTI travel management process, called ISTI Travel Model (ITM).

In order to develop the ITM we followed a storytelling methodology [14], [15]. Through interviews with ISTI personnel and domain experts we collected the most interesting behaviors and critical activities of the travel management process. The method is summarized in Fig. 1, where three main stakeholders are: the *Tellers*, who are asked to describe their activities explicitly through stories; the *Facilitators* who provide support to story tellers for producing coherent stories and to modelers for the definition of the first abstraction of the models; *Modelers* who are the process analysts defining the graphical models on the bases of information collected from the tellers and facilitators. Following the storytelling methodology three specific phases, each one involving all the roles, have been executed as briefly described in the rest of this section.

The **first phase** consisted mainly in meetings targeting the definition of the context and the collection of the most interesting stories useful to describe the ITM. The meeting team was composed by three *Modelers*, 15 *Tellers* and three *Facilitator*. Modelers were researchers with strong background in BP modeling and software engineering; tellers were selected ISTI employees having different experience and belonging to different categories; the facilitators ISTI administrative staff having deep knowledge of the CNR travel management process.

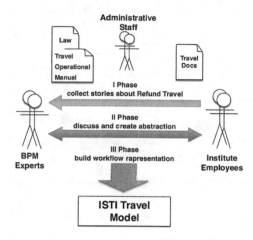

Fig. 1. Methodology to create the model

During the first phase, five meetings have been necessary. To the end of this phase the stories were collected and a set of needs identifies.

In the **second phase** the needs has been refined according to the rules and policies of the CNR travel management documentation [16] and a set of software requirements and the main process elements have been identified. The examination of the stories produces activities, flow, events, business rules, in order to extract the models elements of the process. During this phase the set of quality attributes have been also identified as detailed in Sect. 4. In this phase, two meetings have been necessary.

Finally, in the **third phase**, the elements of the identified processes have been converted into BPMN models. The models have been presented to the participants in order to consolidate them, to implement necessary corrections and generate a final version. Therefore the quality assessment of the BPMN model has been manually performed by domain experts.

At the end of the three phases we have produced one high-level model that describes the main process of the ITM and sixteen lower level models that describe in details the sub-processes. For simplicity we report in Fig. 2 just high-level model of the ITM concerning the reimbursing travel related expenses. As in the figure the actors interact with the COSO framework according to the following procedure: (1) The employee authenticates himself/herself though COSO and starts a request of travel refund expenses; (2) Using an Identity Provider[1] (IdP) COSO identifies the users; (3) GEKO [17], the ISTI internal internet service managing administrative projects funding, sends to COSO the data relative to the selected travel; (4) the employee fills/uploads and accepts travel data and documents. The COSO framework aids the employee in the module completion implementing the rules and policies of the CNR travel management procedure concerning the accomodation, transportation, meal expenses and so on

---

[1] IdP is responsible for providing identifiers for users looking to interact with a system.

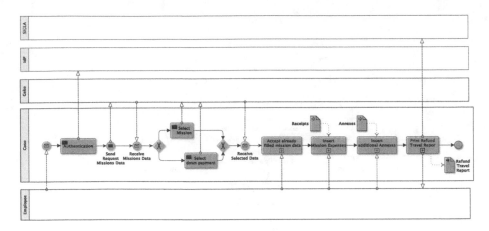

Fig. 2. COSO high-level model

as detailed in Sect. 2; (5) Finally, the Refund request is printed and sent to the SIGLA framework [18], which is the official CNR system for the management of the accounting and financial reporting.

4   Quality Aspects

In this section a quality model useful for the assessment of the proposed framework is presented. It has been developed considering different aspects, such as business, timeless, and usability and performance. It is the result of the integration of: (i) peculiarities of the ISTI travel business management; (ii) the information collected in the second phase of the storytelling methodology (see Sect. 3); (iii) the set of attributes expressed in the ISO/IEC 25010 standard [19]. For space limitation we show in Fig. 3 only the characteristics, and their corresponding subcharacteristics, that have been included from the ISO/IEC 25010 standard [19] into the customized quality model. We refer to [19] for their description.

Additionally to better face the peculiarities ISTI travel business management, the following two quality attributes, not included in the ISO/IEC 25010 standard, have been integrated into the customized the quality model:

Traceability: Degree to which the system can keep track of a given set or type of information to a given degree. Specifically the system should log and trace activities execution according to user defined specific rules. It is measured in terms of number of tracking and storage facilities included into the system.

Customizable data collection: Degree to which the system can provide statistical analysis on the bases of travel data collection. It is measured in terms of the number of user defined statistical analysis the system can produce.

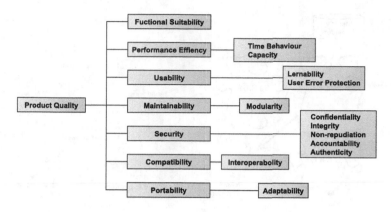

Fig. 3. Customization of ISO/IEC 25010

5   Framework

In this section some details about the automation of the CNR travel management procedure, thought the COSO framework, are provided. The prototype implementation is running on a distributed environment composed of several heterogeneous software and machines. In particular the framework needs to collaborate with the three main software products of ISTI that are SIGLA [18], for the management of the accounting and financial reporting and GEKO [17] for the management of funding and for Identity Provider to manage authentication. However during the development and validation stages, the prototype has been forced to work as a stand-alone framework. In the Fig. 4a the overall architecture of the implemented framework is provided. In the remaining of this section more detailed about the architecture of the COSO component are provided which includes five main components (see Fig. 4b)

- the **editor**: it provides facilities both for creating and modifying the models representing the business process.
- the **front-end**: it is composed of several web-forms and help facilities. It provides both documentations and suggestions to the user and contributes to decrease the number of errors in module fulfilling.
- the **monitoring**: it keeps track of models execution and collects specific travel data useful for statistical analysis.
- the **message broker**: it deals with the communication between different components.
- the **BPM engine**: it executes the BP model relative the CNR travel management process.

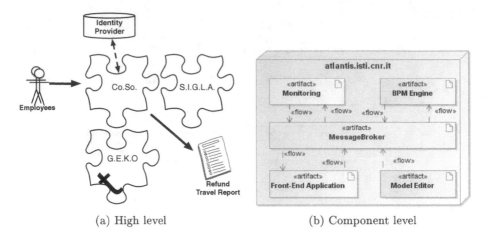

(a) High level   (b) Component level

Fig. 4. Architectural views

6   Assessment

The quality model presented in Sect. 4 has been used to assess the preliminary version of the COSO prototype framework. As described in Sect. 4 we considered different aspects, such as business, timeless, and usability and performance. Here below how and where each aspect and the corresponding attribute of the quality model have been addressed and evaluated is reported.

Considering in particular the business attributes Table 1 presents their assessment.

The attributes related to the security aspects, i.e. confidentiality, integrity, non-repudiation, authenticity, are covered by the ISTI authentication system, and ISTI intranet in general, on which users of must authenticate before using the framework. Specifically, to better focus on these quality aspects, as depicted in Fig. 2, in the BP model a specific task has been entirely dedicated to the security.

From the performance aspects, the automation of a process that was previously completed only manually, guarantees time saving and to speed up the overall refund procedure. In addition the automation assures: a reduction in time required for checking and validate the different costs and expenses; the possibility of simultaneous accesses of from different users so to speed up the administrative tasks and decrease the communications. We are currently collecting data for the evaluation of the precise time behaviour and capacity measures. In particular for time behaviour the overall target is to reduce to at list to one third the mean time required for a completion of a travel authorization and refund that are currently estimated into 3 and 1.5 h. Considering that inside ISTI the average number of travel authorizations and refunds per years is around 1500 this can represent a considerable budget and effort reduction for the overall institute.

Table 1. Business attributes

Attribute	How has been addressed	Where has been addressed
Suitability	During the model creation the requirements list has been definited	Each requirement has been realized into one or more activity or task of the BP model
Learnability	A set of user documentation and help facilities has been defined collaboration with Administrative Staff	We are currently working in on this topic
User error protection	The BP model implements all the rules and policies defined within the [16]	The front-end application has been developed to prevent rules violation
Adaptability	Splitting process in more sub-processes, each one associated to a requirement, makes easy to maintain and adapt the framework	The editor allows to update the models according new requirements.
Modularity	The framework has been developed following Model-View-Controller paradigm	Decoupling with messages, separating front-end from business logic

Finally considering the additional attributes included in quality model, the monitoring component of the framework, lets to log, trace and store activities execution according to specific rules defined in collaboration with ISTI administrative staff. The purpose is to improve costs management and predictions; establish a better distribution of ISTI budget and possibly establish specific (accommodation/transportation) conventions. In addition monitoring component include the possibility to defined customizable rules and store the relative data so to improve user defined statistical analysis. This guarantees a satisfied level of the enhancement quality attribute implementation.

In the rest of this section graphs representing some of statistical analysis considered in the current prototype version are briefly presented. Because the framework is still under development and refinement, the data of the used in the table has been manually derived from the ISTI hard copy documentations. As soon as the framework will be adopted inside ISTI, the data analysis will be completely automated and the considered table immediately available. In this paper for confidentiality reasons the information of the various graphs has been anonymized and represents just example of rules application.

Specifically in Fig. 5a the distribution of cost per travel is reported considering a period of three years of a young researcher. As in the graph the expenditure

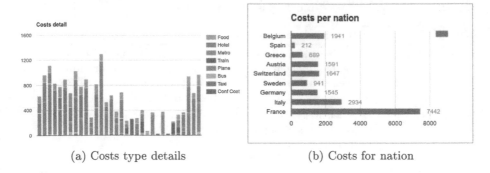

(a) Costs type details   (b) Costs for nation

Fig. 5. Statistical analysis

items that impact more on the overall travel costs are transportations (especially plane) and accommodations. This confirms that a considerable cost reduction could be reached by establishing specific conventions with main airlines and hotel chains.

In Fig. 5b report the average of cost per day and per nation of the ISTI personnel considering travels done in European countries. The data has been collected considering different categories of ISTI employees over a period of three years. As in the table France is the country having the highest frequency while Belgium has the highest cost per day. This data could be exploited again for establish conventions at least with these two countries but also for faithful travel costs planning and for a better schedule the overall travel budget inside for instance project proposals.

7   Related Work

Information technology (IT) has the potential to improve information management and the quality of governmental services. However to take full advantages of IT requires organizations to understand and to overcome several challenges. One of the major challenges is to develop credible business processes for enterprise information management [20]. Although much attention has been given to e-government lately, most of the papers, treat e-government from a customer's point of view and overlook the benefits it brings to governmental institutions.

The most important inhibitors to an efficient realization of BPM in the public administration are the redundant efforts in BPM and an intra-organizational and inter-organizational knowledge deficits because of poor exchange and lack of networking. Based on these findings, they encourage the collaborative creation of a process database that enables the sharing and reuse of process knowledge and process models. [21] presents a platform for reference models exclusively for municipal administrations [22].

Falck in [23] describes the initiation of a virtual community on BPM in the Berlin administration. According to her, the largest obstacles when developing

BPM in the administration are a lack of knowledge off the staff about their administrative processes and the weakly pronounced culture of information dissemination. In this way one of the goal in our research was to share the process model to the stakeholders.

8   Discussion and Conclusion

The introduction of laws/regulations concerning the improvement of automatic documentations management as well as the necessity of costs reduction provide new challenges for the enactment and automation of PA business process. In this paper, considering the travel management process adopted inside the ISTI - CNR public administration, we proposed an automatic support for the authorization and refunding of travel expenses, which provides also statistical analysis of travel data. The implemented framework contributed to cost reductions and improved the overall travel management process in different aspects: it increased the quality of the modules necessary for travel authorization and refunding by drastically reducing the number errors and inconsistencies inside them; it decreased the loss of documentations because made easier their digital collection; it decreased the time and effort required by the ISTI administrative staff to check and validate the different modules and documentations; it provided automatic facility for statistical analysis of travel data so to better plan the annual budget distribution and to make easier the stipulation of conventions with travel or accommodation companies.

The proposed framework evidenced the difficulties in the representation of the natural language rules listed inside the CNR travel management procedure into concise, clear and unambiguous models. The crucial point during the models creation was the definition of the context of the story, useful to properly guide the tellers. The incremental approach of the storytelling methodology, starting from a general description to a detailed one, has been the solution adopted. This allowed all the critical aspects of the stories to be captured and reduced the possible inconsistencies. Nevertheless, since real contexts can have situations where several degrees of freedom can be possible, the models should abstract from not relevant details and aspects, thus a compromise between models and reality had to be found.

Another difficulty was the identification of set of quality attributes to be integrated into the developed software. The stories collected during the interview with ISTI employee and the analysis of the rules and policies of the CNR travel management procedure only evidences some usability aspects but did not go into detail with productivity, timeless, and performance of the proposed framework.

The preliminary use of the proposed framework, evidenced the necessity to integrate specific components for simulating the travel management procedure execution. This would be an important feature for reducing the training cost of new personnel, for decreasing the number of errors encountered in filling the various documents, and helping PA in modify/clarify the most misinterpreted rules.

Even if the main target is the finalization of the current implementation of the COSO framework, we would like also to investigate more in the definition of the suitable set of rules useful for statistical data analysis and extend the validation of the proposed framework considering a larger set of employees, so to collect possible trouble reports or request for improvements.

Acknowledgments. The authors would like to show their gratitude to the Claudio Montani, Director of the Istituto di Scienza e Tecnologie dell'Informazione "A. Faedo" (ISTI) of the Consiglio Nazionale delle Ricerche in Pisa, for his hints, incitements and useful discussions during the course of this experience.

References

1. Parlament, I.: Codice dell'amministrazione digitale. http://www.parlamento.it/parlam/leggi/deleghe/05082dl.htm
2. AirPlus: Il Travel Management nella Pubblica Amministrazione. https://www.airplus.com/it/it/news_153185_172508/
3. Jeston, J., Nelis, J.: Business Process Management. Routledge, Abingdon (2014)
4. OMG: Business Process Model And Notation (BPMN) Version 2.0, January 2011. http://www.omg.org/spec/BPMN/2.0/PDF
5. Calabró, A., Lonetti, F., Marchetti, E.: Monitoring of business process execution based on performance indicators. In: The Euromicro Conference series on Software Engineering and Advanced Applications (SEAA) (2015)
6. Calabrò, A., Lonetti, F., Marchetti, E.: KPI evaluation of the business process execution through event monitoring activity. In: ES (2015)
7. Zribi, S., Calabrò, A., Lonetti, F., Marchetti, E., Jorquera, T., Lorré, J.P.: Design of a simulation framework for model-based learning. In: Proceedings of International Conference on Model-Driven Engineering and Software Development (2016)
8. Spagnolo, G.O., Marchetti, E., Coco, A., Scarpellini, P., Querci, A., Fabbrini, F., Gnesi, S.: An experience on applying process mining techniques to the Tuscan port community system. In: Winkler, D., Biffl, S., Bergsmann, J. (eds.) SWQD 2016. LNBIP, vol. 238, pp. 49–60. Springer, Heidelberg (2016). doi:10.1007/978-3-319-27033-3_4
9. Spagnolo, G.O., Marchetti, E., Coco, A., Gnesi, S.: Modelling and validating an import/export shipping process. ERCIM News **2016**, 105 (2016)
10. de Vreede, G., Guerrero, L.A., Raventós, G.M. (eds.): Groupware: Design, Implementation and Use. LNCS, vol. 3198. Springer, Heidelberg (2004)
11. Carminatti, N., Borges, M.R.S., Gomes, J.O.: Analyzing approaches to collective knowledge recall. Comput. Artif. Intell. **25**(6), 547–570 (2006)
12. van der Aalst, W.M.P., ter Hofstede, A.H.M., Weske, M. (eds.): Business Process Management. LNCS, vol. 2678. Springer, Heidelberg (2003)
13. ISTI: Trattamento missioni del personale. http://www.isti.cnr.it/intranet/unit.php?unit=Mis&section=1
14. Santoro, F.M., Borges, M.R.S., Pino, J.A.: Acquiring knowledge on business processes from stakeholders' stories. Adv. Eng. Inform. **24**(2), 138–148 (2010)
15. de AR Gonçalves, J.C., Santoro, F.M., Baião, F.A.: Business process mining from group stories. In: CSCWD 2009, pp. 161–166 (2009)
16. Tatarelli, R., Carinici, F.: Le spese di trasferta - criteri e modalitá di corresponsione del trattamenti di missione e dei rimborsi spese. http://www.urp.cnr.it/documenti/c14-015-a.pdf

17. ISTI, CNR in Pisa: Gestione Commesse. http://geko.isti.cnr.it:8180/CNR/
18. CNR: Sistema Informativo Gestione Linee di Attivita. http://contab.cnr.it/portale/
19. International Organization for Standardization: Systems and software Quality Requirements and Evaluation (SQuaRE). http://www.iso.org/iso/catalogue_detail.htm?csnumber=35733
20. Williams, S.P., Scifleet, P.A., Hardy, C.A.: Online business reporting: an information management perspective. J. Inf. Manag. **26**(2), 91–101 (2006)
21. Becker, J., Algermissen, L., Delfmann, P., Niehaves, B.: A web based platform for the design of administrational reference process models. In: Zhou, X., Su, S., Papazoglou, M.P., Orlowska, M.E., Jeffery, K. (eds.) WISE 2004. LNCS, vol. 3306, pp. 159–168. Springer, Heidelberg (2004). doi:10.1007/978-3-540-30480-7_18
22. Eid-Sabbagh, R.-H., Kunze, M., Meyer, A., Weske, M.: A platform for research on process model collections. In: Mendling, J., Weidlich, M. (eds.) BPMN 2012. LNBIP, vol. 125, pp. 8–22. Springer, Heidelberg (2012). doi:10.1007/978-3-642-33155-8_2
23. Falck, M.: Business process management - as a method of governance. In: Traunmüller, R., Lenk, K. (eds.) EGOV 2002. LNCS, vol. 2456, pp. 137–141. Springer, Heidelberg (2002). doi:10.1007/978-3-540-46138-8_21

Author Index

Printed in the United States
By Bookmasters

Printed in the United States
By Bookmasters